Focus on Grammar

A **HIGH-INTERMEDIATE** Course for Reference and Practice

SECOND EDITION

Marjorie Fuchs

Margaret Bonner

Longman

To the memory of my parents, Edith and Joseph Fuchs—MF

To my parents, Marie and Joseph Maus, and to my son, Luke Frances—MB

FOCUS ON GRAMMAR: A **HIGH-INTERMEDIATE** COURSE
FOR REFERENCE AND PRACTICE, VOLUME A

Pearson Education, 10 Bank Street, White Plains, NY 10606

Editorial director: Allen Ascher
Executive editor: Louisa Hellegers
Director of design and production: Rhea Banker
Development editor: Françoise Leffler
Production manager: Alana Zdinak
Managing editor: Linda Moser
Senior production editors: Sandra Pike and Virginia Bernard
Senior manufacturing manager: Patrice Fraccio
Manufacturing manager: David Dickey
Photo research: Karen Pugliano
Cover design: Rhea Banker
Cover image: *Elm, Middleton Woods, Yorkshire,*
    7 November 1980. Copyright © Andy Goldsworthy
    from his book *A Collaboration with Nature,*
    Harry N. Abrams, 1990.
Text design: Charles Yuen
Text composition: Preface, Inc.
Illustrators: Ronald Chironna: pp. 41, 113, 160; Brian Hughes:
    pp. 19, 122, 128; Jock MacRae: pp. 72, 214; Paul McCusker:
    p. 17; Andy Myer: pp. 107, 166, 201; Ortelius Design, Inc.:
    p. 321; Dusan Petricic; pp. 66, 78, 143, 167, 168; PC&F:
    pp. 52, 53 (bl, br), 59, 62.
Photo credits: See p. xiv.

ISBN 0-201-38302-0

2 3 4 5 6 7 8 9 10—CRK—04 03 02 01

FOCUS ON GRAMMAR

A **HIGH-INTERMEDIATE** Course for Reference and Practice

CONTENTS

PART IV

GERUNDS AND INFINITIES

PART V

PHRASAL VERBS

PART VI

ADJECTIVE CLAUSES

APPENDICES

ABOUT THE AUTHORS

Marjorie Fuchs has taught ESL at New York City Technical College and LaGuardia Community College of the City University of New York and EFL at the Sprach Studio Lingua Nova in Munich, Germany. She holds a Master's Degree in Applied English Linguistics and a Certificate in TESOL from the University of Wisconsin–Madison. She has authored or co-authored many widely used ESL textbooks, notably *On Your Way: Building Basic Skills in English, Crossroads, Top Twenty ESL Word Games: Beginning Vocabulary Development, Around the World: Pictures for Practice, Families: Ten Card Games for Language Learners, Focus on Grammar: An Intermediate Course for Reference and Practice*, and the workbooks to the *Longman Dictionary of American English*, the *Longman Photo Dictionary*, *The Oxford Picture Dictionary*, and the *Vistas* series.

Margaret Bonner has taught ESL at Hunter College and the Borough of Manhattan Community College of the City University of New York, at Taiwan National University in Taipei, and at Virginia Commonwealth University in Richmond. She holds a Master's Degree in Library Science from Columbia University, and she has done work towards a Ph.D. in English Literature at the Graduate Center of the City University of New York. She has contributed to a number of ESL and EFL projects, including *Making Connections, On Your Way,* and the Curriculum Renewal Project in Oman, where she wrote textbooks, workbooks, and teachers manuals for the national school system. She authored *Step into Writing: A Basic Writing Text,* and co-authored *Focus on Grammar: An Intermediate Course for Reference and Practice* and *The Oxford Picture Dictionary Intermediate Workbook.*

INTRODUCTION

THE **FOCUS ON GRAMMAR** SERIES

Focus on Grammar: A High-Intermediate Course for Reference and Practice, *Second Edition,* is part of the four-level *Focus on Grammar* series. Written by practicing ESL professionals, the series focuses on English grammar through lively listening, speaking, reading, and writing activities. Each of the four Student Books is accompanied by an Answer Key, a Workbook, an Audio Program (cassettes or CDs), a Teacher's Manual, and a CD–ROM. Each Student Book can stand alone as a complete text in itself, or it can be used as part of the series.

BOTH CONTROLLED AND COMMUNICATIVE PRACTICE

Research in applied linguistics suggests that students expect and need to learn the formal rules of a language. However, students need to practice new structures in a variety of contexts to help them internalize and master them. To this end, *Focus on Grammar* provides an abundance of both controlled and communicative exercises so that students can bridge the gap between knowing grammatical structures and using them. The many communicative activities in each unit enable students to personalize what they have learned in order to talk to each other with ease about hundreds of everyday issues.

A UNIQUE FOUR-STEP APPROACH

The series follows a unique four-step approach. In the first step, **grammar in context,** new structures are shown in the natural context of passages, articles, and dialogues. This is followed by a **grammar presentation** of structures in clear and accessible grammar charts, notes, and examples. The third step is **focused practice** of both form and meaning in numerous and varied controlled exercises. In the fourth step, **communication practice,** students use the new structures freely and creatively in motivating, open-ended activities.

A COMPLETE CLASSROOM TEXT AND REFERENCE GUIDE

A major goal in the development of *Focus on Grammar* has been to provide Student Books that serve not only as vehicles for classroom instruction but also as resources for reference and self-study. In each Student Book, the combination of grammar charts, grammar notes, and expansive appendices provides a complete and invaluable reference guide for the student.

THOROUGH RECYCLING

Underpinning the scope and sequence of the series as a whole is the belief that students need to use target structures many times in many contexts at increasing levels of difficulty. For this reason new grammar is constantly recycled so that students will feel thoroughly comfortable with it.

COMPREHENSIVE TESTING PROGRAM

SelfTests at the end of each part of the Student Book allow for continual assessment of progress. In addition, diagnostic and final tests in the Teacher's Manual provide a ready-made, ongoing evaluation component for each student.

THE **HIGH-INTERMEDIATE** STUDENT BOOK

Focus on Grammar: A High-Intermediate Course for Reference and Practice, Second Edition, is divided into ten parts comprising twenty-nine units. Each part contains grammatically related units with each unit focusing on a specific grammatical structure. Where appropriate, contrast units present contrasting forms (for example, the present perfect and the simple past tense). Each unit has a major theme relating the exercises to one another. All units have the same clear, easy-to-follow format:

GRAMMAR IN CONTEXT

Grammar in Context presents the grammar focus of the unit in a natural context. The texts, all of which are recorded, present language in various formats. These include newspaper and magazine excerpts, Web sites, newsletters, advertisements, brochures, and other formats that students encounter in their day-to-day lives. In addition to presenting grammar in context, this introductory section raises student motivation and provides an opportunity for incidental learning and lively classroom discussions. Topics are varied, ranging from people's names, friendship, and saving money to skydiving, body art, and feng shui. Each text is preceded by a pre-reading activity called **Before You Read**. Pre-reading questions create interest, elicit students' knowledge about the topic, help point out features of the text, and lead students to make predictions about the reading.

GRAMMAR PRESENTATION

This section is made up of grammar charts, notes, and examples. The Grammar **charts** focus on the form of the unit's target structure. The clear and easy-to-understand boxes present each grammatical form in all its combinations. Affirmative and negative statements, *yes/no* and *wh-* questions, short answers, and contractions are presented for all tenses and modals covered. These charts provide students with a clear visual reference for each new structure.

The Grammar **notes** and **examples** that follow the charts focus on the meaning and use of the structure. Each note gives a clear explanation of the grammar point, and is always accompanied by one or more examples. Where appropriate, timelines help illustrate the meaning of verb tenses and their relationship to one another. *Be careful!* notes alert students to common ESL/EFL errors. Usage Notes provide guidelines for using and understanding different levels of formality and correctness. Pronunciation Notes are provided when appropriate. Reference Notes provide cross-references to related units and the Appendices.

FOCUSED PRACTICE

The exercises in this section provide practice for all uses of the structure presented in the Grammar Presentation. Each Focused Practice section begins with a "for recognition only" exercise called **Discover the Grammar**. Here, students are expected to recognize either the form of the structure or its meaning without having to produce any language. This activity raises awareness of the structures as it builds confidence.

Following the Discover the Grammar activity are exercises that practice the grammar in a controlled, but still contextualized, environment. The exercises proceed from simpler to more complex. There is a large variety of exercise types including fill-in-the-blanks, matching, multiple choice, question and sentence formation, and editing (error analysis). Exercises are cross-referenced to the appropriate grammar notes so that students can review the notes if necessary. As with the Grammar in Context, students are exposed to many different written formats, including letters, electronic bulletin boards, journal entries, resumes, charts, graphs, schedules, and news articles. Many exercises are art-based, providing a rich and interesting context for meaningful practice. All Focused Practice exercises are suitable for self-study or homework. A complete **Answer Key** is provided in a separate booklet.

COMMUNICATION PRACTICE

The exercises in this section are intended for in-class use. The first exercise is **Listening**. After having had exposure to and practice with the grammar in its written form, students now have the opportunity to check their aural comprehension. Students hear a variety of listening formats, including conversations, television scripts, weather forecasts, interviews, and flight announcements. After listening to the recording (or hearing the teacher read the tapescript, which can be found in the Teacher's Manual), students complete a task that focuses on either the form or the meaning of the structure. It is suggested that students be allowed to hear the text as many times as they wish to complete the task successfully.

The listening exercise is followed by a variety of activities that provide students with the opportunity to use the grammar in open-ended, interactive ways. Students work in pairs or small groups in interviews, surveys, opinion polls, information gaps, discussions, role plays, games, and problem-solving activities. The activities are fun and engaging and offer ample opportunity for self-expression and cross-cultural comparison. The final exercise in this section is always **Writing**, in which students practice using the structure in a variety of written formats.

REVIEW OR SELFTEST

After the last unit of each part, there is a review feature that can be used as a self-test. The exercises in this section test the form and use of the grammar content of the part. These tests include questions in the format of the Structure and Written Expression sections of the TOEFL®. An **Answer Key** is provided after each test, with cross-references to units for easy review.

FROM GRAMMAR TO WRITING

At the end of each part, there is a writing section called From Grammar to Writing in which students are guided to use the grammar structures in a piece of extended writing. Formats include a personal letter, a business letter, a summary, a report, and an essay. Students practice pre-writing strategies such as brainstorming, free writing, constructing a time line, using a Venn diagram, and outlining. Each writing section concludes with peer review and editing.

APPENDICES

The Appendices provide useful information, such as lists of common irregular verbs, common adjective-plus-preposition combinations, and spelling and pronunciation rules. The Appendices can help students do the unit exercises, act as a springboard for further classroom work, and serve as a reference source.

NEW IN THIS EDITION

In response to users' requests, this edition has:

- new and updated texts for Grammar in Context
- pre-reading questions
- a new easy-to-read format for grammar notes and examples
- cross-references that link exercises to corresponding grammar notes
- more photos and art
- more recorded exercises
- more information gap exercises
- more editing (error analysis) exercises
- a writing exercise in each unit
- a From Grammar to Writing section at the end of each part

SUPPLEMENTARY **COMPONENTS**

All supplementary components of *Focus on Grammar, Second Edition,* —the Audio Program (cassettes or CDs), the Workbook, and the Teacher's Manual—are tightly keyed to the Student Book. Along with the CD-ROM, these components provide a wealth of practice and an opportunity to tailor the series to the needs of each individual classroom.

AUDIO PROGRAM

All of the Listening exercises as well as the Grammar in Context passages and other appropriate exercises are recorded on cassettes and CDs. The symbol appears next to these activities. The scripts appear in the Teacher's Manual and may be used as an alternative way of presenting these activities.

WORKBOOK

The Workbook accompanying *Focus on Grammar: A High-Intermediate Course for Reference and Practice, Second Edition,* provides a wealth of additional exercises appropriate for self-study of the target grammar of each unit in the Student Book. Most of the exercises are fully contextualized. Themes of the Workbook exercises are typically a continuation or a spin-off of the corresponding Student Book unit themes. There are also ten tests, one for each of the ten Student Book parts. These tests have questions in the format of the Structure and Written Expression section of the TOEFL®. Besides reviewing the material in the Student Book, these questions provide invaluable practice to those who are interested in taking this widely administered test.

TEACHER'S MANUAL

The Teacher's Manual, divided into five parts, contains a variety of suggestions and information to enrich the material in the Student Book. The first part gives general suggestions for each section of a typical unit. The next part offers practical teaching suggestions and cultural information to accompany specific material in each unit. The Teacher's Manual also provides ready-to-use diagnostic and final tests for each of the ten parts of the Student Book. In addition, a complete script of the Listening exercises is provided, as is an answer key for the diagnostic and final tests.

CD-ROM

The *Focus on Grammar* CD-ROM provides individualized practice with immediate feedback. Fully contextualized and interactive, the activities broaden and extend practice of the grammatical structures in the reading, listening, and writing skill areas. The CD-ROM includes grammar review, review tests, and all relevant reference material from the Student Book. It can also be used alongside the *Longman Interactive American Dictionary* CD-ROM.

CREDITS

ACKNOWLEDGMENTS

Before acknowledging the many people who have contributed to the second edition of *Focus on Grammar: A High-Intermediate Course for Reference and Practice*, we wish to express our gratitude to those who worked on the FIRST EDITION, and whose influence is still present in the new work.

Our continuing thanks to:

- **Joanne Dresner,** who initiated the project and helped conceptualize the general approach of *Focus on Grammar.*

- **Joan Saslow,** our editor, for helping to bring the first edition to fruition.

- **Sharon Hilles,** our grammar consultant, for her insight and advice.

Writing a SECOND EDITION has given us the wonderful opportunity to update the book and implement valuable feedback from teachers who have been using *Focus on Grammar.*

We wish, first of all, to acknowledge the following consultants and reviewers for reading the manuscript and offering many useful suggestions:

- CONSULTANTS: **Marcia Edwards Hijaab**, Henrico County Schools, Richmond, Virginia; **Tim Rees**, Transworld Schools, Boston; **Alison Rice**, Director of the International English Language Institute, Hunter College, New York; **Ellen Shaw**, University of Nevada, Las Vegas.

- REVIEWERS: **Daniel Chapuis**, English Language Institute, Queens College, CUNY; **Jeffrey Di Iuglio**, Harvard I.E.L.; **William Hall**, Houston Community College; **D. Smith**, English Language Institute, University of Pittsburgh; **Mark Stepner**, SCALE, the Somerville Center for Adult Learning Experiences, Somerville, Massachusetts; **Dee Strouse**, English Language Institute, University of Pittsburgh; **Paula Undeweiser**, University of California at Irvine; **Ellen Yaniv**, Boston University, CELOP.

We are also grateful to the following editors and colleagues:

- **Françoise Leffler**, editor *extraordinaire,* for her dedication, her keen ear, and her sense of style. We also appreciate her unstinting attention to detail and her humor, which had us looking forward to her calls. The book is undoubtedly better for her efforts.

- **Louisa Hellegers**, for being accessible and responsive to individual authors while coordinating the many complex aspects of this project.

(continued on next page)

- **Virginia Bernard** and **Sandra Pike**, for piloting the book through its many stages of production.

- **Irene Schoenberg**, author of the Basic level of *Focus on Grammar*, for generously sharing her experience in teaching our first edition and for her enthusiastic support.

Finally, we are grateful, as always, to **Rick Smith** and **Luke Frances**, for their helpful input and for standing by and supporting us as we navigated our way through another *FOG*.

M.F. and M.B.

THE STORY BEHIND THE COVER

The photograph on the cover is the work of **Andy Goldsworthy**, an innovative artist who works exclusively with natural materials to create unique outdoor sculpture, which he then photographs. Each Goldsworthy sculpture communicates the artist's own "sympathetic contact with nature" by intertwining forms and shapes structured by natural events with his own creative perspective. Goldsworthy's intention is not to "make his mark on the landscape, but to create a new perception and an evergrowing understanding of the land."

So, too, *Focus on Grammar* takes grammar found in its most natural context and expertly reveals its hidden structure and meaning. It is our hope that students everywhere will also develop a new perception and an evergrowing understanding of the world of grammar.

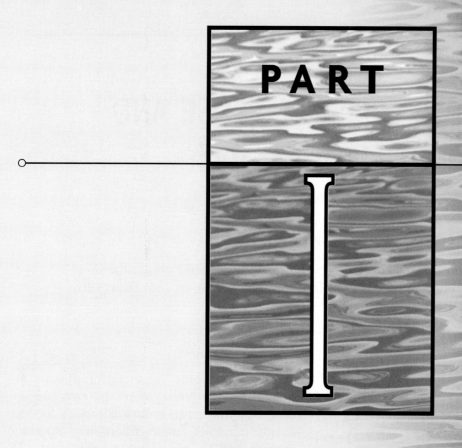

PART

I

PRESENT AND PAST:
REVIEW AND EXPANSION

SIMPLE PRESENT TENSE AND PRESENT PROGRESSIVE

GRAMMAR **IN CONTEXT**

BEFORE YOU READ   Look at the photo. What would you name these babies? What are popular girls' and boys' names in your first culture?

Read this book review.

Books   Section 14

THE NEW AGE BABY NAME BOOK By Sue Browder
Workman Publishing Company, $9.95 (393 pp.)

So, you**'re expecting** a baby, and you**'re** still **choosing** a name. Your child's name is going to affect his or her future, so you **don't want** to make a mistake. You've heard reports that teachers **give** better grades to David and Karen than to Elmer and Gertrude. Relax. Now there**'s** help— Sue Browder's *The New Age Baby Name Book*. Browder **tells** us that those reports about teachers **are** probably wrong. She **believes,** however, that a special name **helps** a child develop self-esteem. (She**'s talking** about a special name, not a weird one—a name like Ima Pigg won't help your child.)

What **are** some new developments in naming children? Many parents **are using** yesterday's nicknames as today's formal given names. Carrie **is becoming** more popular than Caroline, for example. Also, more and more parents **are selecting** unisex names such as Dana, Leslie, or Marty. And many **are turning** to their roots and **choosing** names from their ethnic background. Names like

Lateef (North African: "gentle") and Jonina (Hebrew: "dove") **are showing up** on birth certificates.

Whether you **prefer** trendy names or traditional ones, Browder's book **has** them all. In addition, you will find the meaning, place of origin, and—where necessary— the pronunciation of these names. In short, *The New Age Baby Name Book* **makes** fascinating reading, even if you **aren't becoming** a parent.

—MARTA LOPEZ

THE MOST POPULAR NAMES IN THE U. S.			
GIRLS	BOYS	GIRLS	BOYS
Sarah	Michael	Jessica	Austin
Emily	Matthew	Taylor	Joshua
Kaitlyn	Nicholas	Megan	Zachary
Brianna	Jacob	Hannah	Andrew
Ashley	Christopher	Samantha	Brandon

Source: Russell Ash, *The Top 10 of Everything* © 1999 (New York: DK Publishing, Inc.), 1998.

GRAMMAR **PRESENTATION**

SIMPLE PRESENT TENSE	PRESENT PROGRESSIVE

AFFIRMATIVE STATEMENTS

People often **choose** relatives' names.
Megan always **helps** me.

AFFIRMATIVE STATEMENTS

Today, people **are choosing** unisex names.
Megan **is helping** me today.

NEGATIVE STATEMENTS

They **don't study** together.
John **doesn't read** very often.

NEGATIVE STATEMENTS

They **aren't studying** together now.
John **isn't reading** at the moment.

YES / NO QUESTIONS

Do you usually **get up** early?
Does he **read** the *Times*?

YES / NO QUESTIONS

Are you **getting up** early these days?
Is he **reading** the *Times* now?

SHORT ANSWERS

Yes, I **do**.
Yes, he **does**.

No, I **don't**.
No, he **doesn't**.

SHORT ANSWERS

Yes, I **am**.
Yes, he **is**.

No, I**'m not**.
No, he **isn't**.

WH- QUESTIONS

How **do** they **feel**?
Why **does** she **smile** so much?

WH- QUESTIONS

How **are** they **feeling** these days?
Why **is** she **smiling**?

NOTES

EXAMPLES

1. The **present progressive** describes what is happening <u>right now</u> or <u>in the extended present</u> (for example, *nowadays, this month, these days, this year*).

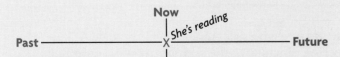

The **simple present tense** describes what <u>generally happens</u> (but not necessarily right now).

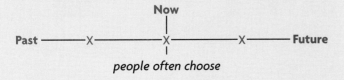

A: Where's Pat?
B: In the den. She**'s reading** a book on baby names.

A: What**'s** Bob **doing** *these days*?
B: He**'s working** on a new project.

- People *often* **choose** names from books.
- We *never* **use** nicknames.
- The paper *usually* **arrives** at 7:00 A.M.

(continued on next page)

2. Remember that **non-action verbs** (also called stative verbs) are <u>not usually used in the progressive</u> even when they describe a situation that exists at the moment of speaking.

Non-action verbs describe emotions (*love*, *hate*), mental states (*remember*, *understand*), wants (*need*, *want*), perceptions (*hear*, *see*), appearance (*look*, *seem*), and possession (*have*, *own*).

(*See Appendix 2 on page A-2 for a list of non-action verbs*.)

- I **want** to choose a special name.
  NOT ~~I'm wanting to choose a special name.~~

- I **hate** my nickname.
- **Do** you **remember** her name?
- Jan **wants** to change her name.
- She **seems** determined.

3. The **simple present tense** is used to talk about situations that are <u>not connected to time</u>—for example, scientific facts, and physical laws.

- Water **freezes** at 32°F / 0°C.
- It **boils** at 212°F / 100°C.
- The Earth **orbits** the sun.

4. The **simple present tense** is often used <u>in summaries</u> such as book or movie reviews.

- In her book, Browder **describes** the meaning of names. She also **explores** the psychological effects of names.

5. The **present progressive** is often used with *always* to express a <u>repeated action</u>.

USAGE NOTE: We often use the present progressive to express a negative reaction to a situation.

- She**'s** *always* **smiling**. That's why we call her "Sunshine."

- He**'s** *always* **calling** me "Sweetie." I wish he'd stop.

REFERENCE NOTES
For **spelling rules** on forming the **present progressive**, see Appendix 17 on page A-7.
For **spelling rules** on forming the third person singular of the **simple present** tense, see Appendix 18 on page A-8.
For **pronunciation rules** for the **simple present** tense, see Appendix 24 on page A-10.

FOCUSED PRACTICE

1 DISCOVER THE GRAMMAR

Read this short review of another baby-name book. Underline all the present progressive verbs and circle all the simple present tense verbs.

<u>Are you looking</u> for an interesting, original name for your baby? (Do you want) to avoid choosing the same name as all the neighbors' kids? Maybe you're writing a romance novel and you need an exciting name for your hero. Or perhaps you're searching for the perfect name for your pet. In any case, *Beyond Jennifer and Jason,* a new book by Marvella Whitman, is the source for you. Along with tried and true names like Tiffany and Adam, the author lists fascinating ones such as Adoracion and Slade. Whitman, a historian, tells stories associated with many names, and she clearly feels their magic. In addition to an alphabetical listing of names, this book includes origins, meanings, and pronunciations. It also gives each name a popularity rating. Whitman is currently working on a history of cross-cultural dating customs.

2 PARTY TALK   Grammar Notes 1–3, 5

Complete the conversations with the correct form of the verbs in parentheses. Choose between the simple present tense and the present progressive.

1. **IANTHA:** Hi, I'm Iantha.

   AL: Nice to meet you, Iantha. I'm Alan, but my friends _____*call*_____ me Al.
   a. (call)

   Iantha is an unusual name. Where _____ it _____ from?
   b. (come)

   IANTHA: It's Greek. It _____ "violet-colored flower."
   c. (mean)

   AL: That's pretty. What _____ you _____, Iantha?
   d. (do)

   IANTHA: Well, I usually _____ computer equipment, but right now
   e. (sell)

   I _____ at a flower shop. My uncle _____ it.
   f. (work)   g. (own)

   AL: You _____! I _____ it's true that names _____
   h. (joke)   i. (guess)   j. (influence)

   our lives!

2. **MARIO:** I _____ to find Greg Costanza. _____ you _____ him?
   a. (try)   b. (know)

   BELA: Greg? Oh, you _____ Lucky. That's his nickname. Everyone
   c. (mean)

   _____ him Lucky because he _____ things.
   d. (call)   e. (always / win)

(continued on next page)

3. **Lola:** I _____ that you _____ a baby. Have you decided on a
a. (hear)   b. (expect)

name yet?

Vanya: We _____ naming the baby Mangena. What _____ you
c. (think of)

_____ that name?
d. (think about)

Lola: It _____ pretty. How _____ you _____ it?
e. (sound)   f. (spell)

4. **Rosa:** Would you like a cup of coffee, Dr. Ho?

Dr. Ho: Oh. No, thanks. It _____ delicious, but I _____ coffee.
a. (smell)   b. (not drink)

Rosa: Well, how about a cup of tea, then? The water _____.
c. (boil)

Dr. Ho: OK. Thanks.

Rosa: Why _____ water _____ so quickly here, Dr. Ho?
d. (boil)

Dr. Ho: In the mountains, water _____ at a lower temperature.
e. (boil)

3 EDITING

*Read this posting to a class electronic bulletin board. Find and correct eleven
mistakes in the use of the present progressive and the simple present tense. The
first mistake is already corrected.*

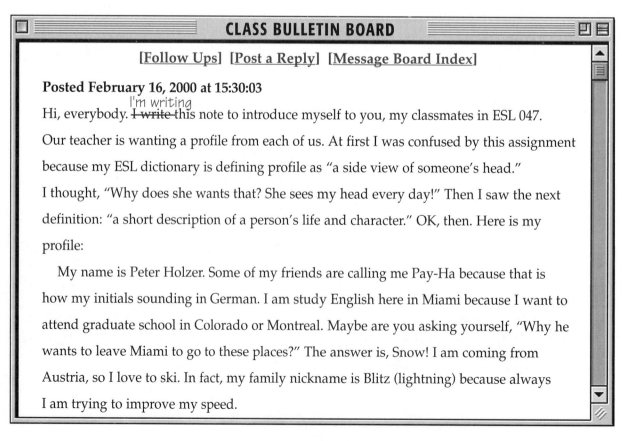

CLASS BULLETIN BOARD

[Follow Ups] [Post a Reply] [Message Board Index]

Posted February 16, 2000 at 15:30:03

Hi, everybody. ~~I write~~ *I'm writing* this note to introduce myself to you, my classmates in ESL 047.

Our teacher is wanting a profile from each of us. At first I was confused by this assignment

because my ESL dictionary is defining profile as "a side view of someone's head."

I thought, "Why does she wants that? She sees my head every day!" Then I saw the next

definition: "a short description of a person's life and character." OK, then. Here is my

profile:

   My name is Peter Holzer. Some of my friends are calling me Pay-Ha because that is

how my initials sounding in German. I am study English here in Miami because I want to

attend graduate school in Colorado or Montreal. Maybe are you asking yourself, "Why he

wants to leave Miami to go to these places?" The answer is, Snow! I am coming from

Austria, so I love to ski. In fact, my family nickname is Blitz (lightning) because always

I am trying to improve my speed.

COMMUNICATION PRACTICE

4 **LISTENING**

Listen to two classmates discuss these photographs. Then listen again and label each photograph with the correct name from the box.

~~Alex~~   Bertha   "Bozo"   Karl   Red   "Sunshine"   Vicki

a. _____

b. _____

c. _____

d. _____Alex_____

e. _____

f. _____

⑤ GETTING TO KNOW YOU

Write down your full name on a piece of paper. Your teacher will collect all the names and redistribute them. Walk around the room. Introduce yourself to other students and try to find the person whose name you have on your piece of paper.

EXAMPLE:

A: Hi. I'm Jelena.
B: I'm Eddy.
A: I'm looking for Kadin Al-Tattany. Do you know him?
B: I think that's him over there.
　　　　OR
　　Sorry, I don't.

When you find the person you are looking for, find out about his or her name. You can ask some of these questions:

What does your name mean?

Which part of your name is your family name?

Do you use a title? (Ms., Miss, Mrs., Mr., . . .)

What do your friends call you?

Do you have a nickname?

What do you prefer to be called?

How do you feel about your name?

Other: _____

EXAMPLE:

A: What does Kadin mean?
B: It means "friend" or "companion." It's Arabic.
　　　　OR
　　I don't know what it means.

You can also ask some general questions such as:

Where do you come from?

Where are you living now?

Why are you studying English?

Other: _____

Finally, introduce your classmate to the rest of the class.

EXAMPLE:

A: This is Henka Krol. Henka comes from Poland.
　　Her name means "ruler of the house or home." . . .

⑥ WRITING

Write a profile to introduce yourself to your class. Write about your name, your interests and hobbies, and your plans. Use the profile in Exercise 3 as a model.

EXAMPLE:

My name is Thuy Nguyen, but my American friends call me Tina.

SIMPLE PAST TENSE AND PAST PROGRESSIVE

GRAMMAR IN CONTEXT

BEFORE YOU READ Look at the photos. Which couples do you recognize?
What do you know about them?

Read this article about four famous couples.

SUPER COUPLES

BEARING LOIS IN HIS ARMS
SUPERMAN HEADS TOWARD
THE CITY — —

Superman
and Lois Lane

Cover Story by DENNIS BROOKS

IT'S A BIRD . . . , it's a plane . . . , it's Superman!
Disguised as Clark Kent, this world-famous
character **met** Lois Lane while the two **were working**
as newspaper reporters for the *Daily Planet*. At first
Lois **wasn't** interested in mild-mannered Kent—she
wanted to cover stories about "The Man of Steel." In
time, she **changed** her mind. When Kent **proposed**,
Lois **accepted**. (And she **didn't** even **know** he was
Superman!)

   Like Superman and Lois Lane, some names just
seem to belong together: Marie and Pierre Curie,
Gloria and Emilio Estefan, or Ekaterina Gordeeva and
Sergei Grinkov. What **were** these other super couples
doing when they **met**? What **did** they **accomplish**
together? Find out on the next page.

(continued on next page)

WHEN SHE **WAS** 24, Maria Sklodowska **left** Poland and **moved** to Paris. While she **was studying** at the Sorbonne, she **met** physicist Pierre Curie. She **was going to return** to her country after her studies, but the two scientists **fell** in love and **got** married. While they **were raising** their two daughters, they **were** also **doing** research on radioactivity. In 1903, the Curies **won** the Nobel Prize in physics for their discoveries. Then, in 1906, a horse-drawn carriage **hit** and **killed** Pierre while he **was** out **walking**. When Marie **recovered** from the shock of his death, she **put** all her efforts into continuing their work. In 1911, she **received** her second Nobel Prize, this time for chemistry.

Marie and Pierre Curie

Gloria and Emilio Estefan

CONGA! In 1985 millions of people **were listening** to this hit song. It **made** singer Gloria Estefan and bandleader Emilio Estefan international stars. Born in Cuba, Gloria **was** only 16 months old when she and her family **moved** to the United States. By that time she **was** already **showing** musical talent. She first **met** Emilio when he **went** to speak to her high school music class. Soon after, he **convinced** her to join his group. The two **married** a few years later. In 1990 while they **were enjoying** their success, Gloria **broke** her back in a traffic accident. She **recovered** and **went on** to win many awards for her Spanish and English songs.

SHE **WAS ONLY** 11 and he **was** 15 when they **met** at a sports school in the former Soviet Union. Their coaches **brought** them together as skating partners, but off the ice Sergei **didn't pay** much attention to "Katia." It **wasn't** until they **won** their first Olympic Gold Medal in 1989 that the two **fell** in love. World-famous skaters Ekaterina Gordeeva and Sergei Grinkov **thrilled** their fans when they **married** two years later. They **had** a baby girl and **won** another Olympic Gold. Their life **seemed** perfect. Then one day Sergei **collapsed** while they **were practicing**. He **died** an hour later. Today Gordeeva is continuing her career as a solo skater.

Ekaterina Gordeeva and Sergei Grinkov

GRAMMAR **PRESENTATION**

SIMPLE PAST TENSE

PAST PROGRESSIVE

AFFIRMATIVE STATEMENTS

Marie **got** her degree in 1893.
Lois and Clark **married** in June.

AFFIRMATIVE STATEMENTS

She **was studying** at the Sorbonne in 1892.
They **were writing** for a newspaper.

NEGATIVE STATEMENTS

Sergei **didn't fall** in love right away.
Lois **didn't like** Clark at first.

NEGATIVE STATEMENTS

He **wasn't paying** attention to Katia.
She **wasn't looking** for a husband.

YES / NO QUESTIONS

Did he **teach** physics?
Did they **work** together?

YES / NO QUESTIONS

Was he **teaching** in 1892?
Were they **doing** research?

SHORT ANSWERS

Yes, he **did**.
Yes, they **did**.

No, he **didn't**.
No, they **didn't**.

SHORT ANSWERS

Yes, he **was**.
Yes, they **were**.

No, he **wasn't**.
No, they **weren't**.

WH- QUESTIONS

Who **introduced** them?
When **did** they **meet**?

WH- QUESTIONS

Who **was coaching** them?
When **were** they **attending** sports school?

SIMPLE PAST AND SIMPLE PAST

They **fell** in love when they **met**.

PAST PROGRESSIVE AND PAST PROGRESSIVE

She **was doing** research while he **was teaching**.

SIMPLE PAST AND PAST PROGRESSIVE

She **met** him while she **was studying**.

PAST PROGRESSIVE AND SIMPLE PAST

She **was studying** when she **met** him.

NOTES	**EXAMPLES**

1. Use the **past progressive** (also called the past continuous) to describe an action that <u>was in progress</u> at a specific time in the past. The action began before the specific time and may or may not continue after the specific time.

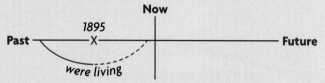

Use the **simple past tense** to describe an action or state that <u>was completed</u> at a specific time in the past.

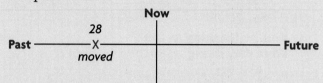

(See Appendix 1 on pages A1–A2 for a list of irregular past tense verbs.)

REMEMBER! Non-action verbs are not usually used in the progressive.

- The Curies **were living** in Paris in 1895.
- She **was expecting** a baby in the fall.

- Marie **moved** to Paris when she was 28.
- They **had** their first child in September.

- Marie **had** a degree in physics. NOT Marie ~~was having~~ a degree in physics.

2. Use the **past progressive** with the **simple past tense** to talk about an action that was <u>interrupted by another action</u>. Use the simple past tense for the interrupting action.

You can use *while* (with the past progressive) or *when* (with the simple past) to connect the two actions.

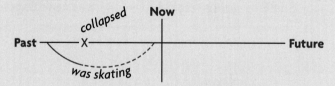

- They **were driving** when the accident **occurred**.

- *While* he **was skating**, he **collapsed**.

  OR

- He **was skating** *when* he **collapsed**.

3. You can use the **past progressive with** *while* **(or** *when***)** to talk about <u>two actions in progress at the same time</u> in the past. Use the past progressive in both clauses.

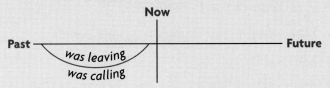

- *While* Clark **was leaving** the newsroom, Lois **was calling** the police.
- *When* she **wasn't looking**, he **was changing** into Superman.

4. **BE CAREFUL!** Sentences with two clauses in the simple past tense have a very different meaning from sentences with one clause in the simple past tense and one clause in the past progressive.

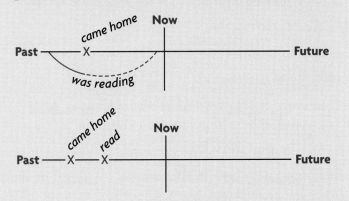

- When he **came** home, she **was reading** the paper.
  (*First she started reading the paper. Then he came home.*)

- When he **came** home, she **read** the paper.
  (*First he came home. Then she read the paper.*)

5. Use *was* or *were going to* to talk about <u>future plans or expectations that existed in the past</u>. (This structure is also known as *future in the past*.)

Notice that we often use *was* or *were going to* when things we expected to happen did not happen.

- It was 1959. Gloria and her family **were going to leave** Cuba.

- Gloria **was going to be** a psychologist, but she became a performer instead.

FOCUSED PRACTICE

1 DISCOVER THE GRAMMAR

*Read these people's descriptions of how they met their friends or spouses. Decide if the statement that follows each description is **True (T)** or **False (F)**.*

1. LUCKY: I was riding home on my bike when I saw Elena on a park bench.

____F____ Lucky saw Elena before he got on his bike.

2. LEE: I was going to rent the apartment alone. Then I met my roommate Cho.

_____ Lee rented the apartment alone.

3. ROD: I was climbing a mountain when I met my best friend, Ian.

_____ Ian was on the mountain.

4. MARIE: How did I meet Philippe? I was sitting at home when the phone rang. When I answered it, it was the wrong number, but we spoke for an hour!

_____ Marie knew Philippe before they spoke on the phone.

5. DON: When I first met Ana, I was working in a restaurant. She was a customer.

_____ Don started his restaurant job after he met Ana.

6. TONY: How did I meet my wife? Actually, it was kind of like a blind date. My cousins invited her to dinner while I was living at their place.

_____ Tony moved in with his cousins after he met his wife.

7. MONICA: I was going to take a morning ESL class, but I changed my mind at the last minute. I'm glad I did, because Dania was taking the afternoon class. That's how we met.

_____ Monica took the afternoon ESL class.

2 HAPPY ENDINGS / SAD ENDINGS   Grammar Notes 1–5

*Complete these conversations. Use the correct form of the verbs in parentheses—past progressive, simple past tense, or **was / were going to**.*

1.   **PAZ:** What _____were_____ you_____looking_____ at just then? You
                                              a. (look)

_____.
   b. (smile)

EVA: I _____ the video of Matt and Nicole's wedding. They're such a
                    c. (watch)

great couple.

PAZ: How _____ they _____?
                                              d. (meet)

EVA: At my daughter's graduation party. It's funny, I _____ Matt. At the
                                                              e. (not invite)

last minute I _____ my mind and _____ him to come.
                      f. (change)   g. (ask)

2. LILY: Guess what! I _____ Gloria Estefan at Club Rio last night.

a. (see)

We _____ in the door while she _____.

b. (go)   c. (leave)

TONY: _____ you _____ her autograph?

d. (get)

LILY: Yes. And when she _____ writing it, she _____ me

e. (finish)   f. (give)

her pen.

3. VAL: Your Superman Web page is great. When _____ you

_____ a Superman fan?

a. (become)

DEE: As a kid I _____ always _____ comics. In fact, I

b. (read)

_____ graphic arts in college, but I _____ change my

c. (study)   d. (have to)

plans when my father _____.

e. (die)

VAL: That's too bad. I _____ on your Web page that you collect comics.

f. (notice)

DEE: That's right. Last week I _____ a first edition for $500!

g. (sell)

4. EVA: Why _____ you _____ when I _____ in?

a. (cry)   b. (come)

MAI: I _____ a really sad movie about the Curies.

c. (watch)

EVA: Oh, I'm sorry. I _____ you.

d. (interrupt)

MAI: No problem. When the doorbell _____, I just _____

e. (ring)   f. (press)

the record button on my VCR.

5. TARO: What _____ you _____ when you _____

a. (do)   b. (break)

your arm?

KIWA: I _____ with my boyfriend. We _____ to be Gordeeva

c. (ice-skate)   d. (pretend)

and Grinkov. Jon _____ me while he _____ to lift me

e. (drop)   f. (try)

over his head!

6. LARA: I _____ you last night, but you _____ home.

a. (call)   b. (not be)

VLAD: Right. I _____ home, but I _____ go to the lab instead.

c. (stay)   d. (decide)

LARA: How come?

VLAD: I _____ a science article when I _____ a great idea for

e. (read)   f. (get)

an experiment.

3 TIME LINE

This time line shows some important events in Monique's life. Use the time line and the cues below to make sentences about her. Use **when** *or* **while.**

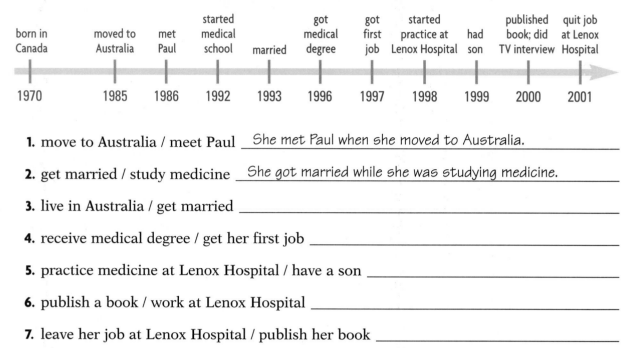

born in Canada	moved to Australia	met Paul	started medical school	married	got medical degree	got first job	started practice at Lenox Hospital	had son	published book; did TV interview	quit job at Lenox Hospital
1970	1985	1986	1992	1993	1996	1997	1998	1999	2000	2001

1. move to Australia / meet Paul <u>She met Paul when she moved to Australia.</u>

2. get married / study medicine <u>She got married while she was studying medicine.</u>

3. live in Australia / get married _____

4. receive medical degree / get her first job _____

5. practice medicine at Lenox Hospital / have a son _____

6. publish a book / work at Lenox Hospital _____

7. leave her job at Lenox Hospital / publish her book _____

8. do a TV interview / publish her book _____

4 EDITING

Read Monique's letter to a friend. Find and correct eleven mistakes in the use of the simple past tense and the past progressive. The first mistake is already corrected.

Dear Crystal,

I was writing chapter two of my new book when I ~~was thinking~~ thought of you. The last time I saw you, you walked down the aisle to marry Dave. That was more than two years ago. How are you? How is married life?

A lot has happened in my life since that time. While I worked at Lenox Hospital, I began writing. In 2000, I was publishing a book on women's health issues. It was quite successful here in Australia. I even got interviewed on TV. When I was getting a contract to write a second book, I decided to quit my hospital job to write full time. That's what I'm doing now. Paul, too, has had a career change. While I was writing, he was attending law school. He was getting his degree last summer.

Oh, the reason I thought of you while I wrote was because the chapter was about rashes. Remember the time you were getting that terrible rash? We rode our bikes when you were falling into a patch of poison ivy. And that's how you met Dave! When you were falling off the bike, he offered to give us a ride home. Life's funny, isn't it?

Well, please write soon, and send my love to Dave. I miss you!

Monique

COMMUNICATION PRACTICE

5 LISTENING

Listen to a woman explain how she met her husband. Then listen again and circle the letter of the series of pictures that illustrate her story.

a.

b.

c.

6 FIRST ENCOUNTERS

Work in small groups. Think about the first time you met someone important to you: a best friend, teacher, boyfriend or girlfriend, husband or wife. Tell your classmates about the meeting. What were you doing? What happened then?

> **EXAMPLE:**
> I was walking to class when this guy came over and asked me for the time. . . .

7 THE TIMES OF YOUR LIFE

Draw a time line with some important events in your life. Show it to a classmate. Answer your classmate's questions.

Event

Year

> **EXAMPLE:**
> **A:** How did you meet your girlfriend?
> **B:** She was working in my school library.

8 WRITING

Write about a relationship that is important to you. How did you meet? What were you doing when you met? Describe some events in the relationship.

Present Perfect, Present Perfect Progressive, and Simple Past Tense

GRAMMAR **IN CONTEXT**

BEFORE YOU READ   Look at the picture. What are the people doing? Have you ever participated in an adventure sport?

Read this personal Web page.

JUMPING FOR JOY

Hi, I'm Jason Barricelli and thanks for visiting my website. I**'ve been building** this site for a while, and I'm almost finished. I**'ve written** this page to introduce myself.

I**'ve** always **been** a work-hard, play-hard kind of guy. I **grew up** in Idaho, and my family **did** a lot of adventure sports like rock climbing and white-water rafting. Lately, people **have named** these activities "extreme sports," but to me they**'ve** always **seemed** just like normal fun.

I**'ve been working** on a master's degree for a couple of years, but I still take time out to play. Since I **moved** to San Diego, I**'ve gone** on six scuba dives, and last year, I finally **learned** how to skydive. This month, I**'ve** already **completed** five jumps.

Yes, I have a social life too. In fact, last month I **got** engaged to a fantastic woman. Here's a picture of the two of us jumping together.

We've been falling for an awfully long time!

Joy **hasn't been skydiving** that long, but she **wanted** to celebrate our engagement with a jump.

I**'ve included** more pictures of this historic jump. Just click on the plane to continue.

My Family   Other Interests   Home   Next . . .

GRAMMAR **PRESENTATION**

SIMPLE PAST TENSE

PRESENT PERFECT
PRESENT PERFECT PROGRESSIVE

AFFIRMATIVE STATEMENTS

I **built** a website last month.

AFFIRMATIVE STATEMENTS

I**'ve built** a website.
I**'ve been building** a website this month.

NEGATIVE STATEMENTS

She **didn't make** a dive last week.

NEGATIVE STATEMENTS

She **hasn't made** many dives.
She **hasn't been making** many dives lately.

YES / NO QUESTIONS

Did they **learn** to skydive?

YES / NO QUESTIONS

Have they **learned** to land safely?
Have they **been learning** to land safely?

SHORT ANSWERS

Yes, they **did**.
No, they **didn't**.

SHORT ANSWERS

Yes, they **have**.
No, they **haven't**.

WH- QUESTIONS

Who **taught** him to dive?

WH- QUESTIONS

Who**'s taught** him to dive?
Who**'s been teaching** him to dive?

NOTES	EXAMPLES
1. The **present perfect** and **present perfect progressive** (also called the present perfect continuous) are used to talk about things that <u>started in the past, continue up to the present,</u> and may continue into the future. 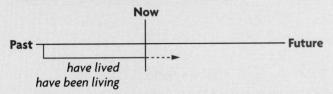	• I**'ve lived** in Idaho my whole life. OR • I**'ve been living** in Idaho my whole life. *(I was born in Idaho, and I'm still living there.)*
We often use the present perfect and the present perfect progressive with *for* or *since*. Use *for* + <u>a length of time</u> to show how long a present condition has been true. Use *since* + <u>a point in time</u> to show when a present condition started.	• He**'s lived** in Idaho *for three years*. • He**'s lived** in Idaho *since 1999*. • He**'s lived** there *since he graduated*.
REMEMBER! Non-action (stative) verbs are not usually used in the progressive. *(See Appendix 1 on pages A1–A2 for a list of irregular past participles used in forming the present perfect.)*	• He**'s known** Joy for a long time. NOT ~~He's been knowing Joy for a long time.~~
2. The **simple past tense** is used to talk about things that happened and were <u>completed in the past</u>. 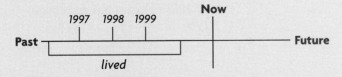	• I **lived** in Idaho for three years. *(I no longer live in Idaho.)*
We often use the simple past tense with *ago* to show when the past condition started. *(See Appendix 1 on pages A1–A2 for a list of irregular past tense verbs.)*	• I **moved** there *ten years ago*.

(continued on next page)

3. The **present perfect** is used to talk about things that happened at an <u>unspecified time in the past</u>.

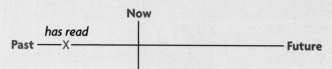

> ▶ **BE CAREFUL!** *She's read a book* and *She's been reading a book* have very different meanings.

The **present perfect** (without *for* or *since*) refers to an activity or state that is <u>finished</u>.

The **present perfect progressive** shows that an activity is <u>unfinished</u>.

The **present perfect progressive** can also indicate that the action is <u>temporary</u>.

- She**'s read** a book about skydiving.
  (*We don't know exactly when she read the book, or the time is not important.*)

- She**'s read** a book about skydiving.
  (*She's finished the book.*)

- She**'s been reading** a book about skydiving.
  (*She's still reading it.*)

- I**'ve been living** in Idaho for three years, but next month I'm moving to San Diego.

4. The **simple past tense** is used to talk about things that happened at <u>a specific time in the past</u>.

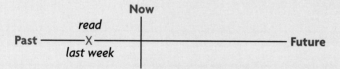

> ▶ **BE CAREFUL!** Do not use the present perfect with specific past time expressions except after *since*.

- I **read** a book about skydiving *last week*.

- She **took** lessons *last year*.
  NOT ~~She has taken lessons last year.~~

- She **has taken** lessons *since 1999*.

5. Use the **present perfect** to talk about things that have happened <u>in a time period that is not finished</u>, such as *today, this month, this year*.

- She**'s had** three cups of coffee *this morning*.
  (It's still this morning, and it is possible that she will have some more.)

▶ **BE CAREFUL!** We don't usually use the present perfect progressive to talk about <u>how many times</u> someone has done something or <u>how many things</u> someone has done.

- She**'s typed** two e-mails this morning.
  NOT ~~She's been typing two e-mails this morning.~~

6. Use the **simple past tense** to talk about things that happened in a <u>time period that is finished</u>, such as *yesterday, last month, last year*.

- She **typed** three e-mails *yesterday*.
  (Yesterday is finished.)

▶ **BE CAREFUL!** Some time expressions such as *this morning, this month,* or *this year* can refer to a finished or unfinished time period.

Use the **present perfect** if the time period is <u>unfinished</u>.

- It's 10:00 A.M. She**'s typed** three e-mails *this morning*.
  (The morning is not over.)

Use the **simple past tense** if the time period is <u>finished</u>.

- It's 1:00 P.M. She **typed** three e-mails *this morning*.
  (The morning is over. It is now afternoon.)

FOCUSED PRACTICE

1 **DISCOVER THE GRAMMAR**

Read this marriage announcement from a newspaper. Underline all the present perfect verbs. Circle all the simple past tense verbs.

Weddings

Joy Anne Margolyes,
Jason Barricelli

Joy Anne Margolyes, a daughter of Rosemary Peck-Margolyes and William J. Margolyes of San Marino, California, married Jason Barricelli, a son of Rose and Anthony Barricelli of Boise, Idaho. The Honorable Mary Riggens, a justice of the peace, performed the ceremony at the Waterside Hotel yesterday in Greenville.

Ms. Margolyes, 29, has chosen to keep her own name. She has been an associate at the Los Angeles law firm of Miles, Shaker, & Lynch for two years. She graduated with honors from the University of California at Los Angeles and received a degree in law from Yale University. Recently, she has been teaching scuba diving in her free time. Her father owned a video corporation for 15 years. Her mother has taught special education at the high-school level for 20 years.

Mr. Barricelli, 27, graduated from the University of Idaho in 1997. He has been studying for a master's degree in social work at the University of California. In his free time he pursues his passion for skydiving. The groom's father has been a senior partner at a Boise accounting firm, Poler & Co., since 1967. His mother, who is retired, worked as a nurse for 30 years. The groom's previous marriage ended in divorce. The couple plan to go on a sky-diving honeymoon in the Caribbean.

Now read the statements and decide if they are **True (T)** *or* **False (F)**.

__F__   **1.** The bride is changing her name.

_____   **2.** Joy Margolyes works for a law firm.

_____   **3.** She teaches scuba diving.

_____   **4.** Her father owns a video corporation.

_____   **5.** Her mother teaches special education.

_____   **6.** Jason Barricelli is attending the University of Idaho.

_____   **7.** He got his master's degree in 1997.

_____   **8.** The groom's father works at an accounting firm.

_____   **9.** The groom's mother works as a nurse.

_____   **10.** This is the groom's first marriage.

2 **TOY STORY**   **Grammar Notes 1–6**

Circle the correct verbs to complete this article.

MOVE OVER, BARBIE AND KEN!

Ty Warner (has been making)/ made toys
                        a.
since 1986. In 1992, he has gotten / got the idea to
                                b.
make animals that children could afford. The first nine

Beanie Babies® have appeared / appeared in stores
                        c.
just one year later. Pattie the Platypus and her eight companions have sold out / sold out
                                                                                d.
immediately. Ever since then, store owners have been having / had a hard time keeping
                                                        e.
Beanies on the shelves. In recent years, the fad has become / has been becoming an interna-
                                                        f.
tional craze. More than 2 billion fans have visited / have been visiting Ty's website, and more
                                                        g.
than one collector has paid / has been paying $3,000 for a rare Beanie. Which reminds me—I'd
                        h.
like to discuss some trades. Have you found / Have you been finding Iggy the Iguana yet?
                                                i.

3 **OTHER PEOPLE, OTHER INTERESTS**   **Grammar Notes 1–6**

*Complete these paragraphs about other people's interests. Use the correct form of
the verbs in parentheses—simple past tense, present perfect, or present perfect
progressive.*

1. May __has been taking__ photos ever since her parents _____ her a
        a. (take)   **b. (buy)**
camera when she _____ only ten. At first she only _____
                        c. (be)   **d. (take)**
color snapshots of friends and family, but then she _____ to black and
                                                        e. (change)
white. Lately she _____ a lot of nature photographs. This year she
                        f. (shoot)
_____ in three amateur photography contests. In fact, last month she
g. (compete)
_____ second prize for her night-time photo of a lightning storm.
h. (win)

(continued on next page)

2. Carlos _____ playing music when he
a. (began)

_____ an electric guitar for his twelfth
b. (get)

birthday. He _____ playing since. In fact, the
c. (not stop)

guitar _____ more than just a way of having
d. (become)

some fun with his friends. Last year he _____
e. (join)

a local band. Since then, they _____ all over
f. (perform)

town. So far this year, they _____ six concerts,
g. (give)

and they have plans for many more.

3. Kate _____ a beautiful old stamp last month. It is now part of the
a. (find)

collection she _____ on for the past two years. At first she just
b. (work)

_____ stamps from letters that she _____ from friends. After
c. (save)   d. (get)

a while, though, she _____ to look more actively for stamps. Lately, she
e. (begin)

_____ them from special stores and _____ stamps with other
f. (buy)   g. (trade)

collectors. So far she _____ over 200 stamps from all over the world.
h. (find)

---

④ EDITING

Read this Web page. Find and correct nine mistakes in the use of the present perfect, present perfect progressive, and the simple past tense. The first mistake is already corrected.

---

have been
I ~~am~~ collecting coins for several years now. I have started three years ago when I made my first

trip abroad. I was in Ecuador, and I have noticed that the coins there were very interesting. On

the day that we have left, I was going to try to spend them all. I changed my mind, though, and

took them home instead. When I have gotten home, I put them in a glass bowl in the living

room. Since that time my collection grew. I have asked everyone I know to bring me back coins

from their travels. My roommate, for example, just got back from China last night. He has been

bringing me more coins for my collection. So far I have been collecting forty coins from fifteen

countries. My goal is to get coins from every country in the world. It's been fun, but I think

I may want to get more serious about collecting. I have read a book about coin collecting.

When I am finished with it, I may join a club.

COMMUNICATION PRACTICE

❺ LISTENING

Joy and Jason have been planning their honeymoon trip. Look at their To Do list and listen to their phone conversation. Then listen again and check the things that they've already done.

To Do
- [ ] renew passports
- [x] pick up plane tickets
- [ ] read skydiving guide
- [ ] make reservations at Hotel Splendor
- [ ] stop mail for two weeks
- [ ] buy bathing suit (Joy)

❻ WHAT HAVE YOU DONE?

Make a list of things that you wanted to accomplish last week. Include things that you did and things that you still haven't done. Do not check any of the items. Exchange lists with a partner. Ask your partner questions about his or her list. Check the things that your partner has already done. Answer your partner's questions about your list. When you are done, check your answers together.

> **EXAMPLE:**
> **A:** Have you written to your aunt?
> **B:** Yes. I wrote her a letter last weekend, but I haven't mailed it yet.

❼ WHAT'S YOUR HOBBY?

Work in small groups. Ask and answer questions about your hobbies and interests.

> **EXAMPLE:**
> **A:** Do you have any hobbies?
> **B:** I collect stamps.
> **C:** How long have you been doing that?
> **B:** Since I came to this country.
> **D:** How many . . .

❽ WRITING

Write a few paragraphs about yourself for a personal Web page like the one on page 26. Tell about your interests and hobbies.

4 PAST PERFECT AND PAST PERFECT PROGRESSIVE

GRAMMAR IN CONTEXT

BEFORE YOU READ Have you ever watched a talk show? What kind of personality should a talk-show host have? What types of topics should the host discuss?

Read this article about talk-show host and actress Oprah Winfrey.

QUEEN OF TALK

Oprah Winfrey began speaking publicly in church when she was two. By the time she was twelve, she **had** already **decided** on a career. She wanted to be "paid to talk." In fact, it wasn't that long before she got her first radio job. Although she **hadn't had** any experience, she became a news reporter.

When Winfrey got her TV talk show in 1986, she **had** already **been** a TV news reporter and **had acted** in a major Hollywood movie, *The Color Purple*. Oprah's warm personality made her TV guests comfortable. Her stories on topics such as child abuse—Oprah, herself, **had been** a victim—touched the hearts of her audience. "The Oprah Winfrey Show" became so popular that by the late 1980s "Oprah" **had become** a household word.

In 1994 Winfrey decided that the quality of talk-show themes **had been getting** worse and worse. She promised to focus on more uplifting, meaningful issues such as runaway teenagers who return home. She also made a personal change. She **had** always **had** a weight problem, but in 1995 TV viewers saw a new Winfrey. She **had been dieting** and working out—and she **had lost** almost 90 pounds! She **had** also successfully **competed** in a Washington, D.C. marathon.

Today Oprah Winfrey is still going strong. In addition to her talk show, she continues to be involved in movies. In 1998 she starred in *Beloved*, which she **had been planning** to produce for ten years. When asked about her future, Winfrey said, "It's so bright it burns my eyes."

TAYLOR LEWIS

GRAMMAR **PRESENTATION**

PAST PERFECT

STATEMENTS		
SUBJECT	*HAD (NOT)* + **PAST PARTICIPLE**	
I You He She We You They	**had (not) decided** on **had (not) chosen***	a career by then.
It	**had (not) been**	a difficult decision.

CONTRACTIONS		
I had	=	**I'd**
you had	=	**you'd**
he had	=	**he'd**
she had	=	**she'd**
we had	=	**we'd**
they had	=	**they'd**
had not	=	**hadn't**

* See Appendix 1 on pages A1–A2 for a list of irregular past participles.

YES / NO QUESTIONS			
HAD	**SUBJECT**	**PAST PARTICIPLE**	
Had	I you he she we you they	**decided** on **chosen**	a career by then?
Had	it	**been**	a difficult decision?

SHORT ANSWERS		
AFFIRMATIVE		
Yes,	you I he she we you they	**had**.
Yes,	it	**had**.

SHORT ANSWERS		
NEGATIVE		
No,	you I he she we you they	**hadn't**.
No,	it	**hadn't**.

WH- QUESTIONS				
WH- **WORD**	*HAD*	**SUBJECT**	**PAST PARTICIPLE**	
Why	**had**	she	**decided**	to be a talk-show host?

(continued on next page)

Past Perfect Progressive

STATEMENTS		
SUBJECT	*HAD (NOT) BEEN + BASE FORM OF VERB + -ING*	
I You He She We You They	**had (not) been exercising***	regularly.
It	**had (not) been getting**	worse.

* See Appendix 17 on page A-7 for the spelling rules for progressive forms.

YES / NO QUESTIONS			
HAD	SUBJECT	*BEEN + BASE FORM OF VERB + -ING*	
Had	I you he she we you they	**been exercising**	regularly?
Had	it	**been getting**	worse?

SHORT ANSWERS		
AFFIRMATIVE		
Yes,	you I he she we you they	**had.**
Yes,	it	**had.**

SHORT ANSWERS		
NEGATIVE		
No,	you I he she we you they	**hadn't.**
No,	it	**hadn't.**

WH- QUESTIONS			
WH- WORD	*HAD*	SUBJECT	*BEEN + BASE FORM OF VERB + -ING*
How long	**had**	he	**been exercising?**

NOTES	EXAMPLES

1. Use the **past perfect** to show that something happened <u>before a specific time in the past</u>.

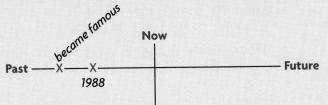

- By 1988 Oprah Winfrey **had become** famous.
- It was 1985. She **had** already **been** in a Hollywood film.

2. Use the **past perfect progressive** (also called the past perfect continuous) to talk about an action that was <u>in progress before a specific time in the past</u>. The progressive emphasizes the <u>process</u>, not the end result.

REMEMBER! Non-action (stative) verbs are not usually used in the progressive.

- It was 1990. Oprah **had been doing** her talk show for four years.

- It was 5:00 P.M. He **had had** a headache all day.
  NOT ~~He had been having a headache all day.~~

3. The **past perfect** and the **past perfect progressive** always show <u>a relationship with another past event</u>.

Use the past perfect or the past perfect progressive for the <u>earlier event</u>. Use the simple past tense for the later event.

- It *was* 1980. She **had been** an author for two years.
  (She was an author before 1980.)

- She **had been studying** at the university when she *got* her first TV job.
  (She was studying at the university. Then she got the job.)

(continued on next page)

▶ **BE CAREFUL!** In these sentences with *when*, notice the difference in meaning between:

a. the simple past tense and the past perfect

- *When* the show ended, she **left**.
  (First the show ended. Then she left.)
- *When* the show ended, she **had left**.
  (First she left. Then the show ended.)

b. the past progressive and the past perfect progressive

- *When* the race started, it **was raining** and the streets were wet.
  (It was still raining during the race.)
- *When* the race started, it **had been raining** and the streets were wet.
  (It wasn't raining during the race. It had already stopped.)

---

4. *Already, yet, ever,* and *never* are often used with the past perfect to <u>emphasize the event which occurred first</u>.

- I saw *The Color Purple* last night. I **had** *never* **seen** it before.
- Jason **had** *already* **seen** it.

---

5. When the <u>time relationship between two past events is clear</u> (as with *before, after,* and *as soon as*), it is common to use the **simple past tense for both events**. The meaning remains clear.

- *After* Oprah **had appeared** in *The Color Purple*, she **got** a part in another movie.
  OR
- *After* Oprah **appeared** in *The Color Purple*, she **got** a part in another movie.

---

6. We often use the past perfect and the past perfect progressive with *by* (a certain time).

- *By 1966* Oprah **had decided** on a career.
- *By the time I got home*, he **had been sleeping** for an hour.

---

7. We often use the **past perfect progressive** to <u>draw conclusions</u> based on evidence.

- She was out of breath. It was clear that she **had been running**.

FOCUSED PRACTICE

1 DISCOVER THE GRAMMAR

Read each numbered situation. Decide if the description which follows is **True (T)** *or* **False (F)**. *If there is not enough information to know, write a question mark* **(?)**.

1. When I got home, "The Oprah Winfrey Show" started.

___F___ First the Oprah show started. Then I got home.

2. When I got home, "The Oprah Winfrey Show" had started.

_____ First the Oprah show started. Then I got home.

3. Oprah invited the guest on her show because he had won the marathon.

_____ The guest won the marathon after his appearance on the show.

4. The guest had been explaining why he had entered the marathon.

_____ The guest's explanation was finished.

5. He had already lost 100 pounds when she interviewed him.

_____ He lost the weight before the interview.

6. By the end of the show, I had fallen asleep.

_____ I fell asleep after the show.

7. It was 7:00. He had been eating dinner.

_____ He finished dinner at 7:00.

8. It was 8:00. She had read the article about Oprah.

_____ She finished the article.

9. When I saw her, her eyes were red. She had been crying.

_____ She wasn't crying when I saw her.

10. When I went to bed, I had turned off the TV.

_____ I turned the TV off after I went to bed.

11. When the phone rang, the baby had been sleeping for an hour.

_____ The phone call woke the baby up.

12. By the time we finished talking, it had already turned light outside.

_____ First we finished talking. Then it turned light outside.

2 TIME LINE

*Look at some important events in Oprah Winfrey's career. Then complete the sentences below. Use the past perfect with **already** or **not yet**.*

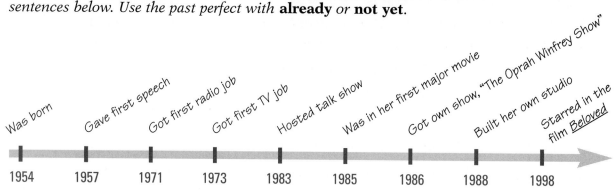

1. By 1958 Oprah _____had already given_____ her first speech.

2. By 1971 she _____ her first TV job.

3. By 1972 she _____ her first radio job.

4. By 1972 she _____ in a major movie.

5. By 1985 she _____ her own TV show, "The Oprah Winfrey Show."

6. By 1986 she _____ in a major movie

7. By 1987 she _____ her own studio, Harpo Productions.

8. By 2000 she _____ in the film *Beloved*.

3 A BUSY DAY

Look at this typical daily schedule for a TV talk-show host. Complete the questions about his schedule. Use the past perfect and give short answers.

7:00 A.M.	Arrive at studio
8:00	Review day's schedule
11:00	Discuss future shows with assistant producers
1:00 P.M.	Talk to wardrobe consultant
2:00	Hair and makeup
2:30	Meet the day's guests
3:00	Tape the show
4:30	Work out with trainer

1. It was 7:45. The host was on schedule.

   A: <u>Had he arrived</u> at the studio yet?

   B: <u>Yes, he had.</u>

2. At 7:30 the host was at his desk.

   A: _____ the day's schedule yet?

   B: _____

3. At 10:30 he was having coffee.

   A: _____ the day's schedule by that time?

   B: _____

4. At 11:30 he was discussing future shows with the assistant producers.

   A: _____ the wardrobe consultant yet?

   B: _____

5. It was 1:00. Everything was going according to schedule.

   A: _____ future shows with the assistant producers?

   B: _____

6. It was 2:00. He was on his way to makeup.

   A: _____ the day's guests by then?

   B: _____

7. It was 3:00. He was still on schedule.

   A: _____ the wardrobe consultant yet?

   B: _____

8. At 4:00 he had a late lunch.

   A: _____ the show yet?

   B: _____

9. He went to bed at 10:30.

   A: _____ with his trainer that day?

   B: _____

4 RUN FOR YOUR LIFE

Complete this story from a magazine article. Use the past perfect progressive form of the verbs in parentheses.

RUN FOR YOUR LIFE

On October 23, I ran the Boston Marathon with a partner, Marcia Davis. We __had been training__ together since
1. (train)
last year, and we _____
2. (plan)
to enter the race ever since we saw

Oprah in the Washington Marathon.

The start of the race was dramatic. Up to that point, we _____, but
3. (joke and laugh)

we were very serious when we lined up. I was so nervous I couldn't breathe. Marcia and

I _____ on those same streets for a couple of weeks, so at the beginning
4. (practice)

we did well. By the time we got to Heartbreak Hill, we _____ for almost four
5. (run)

hours, and I really believed we could finish. Then, halfway up the hill, Marcia stopped. She just

couldn't run anymore. We _____ to this race for so long that I didn't want
6. (look forward)

to go on alone, but Marcia wanted me to finish. When I got to the finish line, I saw Marcia. She

_____ for me for three hours. First we cried. Then we started talking about
7. (wait)

next year's marathon.

---

5 BACKGROUND INFORMATION

A talk-show host is trying to get some background information on a guest she is going to interview. Use time words and the words in parentheses to write questions with the past perfect progressive.

1. She won the marathon. (she / train a long time?)

   Had she been training a long time before she won the marathon?

2. This was her first win. (she / compete long?)

   _____

3. She tripped. (How long / she / run?)

_____

4. Photographers took pictures of her fall. (they / follow her?)

_____

5. She married her trainer. (How long / they / date?)

_____

6. She and her husband moved to Rome. (Where / they / live?)

_____

7. She quit her job to train full-time. (What kind of work / she / do?)

_____

8. At the post-marathon party her eyes were red. (she / cry?)

_____

6 **TROUBLED TEEN**   **Grammar Notes 1–3**

*Complete this psychologist's description of a patient who had appeared as a guest
on a TV talk show. Use the past perfect or past perfect progressive form of the
appropriate verbs in the box. Use the progressive form when possible.*

| arrest | become | bring | have | hurt | leave | lose | recommend | ~~see~~ |

I _____had seen_____ a hundred like him before. He sat on the couch and stared out the
       1.

window. He was only sixteen. His mother sat next to him. She _____ him
                                       2.

to see me. She _____ control of her son. Ever since his father
                 3.

_____ them four years before, she _____ trouble with her son.
    4.   5.

He _____ more and more angry and depressed. Recently he
      6.

_____ someone in a school fight. The police _____ him and
    7.   8.

_____ psychological counseling. The mother was afraid that he was going
    9.

to run away from home.

7 RUNAWAY CHILDREN   Grammar Notes 1–7

A talk-show host is interviewing a teenager. Complete the interview. Determine the correct order of the sentences in parentheses and use the past perfect or past perfect progressive to express the event that occurred first. Use the progressive form where possible.

HOST: When did you decide to run away from home?

GUEST: (I made up my mind to leave home. / I was ten.)

    <u>I had made up my mind to leave home</u> by the time <u>I was ten</u>.
                    1.

HOST: Why did you feel that you had to leave home?

GUEST: (My father beat me for the third time. / I was afraid to stay there.)

    After _____, _____.
                    2.

HOST: I see. Where did you go?

GUEST: To Miami.

    (I made plans with a friend there for a long time. / I left home.)

    Before _____, _____.
                    3.

HOST: But what about money? I mean, you were just ten!

GUEST: Well, my parents gave me a small allowance—about twenty dollars a month.

    (I bought my ticket. / I saved money for months.)

    _____ when _____.
                4.

HOST: So what happened when you arrived in Miami?

GUEST: (I got to Miami. / I already spent all my money.)

    By the time _____, _____.
                    5.

    (I tried not to eat on the trip. / I had very little money.)

    _____ because _____.
                6.

HOST: That's terrible. I want to hear more about that, but first we have to pause for these words.

8 EDITING

Read this short newspaper article about a famous Hispanic talk-show host. Find and correct ten mistakes in the use of the past perfect and the past perfect progressive. The first mistake is already corrected.

TELEVISION   Section 6 / Page 3

OVER THE YEARS, Cristina Saralegui has won a huge and faithful TV audience. By 1999, "El Show de Cristina" ~~has~~ **had** been on the air for ten years and had been winning 100 million faithful viewers. Today they call Cristina "Oprah with salsa." However, the two superstars of talk had very different childhoods.

Oprah with Salsa

Saralegui is from Cuba. Before the revolution, her family had owns several popular magazines there and had control Cuba's paper industry. Before she came to the United States, Saralegui had never watching television or imagined herself as a media star. Like her publisher grandfather, she had "ink in her veins." In the United States, Cristina majored in journalism. She has been working for her B.A. for almost four years when her father had spent her last semester's tuition for her brother's private school. She overcame this setback, however, and became a well-known magazine editor and writer. By the time Univision offered her "El Show," she had being writing and editing for almost twenty years. Like Oprah, Cristina had had a warm personality that gets people to talk. As a girl, she no had planned on becoming the host of the world's most popular talk show, but who could complain about such a fate?

COMMUNICATION PRACTICE

9 LISTENING

A talk-show host is interviewing a successful newspaper reporter. Listen to the reporter talk about some events in his life. Then read the list. Listen again and put the events in the correct chronological order.

_____ Richard and Molly moved to Chicago.

__1__ Richard started reporting crime news for a small-town newspaper.

_____ They found an apartment in Chicago.

_____ They talked about returning to Farmville.

_____ Molly got a part-time teaching job in Chicago.

_____ Richard published his first article about runaways.

10 ACCOMPLISHMENTS

Think about what you did yesterday. Indicate whether it was or wasn't a busy day. Complete the sentences. Then compare your day with a classmate's.

Yesterday was / wasn't a busy day for me.

1. By 9:00 A.M., _____

2. By the time I got to work / school, _____

3. By the time I had lunch, _____

4. By the time I left work / school, _____

5. By the time I had dinner, _____

6. By 9:00 P.M., I _____

7. By the time I went to bed, I had done so much / little that I felt _____

> **EXAMPLE:**
> **A:** By 9:00 A.M., I had made breakfast and taken the kids to school.
> **B:** By 9:00 A.M., I hadn't even gotten up!

11 THERE'S ALWAYS A FIRST TIME

Think about things you had never done before you began living here (or before a certain year). Have a class discussion and write some of the results on the board. Possible topics: food, sports, clothing, entertainment, transportation.

> **EXAMPLE:**
> Before I moved here (or before this year), I had never eaten pizza or popcorn.

12 DRAWING CONCLUSIONS

Work in pairs. Read these descriptions of people who had been at a party the night before. Say what you think had been happening **before** *the party. Use your imagination. Compare your answers with those of the rest of the class.*

EXAMPLE:
Alice's eyes were red.
A: Maybe she'd been crying.
B: Or maybe she'd been slicing onions.

1. Caryn was out of breath.

2. Mr. and Mrs. Jackson were frowning.

3. Carlos greeted everyone in Russian.

4. Margot's hair was all wet.

5. Jack couldn't walk straight.

6. Angela arrived an hour late.

13 THE NIGHT BEFORE

Imagine some friends stayed in your apartment when you were gone. When you came home, this is what you found. Work with a partner. Take turns describing what you saw and making guesses about what had been happening the night before you came home.

EXAMPLE:
There were CDs on the floor. Someone had been listening to music.

14 WRITING

Write a journal entry explaining an achievement, for example, getting your driver's license, learning a new skill, getting a job. In your journal entry, answer some of these questions: What had you been doing before your achievement? How did you prepare for it? Had you considered giving up before you succeeded?

PART
I

REVIEW OR SELFTEST

I. *Complete this magazine article by circling the correct verb forms.*

It's June. Nice weather arrived / (has arrived). And along with it, thoughts
1.

of barbecues. <u>Are you thinking / Do you think</u> of having one? Have you ever
2.

wondered about the origin of the term? According to Jeff Smith, author of

The Frugal Gourmet Cooks American, the term *barbecue* is not strictly an

American one, but only Americans ". . . <u>barbecue / are barbecuing</u>.
3.

The rest of the world simply <u>cooks / is cooking</u> meals over a fire."
4.

People <u>dispute / are disputing</u> the origin of the name. Smith
5.

<u>continues / is continuing</u>: "Some researchers <u>claim / are claiming</u> that the
6.   **7.**

word <u>comes / is coming</u> from Spanish and Haitian origins, and *barbaco*
8.

<u>refers / is referring</u> to a framework of sticks set upon posts." In the past,
9.

people <u>used / were using</u> this rack to roast meat or simply dry it. Other
10.

researchers <u>believe / are believing</u> that the origin of the term is the French
11.

phrase *barbe à queue,* which <u>means / is meaning</u> "from whisker (*barbe*) to
12.

tail (*queue*)." In the eighteenth century, people <u>roasted / have roasted</u> whole
13.

animals outdoors as well as indoors. Native Americans, too, used this

method of cooking outdoors. Whatever the origin of the term, a barbecue

<u>is / has been</u> now not only a means of cooking, but an event. According to
14.

Smith, by 1733 the process <u>had become / had been becoming</u> a party. People
15.

<u>stood / have stood</u> around the fire and <u>drank / had drunk</u> until the food
16.   **17.**

<u>was / had been</u> ready. That, with the addition of barbecue sauce,
18.

<u>sounds / is sounding</u> pretty much like what a barbecue <u>is / has been</u> today.
19.   **20.**

Source: Jeff Smith, *The Frugal Gourmet Cooks American* (New York: William Morrow and Company, 1987).

II. *Complete these conversations that take place at a barbecue by circling the correct verb forms.*

1. **A:** George! How are you? I (haven't seen)/ haven't been seeing you for a long time.
   a.

   What happens / 's been happening?
   b.

   B: Oh. Haven't you heard / Don't you hear? Betty and I moved / have moved last
   c.   **d.**

   month. We bought / were buying a house.
   e.

   A: Congratulations! I didn't know you had looked / had been looking for one. So,
   f.

   where are you now?

   B: In Rockport County. We were going to move / moved to Putnam County, but we
   g.

   have decided / decided on Rockport instead.
   h.

   A: Oh, how come?

   B: The school district is / has been better there.
   i.

   Have you ever been / Had you ever been to Rockport?
   j.

   A: No. It's near Putnam, isn't it?

   B: Uh-huh. Listen, we have / 're having a barbecue almost every weekend. You'll have
   k.

   to come to one.

   A: Thanks. I'd love to.

2. **A:** Have you tried / been trying the hot dogs? They're delicious.
   a.

   B: Yes. I 've already eaten / 've been eating four! The hamburgers smell / are smelling
   b.   **c.**

   good, too. I 'm thinking / think of having some of those.
   d.

   A: Well, just save some room for dessert. When I saw / see Betty in the kitchen a few
   e.

   minutes ago, she was taking some pies out of the oven. They looked / were looking
   f.

   great.

3. **A:** Have you met / Have you been meeting Jack's new wife?
   a.

   B: No. What's her name?

   A: Alice, but everyone calls / is calling her Al.
   b.

   B: What does she do / What is she doing?
   c.

(continued on next page)

A: Well, she's "between jobs." She <u>was working / worked</u> for a health insurance
d.

company when they <u>laid off / had laid off</u> a lot of employees. She was one of the
e.

people who <u>lost / was losing</u> their jobs.
f.

B: A lot of health insurance companies <u>have been cutting / had been cutting</u> their
g.

staff. That's too bad.

A: Yes. And she really <u>likes / liked</u> her job. Now she <u>'s trying / tries</u> to change careers.
h.   i.

4. **A:** <u>Have / Had</u> Al and Jack left for their honeymoon yet?
a.

B: Yes. As a matter of fact, I <u>got / 've gotten</u> a postcard from them yesterday. They
b.

<u>stay / 're staying</u> at the Hotel Splendor. It <u>sounds / 's sounding</u> great.
c.   d.

A: Well, they really <u>need / are needing</u> a vacation. They <u>hadn't been / haven't been</u>
e.   f.

away since they <u>met / were meeting</u> each other.
g.

B: I know. What <u>are they doing / do they do</u> there?
h.

A: Well, they <u>'re taking / take</u> scuba diving lessons, and they also
i.

<u>have been learning / had been learning</u> to water-ski.
j.

B: Sounds like fun.

III. *Circle the letter of the correct word(s) to complete each sentence.*

1. It was 1990, and I _____ in Denver for a year.   A **Ⓑ** C D
   (A) have been living   (C) was living
   (B) had been living   (D) lived

2. I met my wife, Meri, while I _____ some classes at the local college.   A B C D
   (A) was taking   (C) have been taking
   (B) had been taking   (D) am taking

3. She _____ a ski instructor at a resort at that time, and she was   A B C D
   working every weekend.
   (A) is   (C) was
   (B) has been   (D) had been

4. As soon as my friend introduced us, I _____ her about her name.   A B C D
   (A) asked   (C) had asked
   (B) have asked   (D) was asking

5. It _____ from *la mer,* the French word for *sea.*   A B C D
   (A) has come   (C) was coming
   (B) comes   (D) is coming

6. Her parents _____ her after their profession.   **A B C D**
   (A) name   (C) were naming
   (B) are naming   (D) had named

7. Before they _____ , they had both been diving instructors.   **A B C D**
   (A) had retired   (C) have retired
   (B) retired   (D) retire

8. After Meri turned eighteen, they _____ to give her diving lessons.   **A B C D**
   (A) always try   (C) were always trying
   (B) are always trying   (D) have always been trying

9. Meri has loved skiing _____ she was ten.   **A B C D**
   (A) from   (C) since
   (B) for   (D) while

10. When we _____ married, we had been dating about a year.   **A B C D**
   (A) get   (C) have gotten
   (B) had gotten   (D) got

11. We named our first daughter *Neige*, which _____ snow in French.   **A B C D**
   (A) is meaning   (C) means
   (B) meant   (D) has meant

12. Meri _____ our next daughter *Snowflake*, but I changed her mind.   **A B C D**
   (A) has been naming   (C) was going to name
   (B) is going to name   (D) had been naming

13. We _____ our third child now.   **A B C D**
   (A) are expecting   (C) expected
   (B) were expecting   (D) have expected

14. We've been reading baby-name books for weeks, but we _____ a   **A B C D**
name yet.
   (A) didn't choose   (C) hadn't chosen
   (B) don't choose   (D) haven't chosen

IV. *Complete the conversation with the correct form of the verbs in parentheses.*

A: Hi, I __'m_____ Matt Rotell, a friend of Alice's.
      1. (be)

B: Oh, yes. Alice _____ you the other day. Gee, you _____ like a
              2. (mention)   3. (not look)
detective.

A: Well, that's good, I _____ .
                   4. (guess)

B: Tell me, how _____ you _____ to become an undercover cop?
                                 5. (decide)

(continued on next page)

A: Well, when I _____ a kid, I _____ to read detective novels.
    6. (be)   7. (love)

By the time I _____ ten, I _____ every book in the Hardy Boys
      8. (be)   9. (read)

series. I _____ then that I _____ into law enforcement.
    10. (know)   11. (go)

B: But, according to Alice you _____ law school nowadays.
                  12. (attend)

A: Right. I _____ married last month. I _____ being on the police
      13. (get)   14. (not mind)

force when I _____ single, but ever since I _____ Nicole (that's
      15. (be)   16. (meet)

my wife) I _____ to do something less dangerous.
      17. (want)

B: I _____. By the way, _____ you _____ any luck yet
    18. (understand)   19. (have)

with those counterfeiters?

A: Well, I _____ them for more than a month now, but so far I _____
      20. (follow)   21. (not be able to)

catch them in the act. Sometimes I _____ that by the time they're caught,
                        22. (worry)

I'll have my law degree and I'll be defending them!

V. *Read this letter from Al. Find and correct ten mistakes in the use of verb tenses.*
The first mistake is already corrected.

Dear Nicole,
                 have been staying
    Jack and I ~~are staying~~ at the Splendor for almost a week already. We've been spending a
lot of time at the beach swimming and water-skiing, and I was taking scuba lessons in the hotel
pool for several days now. Yesterday, I am going to take my first dive from a boat.
Unfortunately, by the time we left shore, the weather has changed. We had to cancel the dive.
This morning it was still a little cloudy, so we did something different. We were deciding to visit
the Castle, an old pirate stronghold in Hideaway Bay. We had both read about it before we left,
and it sounded fascinating. So we've rented a motorbike and took off. They aren't having any
road signs here outside of town, so by the time we found the Castle, we've been driving for
about an hour. It was fun, though. When we were first seeing the Castle, dark clouds were
drifting over it. It really looked spooky and beautiful.
    Well, the weather has cleared, and Jack gets ready to go for a dive. I think I'll join him.
See you soon.
                                    Love,
                                    Al

▶ *To check your answers, go to the Answer Key on page 50.*

FROM GRAMMAR TO WRITING
EDITING FOR VERB TENSES

In a paragraph that includes more than one time frame (both present and past, for example) keep your meaning clear by using correct verb tenses. You should also use transitional words and phrases such as *now, at that time,* and *since then,* to signal a change in time.

EXAMPLE:
One day I **decided** to change my behavior. *Since then* I **have been** much happier.

1 *Complete this student's paragraph about a* phase *in her life (a temporary period when she had particular kinds of behavior and feelings). Use the correct form of the verbs in parentheses.*

MY "STUPID" PHASE

Today my friends _____think_____ of me as a serious student,
          1. (think)

but they _____ about my "stupid" phase. Until two years
          2. (not know)

ago, I _____ mostly about clothes and makeup, and I
          3. (think)

_____ people by their appearance and possessions. In that
4. (judge)

period of my life, my friends and I used to _____ in
                                              5. (speak)

stereotyped phrases. We _____ "Duhhh!" when anything
                          6. (say)

_____ obvious, and "As if!" when anything _____
7. (seem)   8. (appear)

impossible. I never _____ anyone to realize that I
                      9. (want)

_____ interested in school. I used to _____ the
10. (be)   11. (read)

newspaper secretly and _____ to be unprepared for tests.
                         12. (pretend)

One day, my older brother _____ into my room while I
                            13. (come)

_____ a serious novel. No one _____ ever
14. (read)

_____ me do that before, even though I _____ an
15. (see)   16. (be)

(continued on next page)

avid reader for years. He thought I _____ to be interested
                                          17. (pretend)

in the book in order to impress a new boyfriend. I _____
                                                        18. (get)

angry when he _____ at me, so I _____ a
                  19. (laugh)   20. (make)

decision. I _____ hiding my real interests. Since that day, I
              21. (stop)

_____ my news magazines proudly and _____
     22. (carry)   23. (express)

opinions in class. For the last two years I _____ for tests
                                                24. (prepare)

openly. Now I _____ for college, and I _____
                  25. (apply)   26. (feel)

proud of being a good student.

---

2 *Look at the paragraph in Exercise 1. Find the transitional words and phrases that signal a change.*

a. the simple present to the simple past ___Until two years ago_____

b. the habitual past to the simple past _____

c. the simple past to the present perfect (progressive) _____

d. the present perfect (progressive) to the present progressive _____

---

3 *Complete the chart with information from the paragraph in Exercise 1.*

Paragraph Section	Information	Verb Tense(s)
<u>Topic Sentence</u> • What the writer is like now	a serious student	simple present tense
<u>Body of the Paragraph</u> • habits and feelings during the phase • the event that ended the phase • behavior since the phase ended		
<u>Conclusion</u> • the results of the change		

4 *Before you write . . .*

- Work with a partner. Discuss a phase that each of you has experienced.
- Make a chart like the one in Exercise 3 about your own phase.

5 *Write a paragraph about a phase you went through. Use information from the chart you made in Exercise 3. Remember to use transitional words or phrases when you shift from one time to another.*

6 *Exchange paragraphs with a different partner. Underline the verbs in your partner's paragraph. Circle the transitional words and phrases. Then answer the following questions. Put a question mark (?) in the paragraph where something seems wrong or missing.*

   a. Does each verb correctly express the time the author is writing about?   Yes / No

   b. Is each verb formed correctly?   Yes / No

   c. Are the shifts from one time to another time clearly marked with transitional words or phrases?   Yes / No

7 *Discuss your editing suggestions with your partner. Then rewrite your own paragraph. Make any necessary corrections.*

PART I
REVIEW OR SELFTEST
ANSWER KEY

I. (Units 1–4)

2. Are you thinking
3. barbecue
4. cooks
5. dispute
6. continues
7. claim
8. comes
9. refers
10. used
11. believe
12. means
13. roasted
14. is
15. had become
16. stood
17. drank
18. was
19. sounds
20. is

II. (Units 1–4)

1. b. 's been happening
   c. Haven't you heard
   d. moved
   e. bought
   f. had been looking
   g. were going to move
   h. decided
   i. is
   j. Have you ever been
   k. have

2. a. tried
   b. 've already eaten
   c. smell
   d. 'm thinking
   e. saw
   f. looked

3. a. Have you met
   b. calls
   c. What does she do
   d. was working
   e. laid off
   f. lost
   g. have been cutting
   h. liked
   i. 's trying

4. a. Have
   b. got
   c. 're staying
   d. sounds
   e. need
   f. has been
   g. met
   h. are they doing
   i. 're taking
   j. have been learning

III. (Units 1–4)

2. A
3. C
4. A
5. B
6. D
7. B
8. C
9. C
10. D
11. C
12. C
13. A
14. D

IV. (Units 1–4)

2. mentioned
3. don't look
4. guess
5. did . . . decide
6. was
7. loved
8. was
9. had read
10. knew
11. was going to go OR would go
12. 're attending OR 've been attending
13. got
14. didn't mind
15. was
16. met
17. 've wanted
18. understand
19. have . . . had
20. 've been following
21. haven't been able to
22. worry

V. (Units 1–4)

Jack and I ~~are staying~~ *have been staying* at the Splendor for almost a week already. We've been spending a lot of time at the beach swimming and water-skiing, and I ~~was taking~~ *'ve been taking* scuba lessons in the hotel pool for several days now. Yesterday, I ~~am going to take~~ *was going to take* my first dive from a boat.

Unfortunately, by the time we left shore, the weather ~~has changed~~ *had changed*. We had to cancel the dive. This morning it was still a little cloudy, so we did something different. We ~~were deciding~~ *decided* to visit the Castle, an old pirate stronghold in Hideaway Bay. We had both read about it before we left, and it sounded fascinating. So ~~we've rented~~ *we rented* a motorbike and took off. They ~~aren't having~~ *don't have* any road signs here outside of town, so by the time we found the Castle, ~~we've been driving~~ *we'd been driving* for about an hour. It was fun, though. When we ~~were first seeing~~ *first saw* the Castle, dark clouds were drifting over it. It really looked spooky and beautiful.

Well, the weather has cleared, and Jack ~~gets~~ *is getting* ready to go for a dive. I think I'll join him.

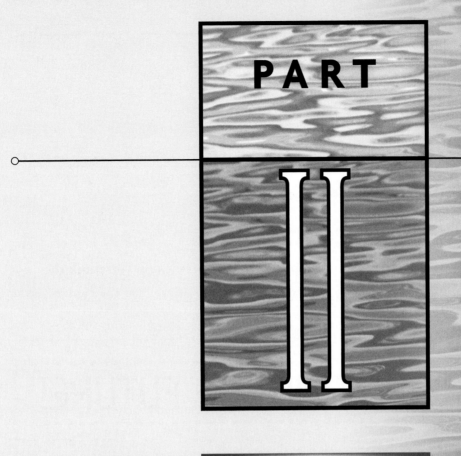

PART

II

FUTURE:
REVIEW AND EXPANSION

FUTURE AND FUTURE PROGRESSIVE

GRAMMAR **IN CONTEXT**

BEFORE YOU READ Look at the pictures. What topics do you think the article will discuss?

 Read this magazine article about the future.

PRESENTING THE FUTURE!

BY TRUONG LENH

The year 2000 was the beginning of a new millennium as well as a new century. With it came a powerful feeling that a new era had begun. Where **will** we **be working** in this new era? How **will** we **be traveling**? What **will** we **be wearing**? Here's what futurists predict.

WORK By the middle of the new millennium, most people **will** probably **be telecommuting**—working at home with computers. As a result, families **will be spending** more time together, and neighborhoods **will become** friendlier.

TRANSPORTATION For those times when you must go to the office, you**'ll** still **be using** a car. However the power sources **will be** a non-polluting combination of hydrogen and electricity. The freeway **will have** a guidance system so you **won't** actually **be driving** most of the distance. You'**ll be** free to listen to music or watch a movie.

(continued on next page)

HOME

Who**'ll be cleaning** house while Mom and Dad **are sitting** in front of their computers? Robots—tiny ones that look like insects and hang around in corners eating the dust. One Massachusetts Institute of Technology designer predicts that in just a few years, small, intelligent robots **are going to be doing** all the household chores.

CLOTHING

Well-dressed men and women **will look** like "Star Trek" officers. They **will be wearing** body suits made of high-tech materials. The suits **will be** cool in the summer and warm in winter. Most likely, people **are going to be wearing** their technology as well— wrist video phones and sunglasses with computer screens on the lenses.

EDUCATION

Some futurists predict that doctors **will be able to place** tiny computer chips into people's brains to increase learning ability. Everyone **will learn** very quickly, and education **will continue** throughout life. Virtual-reality technology **will become** common. On a typical school day, the geography class **will be visiting** Antarctica, while the history class **boards** Sputnik, the ancient Russian space capsule.

NEW NEIGHBORHOODS

For the next several years, astronomers **will be searching** the skies for other civilizations. Meanwhile, the Mars Association, a group of scientists, has already planned the first housing development project on Mars. Get ready. The shuttle **leaves** as soon as they **solve** a few transportation problems.

Many of these changes have already begun, and we**'ll be seeing** others very soon. The future **is arriving** any minute now. Are you ready for it?

GRAMMAR **PRESENTATION**
FUTURE

AFFIRMATIVE STATEMENTS	
We **are going to leave**	
We **will leave**	for Mars soon.
We **are leaving**	
We **leave**	

NEGATIVE STATEMENTS	
We **are not going to leave**	
We **will not leave**	for Mars yet.
We **are not leaving**	
We **don't leave**	

YES / NO QUESTIONS	
Is she **going to leave**	
Will she **leave**	for Mars soon?
Is she **leaving**	
Does she **leave**	

SHORT ANSWERS	
	she **is.**
Yes,	she **will.**
	she **is.**
	she **does.**

SHORT ANSWERS	
	she **isn't.**
No,	she **won't.**
	she **isn't.**
	she **doesn't.**

WH- QUESTIONS	
When **is** she **going to** leave	
When **will** she **leave**	for Mars?
When **is she leaving**	
When **does** she **leave**	

FUTURE PROGRESSIVE

STATEMENTS			
SUBJECT	**BE (NOT) GOING TO / WILL (NOT)**	**BE + BASE FORM + -ING**	
People	**are (not) going to will (not)**	**be living**	on Mars by 2050.

YES / NO QUESTIONS				
BE / WILL	**SUBJECT**	**GOING TO**	**BE + BASE FORM + -ING**	
Are	they	**going to**	**be living**	on Mars by then?
Will	you			

SHORT ANSWERS	
AFFIRMATIVE	
Yes,	they **are.**
	I **will.**

SHORT ANSWERS	
NEGATIVE	
No,	they**'re not.**
	I **won't.**

WH- QUESTIONS					
WH- WORD	**BE / WILL**	**SUBJECT**	**GOING TO**	**BE + BASE FORM + -ING**	
When	**are**	they	**going to**	**be living**	on Mars?
	will	you			

NOTES

EXAMPLES

1. Use *be going to, will*, the **present progressive**, and the **simple present** tense to talk about <u>actions and states in the future</u>.

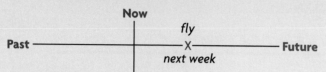

USAGE NOTE: Sometimes only one form of the future is appropriate, but in many cases more than one form is possible.

a. Use *be going to* or *will* to make <u>predictions or guesses</u>.

b. Use *be going to* (not *will*) when <u>something in the present leads to a prediction</u>.

c. Use *be going to, will*, or the **present progressive** to talk about <u>future intentions or plans</u>.

d. We often use *will* when we decide something at the <u>moment of speaking</u>.

e. We often use the **present progressive** when we talk about <u>future plans that have already been arranged</u>. There is usually some reference to the future that shows that the event is not happening now.

f. Use the **simple present tense** to talk about <u>scheduled future events</u> such as timetables, programs, and schedules.

- **I'm going to fly** to Mars next week.

- I **will fly** to Mars next week.

- **I'm flying** to Mars next week.

- I **fly** to Mars next week.

- Virtual reality **is going to make** lessons more fun.

- Virtual reality **will make** lessons more fun.

- Look at that spaceship! It**'s going to land**!
  NOT ~~It will land.~~

- Dr. Granite **is going to speak** tomorrow.

- Dr. Granite **will speak** tomorrow.

- Dr. Granite **is speaking** tomorrow.

A: Dr. Granite is giving a talk tomorrow.

B: Oh! Maybe **I'll go**.

- We**'re buying** a new robot *tomorrow*. We've already chosen the model.

- The shuttle **leaves** at 10:00 A.M.

- It **lands** at midnight.

2. Use the **future progressive** with *be going to* or *will* to talk about actions that will be <u>in progress at a specific time in the future</u>.

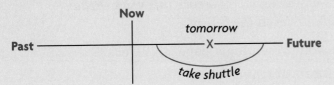

REMEMBER! Non-action (stative) verbs are not usually used in the progressive.

- **I'm going to be taking** the shuttle tomorrow.
- **I'll be taking** the shuttle tomorrow.

- We**'ll have** a robot soon.
  NOT ~~We'll be having a robot soon.~~

---

3. USAGE NOTES

a. The **future** with *be going to*, *will*, the present progressive, and the simple present express that an event <u>will happen</u> in the future.

The **future progressive** emphasizes that an action will be <u>in progress</u> in the future.

b. We often use the **future progressive** instead of the future to <u>make a question more polite</u>.

c. People often use the **future progressive** to <u>hint that they would like someone to do them a favor</u>.

d. Use the **future** with *will* to <u>invite</u> someone.

A: What time **will** you **call**?
B: The lecture **ends** at 8:00. **I'll call** then.

A: Call me at 11:00, OK?
B: I can't. **I'll be sleeping**.

- When **will** you **hand in** your paper? *(teacher to student)*
- When **will** you **be grading** our tests? *(student to teacher)*

A: **Will** you **be going** by the post office tomorrow?
B: Yes. Do you need stamps?
A: Yes. Could you get some?

A: **Will** you **join** us for coffee?
B: Thanks. I'd love to.

---

4. In sentences with a **future time clause**, use the future or the future progressive in the main clause only.
In the time clause, use <u>the simple present or the present progressive</u>. Do not use the future or the future progressive.

- **I'll call** when the robot *finishes*.
  NOT ~~I'll call when the robot will finish.~~

- **I'll be cooking** while the robot *is cleaning*.
  NOT ~~I'll be cooking while the robot will be cleaning.~~

FOCUSED PRACTICE

1 DISCOVER THE GRAMMAR

Professor Granite is a futurist. She's attending a conference this week. Read the conversation and circle all the verbs that refer to the future.

RUSS: Ellen! It's nice to see you. (Are you presenting) a paper this week?

GRANITE: Hi, Rick. Yes. In fact my talk starts at two o'clock.

RUSS: Oh. I think I'll go. Will you be talking about robots?

GRANITE: Yes. I'm focusing on personal robots for household work.

RUSS: I'd like one of those! Where's your son by the way? Is he with you?

GRANITE: No. Tony stays in Denver with his grandparents in the summer. I'm going to visit him when I leave the conference. So, what are you working on these days?

RUSS: I'm still with the Mars Association. In fact, we're going to be holding a news conference next month about the Mars shuttle launch.

GRANITE: That's exciting. Maybe I'll see you there!

2 AT THE CONFERENCE   Grammar Note 1

Circle the most appropriate words to complete these conversations.

1. **GRANITE:** Which project <u>do you work</u> / (are you going to work) on?
    RUSS: I haven't decided for sure. Probably the Spacemobile.

2. **RUSS:** Look at those dark clouds!
    GRANITE: Yes. It looks like <u>it's raining</u> / <u>it's going to rain</u> any minute.

3. **GRANITE:** I'd better get back to my hotel room before it starts to rain.
    RUSS: OK. <u>I'm seeing</u> / <u>I'll see</u> you later.

4. **FRONT DESK:** Professor Granite, your son just called.
    GRANITE: Oh, good. I think <u>I'll call</u> / <u>I'm calling</u> him back right away.

5. **GRANITE:** Hi, honey. How's it going?
    TONY: Great. <u>I go</u> / <u>I'm going</u> fishing with Grandpa tomorrow.

6. **GRANITE:** Have fun, but don't forget. You still have to finish that paper.
    TONY: I know, Mom. <u>I mail</u> / <u>I'm mailing</u> it tomorrow. I already have the envelope.

7. **TONY:** How's the conference?
    GRANITE: Good. <u>I'm giving</u> / <u>I'll give</u> my talk this afternoon.

8. **TONY:** Good luck. When <u>are you</u> / <u>will you be</u> here?
    GRANITE: Tomorrow. My plane <u>lands</u> / <u>will land</u> at 7:00, so <u>I see</u> / <u>I'll see</u> you about 8:00.

3 ROBO'S SCHEDULE

Professor Granite's family uses a robot for household chores. Look at Robo the robot's schedule for tomorrow. Make sentences, using the words in parentheses and the future progressive.

TOMORROW	
8:00	make breakfast
9:00	pay bills
10:00	vacuum
11:00	dust
12:00	do laundry
12:30	make lunch
1:00	shop for food
2:00	recycle the garbage
3:00	give Prof. Granite a massage
5:00	make dinner
6:00	play chess with Tony

1. At 8:05 Robo won't be paying bills. He'll be making breakfast.
   (8:05 / pay bills)

2. _____
   (9:05 / pay bills)

3. _____
   (10:05 / vacuum)

4. _____
   (11:05 / do laundry)

5. _____
   (12:05 / make lunch)

6. _____
   (12:35 / make lunch)

7. _____
   (1:05 / shop for food)

8. _____
   (2:05 / recycle the garbage)

9. _____
   (3:05 / give Prof. Granite a massage)

10. _____
    (5:05 / make dinner)

11. _____
    (6:05 / play cards with Tony)

4 ON CAMPUS

Complete the conversations. Use the future progressive form of the words in parentheses or short answers where appropriate.

1. **STUDENT:** _____Will_____ you _____be having_____ office hours
   (Will / have)
   today? I'd like to talk to you about my term paper.

   PROF. GRANITE: I _____ to lunch at two o'clock. But stop in any time
   (will / go)
   before then.

2. **PROF. GUPTA:** _____ you _____ us for lunch? Dr.
   (Will / join)
   Russ from the Mars Association is going to be there.

   PROF. GRANITE: _____. I've been looking forward to seeing him.

3. **MR. GRANITE:** When _____ you _____ the office?
   (be going to / leave)
   PROF. GRANITE: At two o'clock. Why? Do we need something?

   MR. GRANITE: Would you mind picking up some milk? Robo forgot.

4. **REPORTER:** I'm calling from the *Times-Dispatch*. We've heard that the Mars

   Association _____ a shuttle service to Mars soon.
   (will / start)
   PROF. GRANITE: I can't comment now. But I think we _____ a lot
   (be going to / hear)
   more about it in the next few weeks.

5. **PROF. GRANITE:** _____ you _____ an announcement
   (be going to / make)
   about the Mars shuttle soon? Everyone is very curious.

   PROF. RUSS: _____. We've decided not to say anything until our

   plans are more developed.

6. **DANNY:** Dad? I need some help on my science project. What time

   _____ you _____ home today?
   (will / get)
   PROF. RUSS: I'll be there by 4:00.

7. **TELEMARKETER:** Hi. I'm calling from Robotronics Inc. I _____ your
   (be going to / visit)
   neighborhood soon to demonstrate our new robot.

   ROBO: The Granite family _____ a new robot for a while.
   (will not / buy)

5 LEAVING EARTH

Complete this ad for the Mars shuttle. Use the correct form—the future progressive or the simple present tense—of the verbs in parentheses.

The Sky's Not the Limit

Leave all your earthly problems behind. Call today and in just one week you

_____'ll be flying_____ on the new shuttle to Mars! Imagine—while everyone
1. (fly)

_____ stuck back here on Earth, you _____ gravity in our
2. (be)   3. (defy)

spacious, comfortable, modern spaceship. You _____ in your own com-
4. (float)

partment when one of our friendly flight robots _____ you a freshly
5. (offer)

reconstituted meal. You _____ your complimentary copy of *Star*
6. (read)

Magazine while the gentle swaying of the spacecraft _____ you to
7. (rock)

sleep. And before you know it, you _____ to land on the planet of your
8. (get ready)

dreams. So don't delay! Call for a reservation. Once aboard, we guarantee it—you

_____ about anything except returning again and again and again. . . .
9. (not think)

6 EDITING

Read the flight announcement on the shuttle to Mars. The captain has made seven mistakes in the use of the future and future progressive. Find and correct them. The first mistake is already corrected. (Note: There is often more than one way to correct a mistake.)

"Good evening, ladies and gentlemen. This ~~will be~~ *is* your captain speaking. We are going to be leave the Earth's gravity field in about five minutes. When you will hear the announcement, you'll be able to unbuckle your seat belts and float around the cabin. Host robots take orders for dinner soon. They'll serving from 6:30 to 7:30. The shuttle arrives on Mars tomorrow morning at 9:00. Tonight's temperature on the planet is a mild minus 20 degrees Celsius. When you arrive tomorrow morning, the temperature is 18 degrees, but it will be feeling more like 20 degrees. Enjoy your flight."

COMMUNICATION PRACTICE

7 LISTENING

Four members of the Mars Association are trying to organize a conference on Venus. Listen to their conversation. Then listen again. Mark the chart below to help you figure out when they are all available.

X = not available

Weeks:	JULY				AUGUST			
	1	2	3	4	1	2	3	4
Jennifer							X	X
Brian								
Lorna								
Tranh								

The time that they're all available: _____

8 ROBOTS OF THE FUTURE

Computerized robots will be doing many things in the near future. Look at the list of activities and decide which ones you think robots will or won't be doing. In small groups, share and explain your opinions. Do you think robots will be doing too much for humans? Why?

make dinner

go shopping

write letters

teach English

take care of children

sew clothes

read books

plant gardens

take a vacation

answer the phone

clean house

paint walls

knit sweaters

drive a car

EXAMPLE:

Robots will be cleaning houses, but they won't be taking care of children. Children need human contact to help them develop emotional security.

❾ INFORMATION GAP: PROFESSOR GRANITE'S CALENDAR

Work in pairs (A and B). Student B, look at the Information Gap on page 65 and follow the instructions there. Student A, complete Prof. Granite's calendar below. Get information from Student B. Ask questions and fill in the calendar. Answer Student B's questions.

EXAMPLE:

A: What will Professor Granite be doing on Sunday, the first?

B: She'll be flying to Tokyo.
What about on the second? Will she be attending a conference then?

A: No, she'll be meeting with Professor Kato.

February   2015

Sunday	Monday	Tuesday	Wednesday	Thursday	Friday	Saturday
1 fly to Tokyo	**2** meet with Prof. Kato	**3**	**4** →→→	**5**	**6**	**7** →
8 take Bullet Train to Osaka	**9** sightseeing	**10** →→	**11** →	**12**	**13**	**14** →
15 fly home	**16**	**17**	**18** attend energy seminar →	**19**	**20** →	**21** shop with Tony and Robo
22	**23** →→	**24**	**25**	**26**	**27** →	**28** take shuttle to Mars

When you are finished, compare calendars. Do they have the same information?

🔟 LET'S GET TOGETHER

Complete the schedule below. Write in all your plans for next week. Then work with a partner. Without showing each other your schedules, find a time to get together by asking and answering questions with the future progressive.

	MONDAY	TUESDAY	WEDNESDAY	THURSDAY	FRIDAY
9:00					
11:00					
1:00					
3:00					
5:00					
7:00					

EXAMPLE:

A: What will you be doing at 11:00 on Tuesday?

B: I'll be taking a history test.

1️⃣1️⃣ WRITING

Write a paragraph about your life ten years from now. What will you be doing for a living? What kind of family life will you have? What hobbies will you be enjoying? What will you do to achieve these things?

EXAMPLE:

In ten years, I will be working for the space program. I am going to be planning the first colony on Mars. First I will have to graduate from college.

INFORMATION GAP FOR STUDENT B

Student B, complete Prof. Granite's calendar below. Answer Student A's questions.
Then ask Student A questions and fill in the information.

EXAMPLE:

A: What will Professor Granite be doing on Sunday, the first?

B: She'll be flying to Tokyo.
What about on the second? Will she be attending a conference then?

A: No, she'll be meeting with Professor Kato.

February · 2015

Sunday	Monday	Tuesday	Wednesday	Thursday	Friday	Saturday
1 fly to Tokyo	**2** meet with Prof. Kato	**3** attend World Future Conference	**4** →	**5**	**6**	**7**
8	**9** →	**10**	**11** →	**12** fly to Denver	**13** visit Mom and Dad →	**14** →
15	**16** give speech at Harvard University	**17** meet with Prof. Russ	**18** →	**19**	**20** →	**21**
22 relax!	**23** work at home →	**24**	**25**	**26**	**27** →	**28**

When you are finished, compare calendars. Do they have the same information?

6

FUTURE PERFECT AND FUTURE PERFECT PROGRESSIVE

GRAMMAR **IN CONTEXT**

BEFORE YOU READ Look at the picture and the title of the newsletter. What do you think "penny-pinching" means? What is one way that *you* pinch pennies?

 Read this newsletter.

THE PENNY-PINCHING TIMES

VOLUME 5, NUMBER 1   **January**

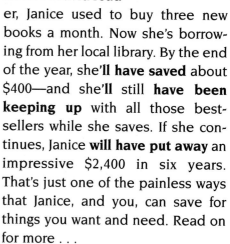

From the Editor's Desk:

Happy New Year! It's time to start talking about savings goals for this year. Start now, and by next year you **will have saved** enough to make some dreams come true. Here's one reader's plan.

Janice Bedford wants to buy a car by the end of the year. A word processor, she takes home about $22,000 a year. After food, clothing, rent, and other essential costs, Janice has $5,000 for optional expenses like entertainment. Of that amount, she plans to save $15 a week. By the end of the year, she **will have met** her savings goal of $780—enough for the down payment on a good used car.

How will she do it? An avid reader, Janice used to buy three new books a month. Now she's borrowing from her local library. By the end of the year, she'**ll have saved** about $400—and she'**ll** still **have been keeping up** with all those best-sellers while she saves. If she continues, Janice **will have put away** an impressive $2,400 in six years. That's just one of the painless ways that Janice, and you, can save for things you want and need. Read on for more . . .

Happy penny pinching!

MARY DOBBS, EDITOR

$ayings worth saving . . .

The safest way to double your money is to fold it over once and put it into your pocket.

(Frank McKinney Hubbard, 1868–1930)

A Penny Saved . . .
Tips from Our Readers

Anne-Marie DuPont wants to pay off a high-interest credit-card debt. By writing letters and sending e-mail instead of making long-distance phone calls, she can pay an additional $50 a month on her card. By June, she**'ll have cut** the debt in half. By a year from June, she**'ll have paid off** the whole thing. This seems like a long time, but remember that all along Anne-Marie **will** also **have been saving** on the 20% that the credit-card company charges for the unpaid balance.

Tom Lu wants a CD player. A student with very little extra money, Tom had to look hard for places to save. By hanging his clothes up to dry, he's saving the cost of the dryer at his laundromat. Two loads a week at $1.50 per load—Tom **will have saved** $156 by this time next year. That's enough to buy the CD player he wants.

$ $ $

Write to us with your own penny-pinching tips. If we publish yours, you'll receive a FREE copy of our popular booklet, *More Bang for the Buck*—AND you**'ll have helped** others pinch a penny.

Here's this month's Penny-Pincher problem:

A 15-ounce box of Boast Cereal costs $3.99. The same brand costs $4.79 for 20 ounces. Which is the better buy? If you buy two boxes a month of the better buy, how much **will** you **have saved** by the end of twelve months?

Answer: The 20-ounce box at 24 cents an ounce is a better buy than the 15-ounce box at 27 cents an ounce. By buying the 20-ounce box, you'll have saved $12.72 by next January.

67

GRAMMAR **PRESENTATION**
FUTURE PERFECT

STATEMENTS

SUBJECT	WILL (NOT)	HAVE + PAST PARTICIPLE	
I You He She We They	will (not)	have saved	enough by then.
It	will (not)	have earned	interest by then.

YES / NO QUESTIONS

WILL	SUBJECT	HAVE + PAST PARTICIPLE	
Will	I you he she we they	have saved	enough by then?
Will	it	have earned	interest by then?

SHORT ANSWERS

AFFIRMATIVE

Yes,	you I he she we they	will (have).
	it	

SHORT ANSWERS

NEGATIVE

No,	you I he she we they	won't (have).
	it	

WH- QUESTIONS

WH- WORD	WILL	SUBJECT	HAVE + PAST PARTICIPLE	
When	will	she	have saved	enough?

FUTURE PERFECT PROGRESSIVE

STATEMENTS

SUBJECT	*WILL (NOT)*	*HAVE BEEN + BASE FORM + -ING*	
I You He She We They	will (not)	have been living	there for ten years.
It	will (not)	have been earning	interest for ten years.

YES / NO QUESTIONS

WILL	SUBJECT	*HAVE BEEN + BASE FORM + -ING*	
Will	I you he she we they	have been living	there for ten years?
Will	it	have been earning	interest for ten years?

SHORT ANSWERS

AFFIRMATIVE

Yes,	you I he she we they	will (have).
	it	

SHORT ANSWERS

NEGATIVE

No,	you I he she we they	won't (have).
	it	

WH- QUESTIONS

WH- WORD	*WILL*	SUBJECT	*HAVE BEEN + BASE FORM + -ING*	
How long	will	she	have been living	there?

NOTES	**EXAMPLES**

1. Use the **future perfect** to talk about a future action that <u>will already be completed by a certain time in the future</u>.

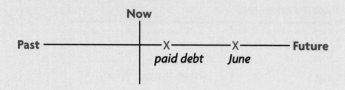

- By June, he **will have paid** his debt.
- She**'ll have bought** a new car by May.
- We**'ll have saved** enough by then.

2. Use the **future perfect progressive** to talk about an action that <u>will still be in progress at a certain time in the future</u>. The action may start sometime in the future or it may have already started.

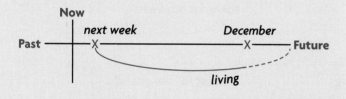

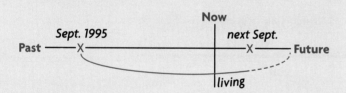

A: You're moving to L.A. next week? Great! Can I come for a visit in December?

B: Sure, by then we**'ll have been living** there for three months. It should be fine.

- They moved to Atlanta in September 1995. So by next September, they**'ll have been living** there for six years.

▶ **BE CAREFUL!** Non-action (stative) verbs are not usually used in the progressive.

- By the spring, he**'ll have owned** that car for five years.

  NOT ~~he'll have been owning that car for five years.~~

3. Use the future perfect or the future perfect progressive **with the simple present tense** to show <u>the relationship between two future events</u>. The event that will happen first uses the perfect. The event that will happen second uses the simple present tense.

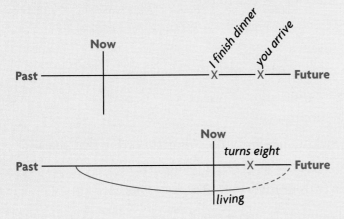

- By the time you ***arrive***, I **will have finished** dinner.
  NOT ~~By the time you will arrive, I will have finished dinner.~~

- When my daughter ***turns*** eight, we **will have been living** here for ten years.

4. We often use ***already*** and ***yet*** with the future perfect to emphasize <u>which event will happen first</u>.

- By the time he graduates, he**'ll have *already* saved** $1,000.
- By the time he graduates, he **won't have saved** $5,000 ***yet***.

FOCUSED PRACTICE

1 DISCOVER THE GRAMMAR

*Read each numbered statement. Then choose the sentence (**a** or **b**) that best describes the situation.*

1. By this time tomorrow, I'll have decided which car to buy.
   a. I know which car I'm going to buy.
   (b.) I haven't decided yet.

2. By the time you get home, we'll have finished the grocery shopping.
   a. You will get home while we are shopping.
   b. You will get home after we finish shopping.

3. By next year, Mary will have been working at *Penny-Pinching Times* for five years.
   a. Next year, Mary will no longer be working at *Penny-Pinching Times*.
   b. Next year, Mary can celebrate her fifth anniversary at *Penny-Pinching Times*.

4. She won't have finished writing her column by ten o'clock.
   a. She will still be writing at ten o'clock.
   b. She will finish writing at ten o'clock.

5. By the year 2010, we will have moved to a larger office.
   a. We will move to a larger office before the year 2010.
   b. We will move to a larger office after the year 2010.

6. They will have finished mailing the newsletter by five o'clock.
   a. They'll be finished by five o'clock.
   b. They'll still be working at five o'clock.

2 FUTURE PLANS   Grammar Note 1

Look at the time line. Write sentences describing what Tom Lu will have done or won't have done by the year 2010.

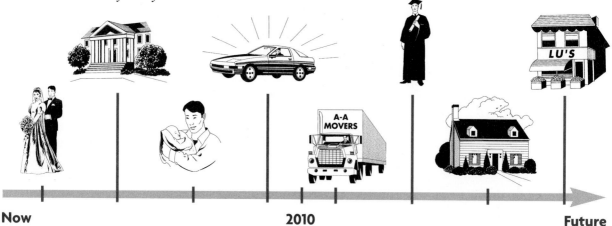

Now   **2010**   **Future**

1. (start college)

By 2010 Tom will have started college.

2. (graduate from college)

_____

3. (get married)

_____

4. (become a parent)

_____

5. (buy a car)

_____

6. (buy a house)

_____

7. (move to Phoenix)

_____

8. (start his own business)

_____

3 **BY THE TIME . . .**   Grammar Notes 3 and 4

Look again at the time line in Exercise 2. Now relate two events in the future.
*What will or won't have happened by the time the first event occurs? Use **already***
*and **yet**.*

1. start college / get married

By the time Tom starts college, he'll have already gotten married.

2. graduate from college / become a parent

_____

3. buy a car / graduate from college

_____

(continued on next page)

4. move to Phoenix / graduate from college

_____

5. buy a house / get married

_____

6. move to Phoenix / start his own business

_____

7. start his own business / graduate from college

_____

4 ACCOMPLISHMENTS Grammar Notes 1 and 2

Ask and answer questions about these people's accomplishments. Choose between the future perfect and the future perfect progressive. Use the calendar to answer the questions.

January	February	March
S M T W T F S	S M T W T F S	S M T W T F S
· · · · · 1 2	· 1 2 3 4 5 6	· 1 2 3 4 5 6
3 4 5 6 7 8 9	7 8 9 10 11 12 13	7 8 9 10 11 12 13
10 11 12 13 14 15 16	14 15 16 17 18 19 20	14 15 16 17 18 19 20
17 18 19 20 21 22 23	21 22 23 24 25 26 27	21 22 23 24 25 26 27
24 25 26 27 28 29 30	28	28 29 30 31
31		

April	May	June
S M T W T F S	S M T W T F S	S M T W T F S
· · · · 1 2 3	· · · · · · 1	· · 1 2 3 4 5
4 5 6 7 8 9 10	2 3 4 5 6 7 8	6 7 8 9 10 11 12
11 12 13 14 15 16 17	9 10 11 12 13 14 15	13 14 15 16 17 18 19
18 19 20 21 22 23 24	16 17 18 19 20 21 22	20 21 22 23 24 25 26
25 26 27 28 29 30	23 24 25 26 27 28 29	27 28 29 30
	30 31	

July	August	September
S M T W T F S	S M T W T F S	S M T W T F S
· · · · 1 2 3	1 2 3 4 5 6 7	· · · 1 2 3 4
4 5 6 7 8 9 10	8 9 10 11 12 13 14	5 6 7 8 9 10 11
11 12 13 14 15 16 17	15 16 17 18 19 20 21	12 13 14 15 16 17 18
18 19 20 21 22 23 24	22 23 24 25 26 27 28	19 20 21 22 23 24 25
25 26 27 28 29 30 31	29 30 31	26 27 28 29 30

October	November	December
S M T W T F S	S M T W T F S	S M T W T F S
· · · · · 1 2	· 1 2 3 4 5 6	· · · 1 2 3 4
3 4 5 6 7 8 9	7 8 9 10 11 12 13	5 6 7 8 9 10 11
10 11 12 13 14 15 16	14 15 16 17 18 19 20	12 13 14 15 16 17 18
17 18 19 20 21 22 23	21 22 23 24 25 26 27	19 20 21 22 23 24 25
24 25 26 27 28 29 30	28 29 30	26 27 28 29 30 31
31		

1. On January 1, Anne-Marie DuPont started saving $5 a week.

QUESTION: (By February 19 / how long / save?)

By February 19, how long will Anne-Marie have been saving?

ANSWER: By February 19, she'll have been saving for seven weeks.

2. On January 1, Valerie Morgan started saving $5 a week.

QUESTION: (By February 18 / how much / save?)

_____

ANSWER: _____

3. On March 3, Tom Lu began reading a book a week.

QUESTION: (By June 16 / how many books / read?)

_____

ANSWER: _____

4. On November 24, Don Caputo began running two miles a day.

QUESTION: (How long / run / by December 29?)

_____

ANSWER: _____

5. On November 24, Tania Zakov began running two miles a day.

QUESTION: (How many miles / run / by December 29?)

_____

ANSWER: _____

6. On May 6, Rick Gregory began saving $10 a week.

QUESTION: (save $100 / by July 1?)

_____

ANSWER: _____

7. On October 4, Tim Rigg began painting two apartments a week.

QUESTION: (How many apartments / paint / by October 25?)

_____

ANSWER: _____

8. Tim's building has twelve apartments.

QUESTION: (finish / by November 15?)

_____

ANSWER: _____

5 EDITING

Read this journal entry. Find and correct nine mistakes in the use of the future perfect and future perfect progressive. The first mistake is already corrected.

                                                                    January 1

                have been
By August, I'll ~~be~~ a word processor for ten years. And I'll

earn almost the same salary for three years! That's why

I've just made a New Year's resolution to go back to

school this year. First I'm going to write for school

catalogs and start saving for tuition. By March, I'll have

figure out how much tuition will cost. Then I'll start

applying. By summer, I had received acceptance letters. In

August, when I will have my annual review with my

boss, I'll have already been decided on a school. I will talk

to her about working part-time and going to school

part-time. By that time, I'll also have saving enough to

pay for a semester's tuition. My cousin will had

graduated by that time, so she might move in with me

and share the rent. By next New Year's Day, I'll have

been study for one whole semester!

COMMUNICATION PRACTICE

6 LISTENING

Don and Thea Caputo want to save for a summer vacation with their two children. Listen to their conversation about how to cut back on their spending. Then listen again and write the amount they will have saved in each category by next summer.

Amount They Will Have Saved by Next Summer

food _____*$500*_____ transportation _____

clothing _____ entertainment _____

Total all the categories. How much will they have saved by the end of the year? _____

With their savings, where can they go for a two-week vacation?

1. ☐ a car trip to British Columbia, camping on the way $ 800
2. ☐ a car trip to British Columbia, staying in motels $1,450
3. ☐ a trip to Disneyland $2,300
4. ☐ a trip by airplane to Mexico and two weeks in a hotel $3,800

7 GOALS

Work in small groups. Conduct a survey to find out how many of your classmates will have done the following things by a year from now. Fill out this chart. In groups, report back to the class.

Event	Number of People	Event	Number of People
1. take a vacation	_____	6. graduate	_____
2. get married	_____	7. get a new job	_____
3. become a parent or grandparent	_____	8. turn sixty	_____
		9. decide on a career	_____
4. move	_____	10. start a business	_____
5. buy a new car	_____		

EXAMPLE:
None of the students in our group will have moved. Three of the students will have gotten new jobs by next year.

8 SAVVY CONSUMERS

Write down some tips for saving money and then share your tips with a group.
Choose the best tips for yourself and figure how much you will have saved by the
end of the year if you use the tips. Tell your group.

EXAMPLE:

I can save $10 a week by parking farther from my office.
By the end of the year I'll have saved $500.

9 WRITING

Write a paragraph about a goal that you are working toward. What steps will you
take to achieve your goal? When will you have completed each step?

EXAMPLE:

I'm going to buy a used car next year. Right now I'm reading consumer
information. In about two months I'll have decided which type of car I'll buy.

REVIEW OR SELFTEST

I. *Circle the most appropriate words to complete each conversation.*

1. A: *You've Got Mail* is playing at the Ciné tonight.

    B: Great. I think <u>I go</u> / <u>I'll go</u>.

2. A: Please don't forget to pay the phone bill.

    B: <u>I'll mail</u> / <u>I mail</u> the check when I leave for work today.

3. A: What are your plans for the weekend?

    B: <u>We'll attend</u> / <u>We're going to attend</u> the Moe concert. We just got our tickets.

4. A: What's wrong?

    B: Those two cars! <u>They will crash</u> / <u>They're going to crash</u>!

5. A: You look happy. What's up?

    B: <u>I'm graduating</u> / <u>I will graduate</u> next week.

6. A: What are you going to do after graduation?

    B: I'm starting a new job as soon as <u>I'm getting</u> / <u>I get</u> my degree.

7. A: I'd better get back to the library.

    B: OK. <u>I'll see</u> / <u>I'm seeing</u> you later.

8. A: I'll call you after <u>I finished</u> / <u>I finish</u> my exams.

    B: Great. I'm going to stay in town until <u>I start</u> / <u>I'll start</u> my new job.

II. *Circle the correct words to complete the conversation.*

A: Graduation ceremonies were this afternoon. I can't believe this year is

    over already.

B: Me neither. Do you realize that in September

    <u>we'll live</u> / <u>we'll have been living</u> in this apartment for two years?
      1.

A: Amazing! And <u>you'll have been studying</u> / <u>you'll be studying</u> here for
                    2.

    four years.

B: I know. Next year at this time

    <u>I'll have been graduating</u> / <u>I'll have graduated</u> already.
           3.

(continued on next page)

A: So, <u>what'll you be doing / what'll you have done</u> next June? Any plans?
4.

B: That's easy. Next June <u>I'll be looking / I'll have been looking</u> for a job. How about you?
5.

A: <u>I won't have graduated / I'll have graduated</u> yet. I plan to go home
6.

at the beginning of July next year, so during June, I guess

<u>I'm going to be getting ready / I'll have gotten ready</u> to travel to Greece.
7.

B: Lucky you. Next summer <u>you sit / you'll be sitting</u> on beautiful beaches while
8.

<u>I go / I'll go</u> job interviews.
9.

A: But just think. By the time <u>I'll be getting / I get</u> back, <u>you'll find / you'll have found</u> a
10.   11.

good job. So while <u>I'm learning / I will learn</u> about verb tenses,
12.

<u>you start / you'll be starting</u> your career.
13.

III. *Circle the letter of the correct words to complete each sentence.*

1. —Are you free tonight? The NBA playoffs are on TV at nine.   **A** **Ⓑ** **C** **D**

—I have to study first, but I _____ by then.

(A) finished   (C) finish
(B) 'll have finished   (D) 'll have been finishing

2. —How will I recognize your brother when I get to the airport?   **A** **B** **C** **D**

—He has short dark hair, and he _____ a black leather jacket.

(A) 'll be wearing   (C) 'll have been wearing
(B) wore   (D) 'll have worn

3. —Do you think Mustafa should take the TOEFL in June?   **A** **B** **C** **D**

—Sure. By that time, he _____ for more than six months.

(A) 'll prepare   (C) 's prepared
(B) prepared   (D) 'll have been preparing

4. —Are you still reading Jack Francis novels?   **A** **B** **C** **D**

—Yes, but when I _____ this one, I'll have read all his books.

(A) 'll finish   (C) finished
(B) finish   (D) 'll have finished

5. —Will we be delayed here in Boston for long?   **A** **B** **C** **D**

—I'm afraid so. The train _____ the station for an hour.

(A) won't be leaving   (C) won't have been leaving
(B) won't have left   (D) didn't leave

6. —Should I call Anna and tell her we're going to be late?   **A   B   C   D**

—No. By the time you find a phone, she _____ already.

(A) leaves   (C) 'll leave
(B) 'll have left   (D) has left

7. —I need to buy new skates. Could you pay me to do some chores?   **A   B   C   D**

—Sure. By next month, you _____ enough for new ones.

(A) 'll have been saving   (C) saved
(B) save   (D) 'll have saved

8. —It's your turn to do the dishes, right?   **A   B   C   D**

—I _____ them in a minute. I'm busy right now.

(A) do   (C) 'll do
(B) 'll have done   (D) 've done

9. —Have you heard a weather report?   **A   B   C   D**

—Yes. It _____ this afternoon.

(A) 's going to snow   (C) snows
(B) 's going to have been   (D) 's snowing
    snowing

10. —This job is endless.   **A   B   C   D**

—I know. By the end of May, we _____ the house for two months.

(A) 'll have painted   (C) 'll have been painting
(B) 'll paint   (D) painted

IV. *Complete the conversation with the future progressive, future perfect, or future perfect progressive form of the verbs in parentheses.*

A: It says in this article that by the year 2020, scientists _____will have perfected_____ an
                                                        1. (perfect)

electric car. That means we _____ gasoline-powered cars in just
                                       2. (not drive)

another few years.

B: Too bad. We _____ paying for our gasoline-powered car by then.
                              3. (finish)

Just in time to sell it and buy another one.

A: Oh, come on. Think of the benefit to the environment. We _____
                                                 4. (not pollute)

the atmosphere the way we do now. And we _____ all that
                                       5. (not spend)

money for fuel every year.

B: I guess you're right. Speaking of driving, _____ you _____ by
                                                     6. (go)

the post office tomorrow?

(continued on next page)

A: Probably. Why? Do you need stamps?

B: No, but I promised to get this report in this week. I _____ on it

7. (work)

all night tonight. With luck, I _____ it by the time you leave for
8. (finish)

work tomorrow.

A: I can send it overnight mail for you. No problem.

B: You know, this is an anniversary for me. I _____ for five years as
9. (telecommute)

of tomorrow.

A: I'll be home at seven. Let's go out for dinner and celebrate.

B: I've got to work all night tonight. I'm afraid I _____ by seven
10. (sleep)

tomorrow evening.

A: OK. The next day then.

V. *Each sentence has four underlined words or phrases. The four underlined
parts of the sentences are marked A, B, C, or D. Circle the letter of the one
underlined word or phrase that is NOT CORRECT.*

1. <u>By the time</u> you <u>will read</u> this, we<u>'ll</u> <u>already</u> have left.   **A** **Ⓑ** **C** **D**
       A   B   C   D

2. We'll <u>traveling</u> <u>for</u> a couple of days, so you <u>won't</u> <u>be able to</u> call us.   **A** **B** **C** **D**
          A   B   C   D

3. We<u>'ll call</u> you <u>as soon as</u> we<u>'re going to</u> <u>get home</u>.   **A** **B** **C** **D**
      A   B   C   D

4. By then, we<u>'ll have been</u> <u>traveled</u> since July, so we<u>'ll</u> <u>be</u> tired.   **A** **B** **C** **D**
               A   B   C D

5. Yukio <u>finished</u> school <u>by</u> next summer, so we<u>'re going to</u> <u>visit</u> her.   **A** **B** **C** **D**
           A   B   C   D

6. You<u>'ll have been</u> <u>studying</u> Japanese <u>for</u> three years, so   **A** **B** **C** **D**
         A   B   C

   you<u>'re speaking</u> fluently by then.
      D

7. We<u>'ll</u> <u>be having</u> a great time <u>when</u> we <u>get</u> together.   **A** **B** **C** **D**
     A   B   C   D

▶*To check your answers, go to the Answer Key on page 86.*

From Grammar to Writing
Avoiding Sentence Fragments

PART
II

Time clauses begin with time words and phrases such as *by the time, when, as soon as, before,* and *after.* A time clause by itself is not a complete sentence. When you write sentences with time clauses, avoid sentence fragments (incomplete sentences) by connecting the time clause to a main clause.

EXAMPLE:

SENTENCE FRAGMENT	COMPLETE SENTENCE
time clause	time clause + main clause
~~As soon as I find a job.~~ →	As soon as I find a job, I will move.
time clause	main clause + time clause
~~Since I moved.~~ →	I have been much happier since I moved.

Note that a comma comes after the time clause when the time clause comes first.

1 *Correct any sentence fragments in this letter by connecting the time clause to a main clause. Use appropriate punctuation and capitalization.*

December 10, 2000

Dear Jamie,

By the time you get this letter,

As of today, I'm a working man! ~~By the time you get this letter.~~ *I'll have been taking tickets at Ciné Moderne for more than a week. It's going to be hard to work and go to school full time, but you'll understand why I'm doing it. When you hear my plans.*

As soon as school ends. My brother Alex and I are going to take a trip to Greece and Turkey. I plan to buy a used car, and we'll camp most of the way. By the end of January, I'll have been saving for more than a year for this trip—and I'll have enough to buy a car.

Why don't you come with us? I don't finish my finals until June 10. You'll already have finished your exams. While I'm still taking mine. Maybe you can come early and do some sightseeing until I'm ready to leave. Alex

---

(continued on next page)

83

has some business to complete. Before he goes on vacation. He won't have finished until July 15, but he can join us then.

I'm leaving Paris on June 17. I'll drive through Italy and take the ferry from Brindisi to Greece. I'll stay in Greece. Until Alex joins me. Just think—while your friends are in summer school, you could be swimming in the Aegean! We'll be leaving Greece. As soon as Alex arrives so we'll have a month in Turkey. We'll start back around August 20. Your classes won't have started by then, will they?

I hope you will be able to join us for this trip. Alex is looking forward to seeing you again, too.

Your friend,

Philippe

2 *Complete the time line with information from the letter in Exercise 1.*

December 10	—	Philippe starts his new job.
January 30	—	_____
May 31	—	_____
June 10	—	_____
June 17	—	_____
July 15	—	_____
August 20	—	_____

3 *Before you write . . .*

• Make a time line that shows plans you are making for the future.

• Tell your plans to a partner. Use time clauses to connect events in your time line. Answer your partner's questions.

4 *Write a letter to a friend about some plans you are making. Use information from your time line. Connect some of the events with time clauses.*

5 *Exchange your letter with a different partner. Underline the time clauses. Put a question mark (?) above any that seem wrong. Then answer the following questions.*

    a. Are the time clauses parts of complete sentences?   Yes / No

    b. Are the sentences with time clauses punctuated correctly?   Yes / No

    c. Are the verb tenses correct in the sentences with time clauses?   Yes / No

    d. Is the sequence of events clear?   Yes / No

    e. List some details you would like to know about. _____

    _____

6 *Discuss the chart with your partner. Rewrite your own letter and make any necessary corrections.*

Review or SelfTest
Answer Key

I. **(Unit 5)**
2. I'll mail
3. We're going to attend
4. They're going to crash
5. I'm graduating
6. I get
7. I'll see
8. I finish, I start

II. **(Units 5–6)**
2. you'll have been studying
3. I'll have graduated
4. what'll you be doing
5. I'll be looking
6. I won't have graduated
7. I'm going to be getting ready
8. you'll be sitting
9. I go
10. I get
11. you'll have found
12. I'm learning
13. you'll be starting

III. **(Units 5–6)**
2. A
3. D
4. B
5. A
6. B
7. D
8. C
9. A
10. C

IV. **(Units 5–6)**
2. won't be driving
3. 'll have finished
4. won't be polluting
5. won't be spending
6. will . . . be going
7. 'll be working
8. 'll have finished
9. 'll have been telecommuting OR 'll have telecommuted
10. 'll be sleeping

V. **(Units 5–6)**
2. A
3. C
4. B
5. A
6. D
7. B

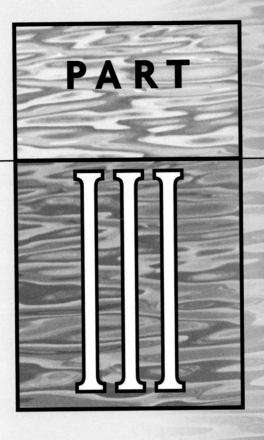

PART

III

NEGATIVE QUESTIONS AND TAG QUESTIONS, ADDITIONS AND RESPONSES

NEGATIVE *YES/NO* QUESTIONS AND TAG QUESTIONS

GRAMMAR **IN CONTEXT**

BEFORE YOU READ What do you like about the town or city where you live? What don't you like?

Read these on-the-street interviews reported in a popular magazine.

AROUND TOWN

IT'S A NICE PLACE TO LIVE, ISN'T IT?

LA COSTA: Excuse me. I'm conducting a survey to find out how people feel about living in L.A. Would you mind answering a few questions?

TOM MOFFETT:
"I'm a screenplay writer, and so Hollywood's the place to be."

MOFFETT: Hey, **aren't you** Jackie La Costa from Channel 7?

LA COSTA: That's right.

MOFFETT: I watch you all the time!

LA COSTA: Thanks. You're not originally from California, **are you?**

MOFFETT: No. You could tell by my accent, **couldn't you?** Actually, I moved here two years ago from New York.

LA COSTA: So, how do you like it here?

MOFFETT: Well, I'm a screenplay writer, and so Hollywood's the place to be.

LA COSTA: But **hasn't it** gotten harder to sell scripts?

MOFFETT: Uh-huh. It's not like a few years ago when . . . I'm sorry. Will you excuse me? I think I see my agent over there . . .

LA COSTA: No problem. Thanks.

LA COSTA: Excuse me, ma'am. Can I ask a few questions?

AGUIRRE: Sure.

MARTA AGUIRRE:
*"Two hundred and fifty-eight days of sunshine a year. You can't beat that, **can you?**"*

(continued on next page)

LA COSTA: Are you from L.A.?

AGUIRRE: No. I'm from New York.

LA COSTA: Hey, **wasn't anyone** born here? How long have you been in L.A.?

AGUIRRE: Almost twenty years.

LA COSTA: That's a pretty long time, **isn't it?** Why did you move here?

AGUIRRE: The weather. Two hundred and fifty-eight days of sunshine a year. You can't beat that, **can you?**

LA COSTA: Not if you don't mind the smog!

AGUIRRE: Well, New York has its problems with air pollution, too.

LA COSTA: That's true.

LA COSTA: So, why did *you* move to L.A.?

MITSUMA: I work in the computer industry. My company does a lot of business in Asia, and I have to fly to Japan at least once a month.

KAZUHIKO MITSUMA:
"I have to fly to Japan at least once a month."

LA COSTA: L.A. *is* a lot closer to Japan, **isn't it?**

MITSUMA: Yes, it is. I save a lot of time traveling. And our customers from Asia come here, too.

LA COSTA: L.A. has really become an international center, **hasn't it?**

MITSUMA: It really has.

LA COSTA: Excuse me, miss. You're not from L.A., by any chance, **are you?**

ROBERTA WILSON:
*"It's a nice city to live in, **isn't it?**"*

WILSON: I'm from L.A.

LA COSTA: Oh. I was beginning to think that no one was born here! I'm trying to find out how people feel about living here.

WILSON: That's funny.

LA COSTA: Funny?

WILSON: Yes. I've lived here all my life, but I'm moving next month. I just got laid off, so I'm moving east. I got a job in New York.

LA COSTA: It seems like everyone I speak to is either going to or coming from New York.

WILSON: Small world, **isn't it?**

LA COSTA: Well, how *did* you like living in L.A.?

WILSON: Except for the traffic on the freeway, I liked it a lot. I'm not even going to have a car in New York.

LA COSTA: **Won't you** miss L.A.?

WILSON: Sure. It's a nice city to live in, **isn't it?**

GRAMMAR **PRESENTATION**
NEGATIVE *YES/NO* QUESTIONS

WITH *BE* AS THE MAIN VERB

QUESTIONS	SHORT ANSWERS	SHORT ANSWERS
BE + NOT + SUBJECT	AFFIRMATIVE	NEGATIVE
Aren't you from L.A.?	**Yes**, I **am**.	**No**, I'm **not**.

WITH ALL AUXILIARY VERBS EXCEPT *DO*

QUESTIONS	SHORT ANSWERS		SHORT ANSWERS	
AUXILIARY + NOT + SUBJECT + VERB	AFFIRMATIVE		NEGATIVE	
Aren't you moving?	**Yes**,	I **am**.	**No**,	I'm **not**.
Hasn't he been here before?		he **has**.		he **hasn't**.
Can't they move tomorrow?		they **can**.		they **can't**.

WITH *DO* AS AN AUXILIARY VERB

QUESTIONS	SHORT ANSWERS		SHORT ANSWERS	
DO + NOT + SUBJECT + VERB	AFFIRMATIVE		NEGATIVE	
Don't you live here?	**Yes**,	I **do**.	**No**,	I **don't**.
Didn't they decide to move?		they **did**.		they **didn't**.

TAG QUESTIONS

WITH *BE* AS THE MAIN VERB

AFFIRMATIVE STATEMENT	NEGATIVE TAG
SUBJECT + *BE*	*BE* + *NOT* + SUBJECT
You're from L.A.,	**aren't you?**

NEGATIVE STATEMENT	AFFIRMATIVE TAG
SUBJECT + *BE* + *NOT*	*BE* + SUBJECT
You're not from L.A.,	**are you?**

WITH ALL AUXILIARY VERBS EXCEPT *DO*

AFFIRMATIVE STATEMENT	NEGATIVE TAG
SUBJECT + AUXILIARY	AUXILIARY + *NOT* + SUBJECT
You're moving,	**aren't you?**
He's been here before,	**hasn't he?**
They can move tomorrow,	**can't they?**

NEGATIVE STATEMENT	AFFIRMATIVE TAG
SUBJECT + AUXILIARY + *NOT*	AUXILIARY + SUBJECT
You're not moving,	**are you?**
He hasn't been here before,	**has he?**
They can't move tomorrow,	**can they?**

WITH *DO* AS AN AUXILIARY VERB

AFFIRMATIVE STATEMENT	NEGATIVE TAG
SUBJECT + VERB	*DO* + *NOT* + SUBJECT
You live here,	**don't you?**
They decided to move,	**didn't they?**

NEGATIVE STATEMENT	AFFIRMATIVE TAG
SUBJECT + *DO* + *NOT* + VERB	*DO* + SUBJECT
You don't live here,	**do you?**
They didn't decide to move,	**did they?**

NOTES	EXAMPLES

1. We often use **negative *yes/no* questions** and **tag questions** to:

a. <u>check information</u> we believe to be true

OR

b. <u>comment on</u> a situation.

The purpose of these two types of questions is similar, but they have different forms.

NEGATIVE *YES/NO* QUESTION
- **Doesn't Tom** live in L.A.?

TAG QUESTION
- Tom lives in L.A., **doesn't he**?
  (In both sentences the speaker believes that Tom lives in L.A. and wants to check this information.)

NEGATIVE *YES/NO* QUESTION
- **Isn't** it a nice day?

TAG QUESTION
- It's a nice day, **isn't it**?
  (In both sentences the speaker is commenting on the weather.)

---

2. Like affirmative *yes/no* questions, **negative *yes/no* questions** begin with a form of <u>be or an auxiliary verb</u> (a form of *be, have, do,* or *will,* or modal verbs such as *can, could, should,* or *would*).

USAGE NOTE: We almost always use contractions in negative questions.

▶ **BE CAREFUL!** Use *are* (not *am*) in negative questions with *I* and a contraction. Without a contraction, use *am.* Notice the different word order.

- **Aren't you** Jackie La Costa?
- **Haven't I** seen you on TV?
- **Don't you** like the weather here?
- **Won't you** be sorry to leave?
- **Shouldn't we** think about moving?
  RARE ~~Should we not think . . .~~

- **Aren't** I right?
  NOT ~~Am'nt I right~~?
- **Am** I **not** right?

---

3. Tag questions consist of a statement and a tag.

Forms of tag questions vary, but their meaning is always similar. The statement expresses an <u>assumption</u>. The tag means *Isn't it true?* OR *Right?*

a. If the <u>statement verb is affirmative</u>, the <u>tag verb is negative</u>.

b. If the <u>statement verb is negative</u>, the <u>tag verb is affirmative</u>.

statement   tag
- You're not from California, **are you?**

- You're Jackie La Costa, **aren't you?**
  (You're Jackie La Costa, right?)
- You're not from New York, **are you?**
  (You're not from New York. Isn't that true?)

affirmative   negative
- You **work** on Fridays, **don't** you?

negative   affirmative
- You **don't** work on Fridays, **do** you?

Like *yes/no* questions, the tag always uses a form of <u>*be* or an auxiliary verb</u> (a form of *be, have, do,* or *will,* or modal verbs such as *can, could, should,* or *would*).

- It**'s** a nice day, **isn't** it?

- You**'ve** lived here a long time, **haven't** you?

- You **come** from New York, **don't** you?

- You**'ll** be here tomorrow, **won't** you?

- You **can** drive, **can't** you?

▶ **BE CAREFUL!** In the tag, only use pronouns.

- *Tom* works here, doesn't **he**?
  NOT ~~Tom works here, doesn't Tom?~~

When the subject of the statement is *that,* the subject of the tag is *it.*

- *That's* a good idea, isn't **it**?
  NOT ~~That's a good idea, isn't that?~~

---

4. Use **tag questions** in conversations when you <u>expect the speaker to agree with you</u>. In this type of tag question, the <u>voice falls</u> on the tag. Use this type of tag question to:

a. <u>check information you believe is correct</u>. You expect the listener to answer (and agree).

b. <u>comment on a situation</u>. This type of tag question is more like a statement than a question. The listener can just nod or say *uh-huh* to show that he or she is listening and agrees.

A: It's getting warmer, **isn't it?**

B: Uh-huh. Seems more like spring than winter.

A: It doesn't snow here, **does it?**

B: No, never. That's why I love it.

A: Beautiful day, **isn't it?**

B: Uh-huh. More like spring than winter.

---

5. Tag questions can be used to <u>get information</u>. This type of tag question is more like a *yes/no* question. You want to confirm your information because you are not sure it is correct. Like a *yes/no* question, the <u>voice rises</u> at the end, and you usually get an answer.

A: You're not moving, **are you?**
(Are you moving?)

B: Yes. We're returning to L.A.

OR

No. We're staying here.

---

6. Answer negative *yes/no* questions and tag questions the same way you answer affirmative *yes/no* questions. The answer is *yes* if the information is correct and *no* if the information is not correct.

A: Don't you work in Hollywood?

B: Yes, I do. I work there.

A: You work in Hollywood, **don't you?**

B: No, I don't. I work in Burbank.

FOCUSED PRACTICE

1 DISCOVER THE GRAMMAR

Read the conversation between Tom and a friend. Underline all the negative questions. Circle all the tags.

KAY: Hi, Tom. Nice day, (isn't it?)

TOM: Sure is. What are *you* doing home today? <u>Don't you usually work on Fridays?</u>

KAY: I took the day off to help my son. He's looking for an apartment. You don't know of any vacant apartments, do you?

TOM: Isn't he staying with you?

KAY: Well, he just got a new job, and he wants a place of his own. Do you know of anything?

TOM: As a matter of fact, I do. You know the Mitsumas, don't you? They're moving to New York next month.

KAY: Are they? What kind of apartment do they have?

TOM: A one-bedroom.

KAY: It's not furnished, is it?

TOM: No. Why? He doesn't need a furnished apartment, does he?

KAY: Well, he doesn't have much furniture.

TOM: Can't he rent some? I did that in my first apartment.

KAY: I don't know. Isn't it less expensive to buy?

2 ISN'T IT NICE?   Grammar Notes 1–2 and 6

Kay's son is looking at an apartment. Complete these negative yes/no *questions.*
Add short answers.

1. **OWNER:** _Isn't your name_ Alex Brown?

   JIM: _No, it isn't._ My name is Jim Robertson.

2. **OWNER:** You look familiar. _____ this apartment before?

   JIM: _____ This is the first time I've seen it.

3. **JIM:** _____ an ad in Sunday's paper?

   OWNER: _____ I put an ad in the *Times*.

4. **JIM:** _____ an air-conditioner?

   OWNER: _____ It has a fan. It really keeps it cool enough.

5. **JIM:** I notice that there are marks on the walls. _____ it?

    OWNER: _____ I haven't had time yet. I'm going to paint it next week.

6. **OWNER:** _____ a nice apartment?

    JIM: _____ It's a lovely apartment.

7. **OWNER:** _____ it?

    JIM: _____ I like it a lot, but I can't afford it.

8. **OWNER:** _____ a roommate?

    JIM: _____ I'm sure I can find one, but I really want to live alone.

❸ GETTING READY TO MOVE   Grammar Note 3

Roberta and her husband are talking about their move. Match the statements with the tags.

	Statement	**Tag**
_i_	**1.** You've called the movers,	**a.** can we?
_____	**2.** They're coming tomorrow,	**b.** do we?
_____	**3.** This isn't going to be cheap,	**c.** is he?
_____	**4.** You haven't finished packing,	**d.** isn't it?
_____	**5.** We don't need any more boxes,	**e.** aren't they?
_____	**6.** Paul is going to help us,	**f.** have you?
_____	**7.** We can put some things in storage,	**g.** isn't he?
_____	**8.** Jack isn't buying our bookcases,	**h.** is it?
_____	**9.** We need to disconnect the phone,	**i.** haven't you?
_____	**10.** The movers aren't packing the books for us,	**j.** don't we?
_____	**11.** We can't turn off the electricity yet,	**k.** can't we?
_____	**12.** Moving is hard,	**l.** are they?

❹ A TV INTERVIEW   Grammar Notes 3–5

Complete this interview with appropriate tags.

HOST: You've lived in Hollywood for many years, ___haven't you___?
                                                    1.

GUEST: Since I was eighteen and came here to write my first screenplay. Seems like ages

ago. Looking back now, I can't believe I just packed one suitcase and got on a plane.

(continued on next page)

HOST: You didn't know anyone here either, _____?
2.

GUEST: No. And I didn't have a cent to my name. Just some ideas and a lot of hope. It

sounds crazy, _____?
3.

HOST: Not when you look at all the movies you've done. Things have sure worked out for

you, _____? You've already written four major hits, and you've done
4.

some work for television as well. You're working on another screenplay now,

_____?
5.

GUEST: Yes. It's a comedy about some kids who become invisible.

HOST: Sounds like a good movie for the whole family. I know I'll certainly take my kids to

see it. Speaking of kids, you have some of your own, _____?
6.

GUEST: Two boys and a girl—all very visible!

HOST: I know what you mean. Do you ever wish they were invisible?

GUEST: Hmmm. That's an interesting thought, _____?
7.

5 EDITING

*Read part of this movie script. Find and correct nine mistakes in the use of
negative questions, tag questions, and short answers. The first mistake is already
corrected.*

BEN: It's been a long time, Joe, ~~haven't~~ it?
      hasn't

JOE: That depends on what you mean by a long time, doesn't that?

BEN: Are not you afraid to show your face around here?

JOE: I can take care of myself. I'm still alive, amn't I?

BEN: Until someone recognizes you. You're still wanted by the police, are you?

JOE: I'll be gone by morning. Look, I need a place to stay. Just for one night.

BEN: I have to think about my wife and kid. Don't you have any place else to go?

JOE: Yes, I do. There's no one to turn to but you. You have to help me.

BEN: I've already helped you plenty. I went to jail for you, haven't I? And didn't I kept my

mouth shut the whole time?

JOE: Yeah, OK, Ben. Don't you remember what happened in Vegas, do you?

BEN: Don't ever think I'll forget that! OK, OK. I can make a call.

6 L.A. PEOPLE
Grammar Notes 1–3 and 6

Read the information about film director Tim Burton. Imagine you are going to interview him, and you are not sure of the information in parentheses. Write negative yes/no questions or tag questions to check that information.

1. TIM BURTON: Film director, screenplay writer, (cartoonist?)
2. born in Burbank, a suburb of L.A. (grew up in Burbank?)
3. made home movies as a child (has always loved horror films?)
4. worked for Disney Studio, but they didn't want to show his films (work was too unusual for them?)
5. directed <u>Batman</u> in 1989—it was a huge success, but Burton was unhappy because he had very little time to complete the film (wasn't satisfied with <u>Batman</u>?)
6. finished <u>Batman Returns</u> in 1992. (Burton liked <u>Batman Returns</u> better?)
7. enjoys making films, but is a very private person (doesn't like publicity?)
8. hates the way Hollywood does things (just opened his own company?)

1. You're a cartoonist, aren't you? OR Aren't you a cartoonist?

2. _____

3. _____

4. _____

5. _____

6. _____

7. _____

8. _____

COMMUNICATION PRACTICE

7 LISTENING

Listen to these people ask questions. Notice if their voices rise or fall at the end of each question. Listen again and decide in each case if they are really asking a question (and expect an answer) or if they are just making a comment (and don't expect an answer). Check the correct column.

	Expect an answer	Don't expect an answer		Expect an answer	Don't expect an answer
1.	☐	☑	6.	☐	☐
2.	☐	☐	7.	☐	☐
3.	☐	☐	8.	☐	☐
4.	☐	☐	9.	☐	☐
5.	☐	☐	10.	☐	☐

8 WHO KNOWS WHO BETTER?

How well do you know your classmates? Work with a partner. Complete the first ten questions with information about your partner that you think is correct. Add two questions of your own. Then ask the questions to check your information. Put a check next to each question that has correct information. Which one of you knows the other one better?

1. _____, aren't you?

2. _____, can you?

3. Don't you _____?

4. _____, haven't you?

5. _____, did you?

6. _____, do you?

7. Aren't you _____?

8. _____, will you?

9. Didn't you _____?

10. _____, can't you?

11. _____, _____?

12. _____?

EXAMPLES:

A: You're from Venezuela, aren't you?

B: That's right. OR No, I'm from Colombia.

A: Don't you play the guitar?

B: Yes. I play the guitar and the drums.

❾ INFORMATION GAP: LOS ANGELES AND NEW YORK

Work in pairs (A and B). Student B, look at the Information Gap on page 100 and follow the instructions there. Student A, look at the questions below. What do you know about Los Angeles? Complete the questions by circling the correct words and writing the tags.

1. Los Angeles is one of the (largest)/ smallest cities in the United States, ___isn't it___?

2. Los Angeles <u>is / isn't</u> the capital of California, _____?

3. Los Angeles is located on the <u>Pacific / Atlantic</u> Ocean, _____?

4. There <u>are / aren't</u> a lot of famous movie studios in L.A., _____?

5. The city <u>has / doesn't have</u> a problem with air pollution, _____?

6. There <u>are / aren't</u> a lot of cars in L.A., _____?

Ask Student B the questions. He or she will read a paragraph about Los Angeles and tell you if your information is correct or not.

EXAMPLE:
A: Los Angeles is one of the largest cities in the United States, isn't it?
B: That's right.

Now read about New York City and answer Student B's questions.

NEW YORK CITY

New York is the largest city in the United States. Located at the mouth of the Hudson River, New York consists of five separate "boroughs," or parts: the Bronx, Brooklyn, Manhattan, Queens, and Staten Island. With its ninety-four universities and colleges, it is one of the major educational centers in the country. New York's historical importance, as well as its fine cultural life, make it a major tourist attraction.

EXAMPLE:
B: New York City is the largest city in the United States, isn't it?
A: Yes, it is.

⑩ WRITING

You are going to interview a classmate about his or her city or school. Write eight questions. Include negative yes/no questions and tag questions. Ask your questions and write your classmate's answers.

INFORMATION GAP FOR STUDENT B

Student B, read about Los Angeles and answer Student A's questions.

Los Angeles

Although Los Angeles isn't the capital of California, it is the state's largest city and the third largest city in the United States. Located on the Pacific Ocean, L.A. is famous for its climate and its beaches. Tourists are also attracted to Hollywood, a section of L.A. which is home to many movie studios. Unfortunately, L.A. is also famous for its smog—air pollution caused by the city's large number of cars.

EXAMPLE:

A: Los Angeles is one of the largest cities in the United States, isn't it?

B: That's right.

Now look at the questions below. What do you know about New York City? Circle the correct words and complete the tag questions.

1. New York City (is)/ isn't the largest city in the United Sates, _____isn't it_____ ?

2. New York City is / isn't located on a river, _____ ?

3. It consists of <u>five / two </u>separate "boroughs," or parts, _____ ?

4. It <u>has / doesn't have</u> over ninety universities and colleges, _____ ?

5. It played a <u>small / big</u> role in early U.S. history, _____ ?

6. <u>Many / Not many</u> tourists visit New York, _____ ?

Ask Student A these same questions. He or she will read a paragraph about New York City and tell you if your information is correct or not.

EXAMPLE:

B: New York City is the largest city in the United States, isn't it?

A: Yes, it is.

ADDITIONS AND RESPONSES WITH *SO, TOO, NEITHER, NOT EITHER,* AND *BUT*

GRAMMAR **IN CONTEXT**

BEFORE YOU READ   Look at the pictures of twins. Find the things that are different about them and the things that are the same.

Read this magazine article about identical twins.

THE TWIN QUESTION: NATURE OR NURTURE?

by RUTH SANBORN, *Family Life* Editor

MARK AND GERALD are identical twins. Mirror images of each other, they also share many similarities in lifestyle. Mark is a firefighter, and **so is Gerald**. Mark has never been married, and **neither has Gerald**. Mark likes hunting, fishing, and Chinese food. **Gerald does too**.

These similarities might not be unusual in identical twins, except for one fact: Mark and Gerald were separated when they were five days old. They grew up in different states with different families. Neither one knew that he had a twin until they found each other accidentally at age thirty-one.

Average people are fascinated by twins, and **so are scientists**. Identical twins share the same genes. Therefore, they offer researchers the chance to study the effect of genetic inheritance on health and personality.

However, when identical twins grow up together, they also experience the same environment. How can researchers separate these environmental factors from genetic factors? By looking at identical twins who are separated at birth! Twins with completely different childhoods give researchers the chance to study the age-old question: Which has more effect on our lives, heredity (the genes we receive from our parents) or environment (the social influences in our childhood)?

MARK AND GERALD

(continued on next page)

JIM AND JIM

Some startling coincidences have turned up in these studies. One astonishing pair is the Springer and Lewis brothers, who were adopted by different families soon after birth. The Springer family named their adopted son Jim. **So did the Lewis family**. When the two Jims met for the first time as adults, they discovered more surprising similarities. Jim Lewis had worked as a gas station attendant and a law enforcement agent. **So had Jim Springer**. Both men had had dogs. Lewis had named his Toy; **so had Springer**. And believe it or not, Lewis had married a woman named Linda, divorced her, and later married a woman named Betty. **So had Springer**.

Do our genes really determine our names, our spouses, our jobs, even our pets? The lives of other twins indicate that the question of nature or nurture is even more complicated than that.

Identical twins Andrea and Barbara, for example, were born in Germany and separated shortly after birth.

Andrea stayed in Germany, **but Barbara didn't**. She moved to the United States with her adoptive American family. The twins grew up in different cultures, speaking different languages. Barbara didn't know she had a twin, **but Andrea did**, and she searched for her sister. When they met, they discovered amazing similarities. Each had a scar on her lip from an accident. Each had had a tonsillectomy —on the same day!

Nevertheless, there were important differences. Andrea is outgoing and expressive, **but Barbara isn't**, despite her identical genetic heritage. Both sisters got married and had two children. Andrea stayed married, but Barbara married and divorced several times.

Clearly, heredity doesn't completely govern our lives. **Our environment doesn't either**. The lives of twins separated at birth suggest that we have a lot to learn about the complex role these two powerful forces play in shaping human lives.

BARBARA AND ANDREA

This photograph was taken on the day Barbara and Andrea were reunited. The man standing between them, Thomas Gulotta, helped bring them together.

GRAMMAR **PRESENTATION**
ADDITIONS WITH *SO, TOO, NEITHER, NOT EITHER*

WITH *BE* AS THE MAIN VERB

AFFIRMATIVE		NEGATIVE	
SUBJECT + *BE*	(*AND*) + *SO* + *BE* + SUBJECT	SUBJECT + *BE* + *NOT*	(*AND*) + *NEITHER* + *BE* + SUBJECT
Amy **is** a twin,	**and so is** Sue.	Amy **isn't** very tall,	**and neither is** Sue.

AFFIRMATIVE		NEGATIVE	
SUBJECT + *BE*	(*AND*) + SUBJECT + *BE* + *TOO*	SUBJECT + *BE* + *NOT*	(*AND*) + SUBJECT + *BE* + *NOT EITHER*
Amy **is** a twin,	**and** Sue **is too**.	Amy **isn't** very tall,	**and** Sue **isn't either**.

WITH ALL AUXILIARY VERBS EXCEPT *DO*

AFFIRMATIVE		NEGATIVE	
SUBJECT + AUXILIARY	(*AND*) + *SO* + AUXILIARY + SUBJECT	SUBJECT + AUXILIARY + *NOT*	(*AND*) + *NEITHER* + AUXILIARY + SUBJECT
Amy **has** had two sons,	**and so has** Sue.	Amy **can't** ski,	**and neither can** Sue.

AFFIRMATIVE		NEGATIVE	
SUBJECT + AUXILIARY	(*AND*) + SUBJECT + AUXILIARY + *TOO*	SUBJECT + AUXILIARY + *NOT*	(*AND*) + SUBJECT + AUXILIARY + *NOT EITHER*
Amy **has** had two sons,	**and** Sue **has too**.	Amy **can't** ski,	**and** Sue **can't either**.

WITH *DO* AS AUXILIARY VERB

AFFIRMATIVE		NEGATIVE	
SUBJECT + VERB	(*AND*) + *SO* + *DO* + SUBJECT	SUBJECT + *DO* + *NOT* + VERB	(*AND*) + *NEITHER* + *DO* + SUBJECT
Amy **likes** dogs,	**and so does** Sue.	Amy **doesn't** like cats,	**and neither does** Sue.

AFFIRMATIVE		NEGATIVE	
SUBJECT + VERB	(*AND*) + SUBJECT + *DO* + *TOO*	SUBJECT + *DO* + *NOT* + VERB	(*AND*) + SUBJECT + *DO* + *NOT* + *EITHER*
Amy **likes** dogs,	**and** Sue **does too**.	Amy **doesn't** like cats,	**and** Sue **doesn't either**.

(continued on next page)

ADDITIONS WITH *BUT*

WITH *BE* AS THE MAIN VERB

AFFIRMATIVE	NEGATIVE		NEGATIVE	AFFIRMATIVE
SUBJECT + *BE*	*BUT* + SUBJECT + *BE* + *NOT*		SUBJECT + *BE* + *NOT*	*BUT* + SUBJECT + *BE*
Amy **is** outgoing,	**but** Sue **isn't**.		Amy **isn't** quiet,	**but** Sue **is**.

WITH ALL AUXILIARY VERBS EXCEPT *DO*

AFFIRMATIVE	NEGATIVE		NEGATIVE	AFFIRMATIVE
SUBJECT + AUXILIARY	*BUT* + SUBJECT + AUXILIARY + *NOT*		SUBJECT + AUXILIARY + *NOT*	*BUT* + SUBJECT + AUXILIARY
Amy **has** traveled,	**but** Sue **hasn't**.		Amy **couldn't** swim,	**but** Sue **could**.

WITH *DO* AS AUXILIARY VERB

AFFIRMATIVE	NEGATIVE		NEGATIVE	AFFIRMATIVE
SUBJECT + VERB	*BUT* + SUBJECT + *DO* + *NOT*		SUBJECT + *DO* + *NOT*	*BUT* + SUBJECT + *DO*
Amy **lives** here,	**but** Sue **doesn't**.		Amy **doesn't** drive,	**but** Sue **does**.

NOTES	EXAMPLES
1. Additions are phrases or short sentences that follow a statement. They express <u>similarity</u> to or <u>contrast</u> with the information in the statement without repeating the information.	**SIMILARITY** • Lewis bites his fingernails, **and so does Springer**. *(Lewis bites his fingernails. Springer bites his fingernails, too.)* **CONTRAST** • Barbara's marriage ended, **but Andrea's didn't**. *(Barbara's marriage ended. Andrea's marriage didn't end.)*
2. Use *so, too, neither*, or *not either* in additions of <u>similarity</u>. In the examples, note that additions of similarity can either be clauses or separate sentences.	• Mark is a firefighter, **and *so* is Gerald**. OR • Mark is a firefighter, **and Gerald is *too***. *(Mark is a firefighter. Gerald is a firefighter.)* • Mark isn't married. ***Neither* is Gerald.** OR • Mark isn't married. **Gerald *isn't either*.** *(Mark isn't married. Gerald isn't married.)*
3. Use *so* or *too* if the addition follows an <u>affirmative</u> statement. Use *neither* or *not either* if the addition follows a <u>negative</u> statement. ▶ **BE CAREFUL!** Notice the <u>word order</u> after *so* and *neither*. The verb comes before the subject.	• Mark **is** a firefighter, and *so* **is** Gerald. OR • Mark **is** a firefighter, and Gerald **is** *too*. • Mark **didn't** get married. ***Neither* did** Gerald. OR • Mark **didn't** get married. Gerald **did*n't* either**. • So **is Gerald**. NOT ~~So Gerald is.~~ • Neither **did Gerald**. NOT ~~Neither Gerald did.~~

(continued on next page)

4. Use *but* in additions of <u>contrast</u>.

If the statement is affirmative, the addition is negative.

- Amy **lived** in Germany, *but* Sue **didn't**.

If the statement is negative, the addition is affirmative.

- Amy's family **didn't speak** English, *but* Sue's **did**.

---

5. Additions always use a form of <u>be or an auxiliary verb</u> (a form of *be, have, do,* or *will* or a modal verb such as *can, could, should,* or *would*). The verb used in the addition depends on the verb used in the preceding statement.

a. If the statement uses *be*, use ***be*** in the addition, too.

- I**'m** a twin, and so **is** my cousin.

b. If the statement uses an auxiliary verb, <u>use the same auxiliary verb</u> in the addition.

- Jim Lewis **had** worked in a gas station, and so **had** Jim Springer.
- I **can't** drive, and neither **can** my twin.

c. If the statement doesn't use *be* or an auxiliary verb, <u>use an appropriate form of *do*</u> in the addition.

- Lewis **bought** a Chevrolet, and so **did** Springer.
- Lewis **owns** a dog, and so **does** Springer.

---

6. In conversation, you can use short **responses** with *so, too, neither,* and *not either* to express <u>agreement</u> with another speaker. These short responses are sometimes called "rejoinders."

A: I **have** a twin sister.
B: *So do I.* OR **I do** *too*.

A: I **don't have** any brothers or sisters.
B: *Neither do I.* OR **I don't** *either*.

USAGE NOTE: In informal speech people say *Me too* to express agreement with an affirmative statement and *Me neither* to express agreement with a negative statement.

A: I **think** twin studies are fascinating.
B: *Me too*.

A: I**'ve never heard** of the Jim twins.
B: *Me neither*.

---

7. In conversation, use short **responses** with *but* to express <u>disagreement</u> with another speaker. You can often omit *but*.

A: I **wouldn't like** to have a twin.
B: Oh, *(but)* **I would**.

FOCUSED PRACTICE

1 DISCOVER THE GRAMMAR

Read these short conversations between reunited twins. Decide if the statement that follows each conversation is **True (T)** *or* **False (F)**.

1. **MARK:** I like Chinese food.
   GERALD: So do I.
   ___T___ Gerald likes Chinese food.

2. **ANDREA:** I don't want to go out tonight.
   BARBARA: Neither do I.
   _____ Barbara wants to go out tonight.

3. **AMY:** I didn't understand that article.
   KERRIE: Oh, I did.
   _____ Kerrie understood the article.

4. **JEAN:** I'm not hungry.
   JOAN: I'm not either.
   _____ Jean and Joan are hungry.

5. **ANDREA:** I was born in Germany.
   BARBARA: So was I.
   _____ Barbara was born in Germany.

6. **AMY:** I've always felt lonely.
   KERRIE: So have I.
   _____ Kerrie has felt lonely.

7. **MARK:** I'm ready to get married.
   GERALD: I'm not.
   _____ Gerald is ready to get married.

8. **DEWAYNE:** I can meet at eight o'clock.
   PAUL: I can too.
   _____ Paul can meet at eight o'clock.

9. **JIM:** I have a headache.
   JIM: So do I.
   _____ Both Jims have headaches.

10. **DEWAYNE:** I'm not looking forward to the TV interview.
    PAUL: I am.
    _____ Paul isn't looking forward to the TV interview.

② DOUBLE TROUBLE

Circle the correct words to complete this paragraph.

Sometimes being a twin can cause trouble. In high school, I was in Mr. Jacobs's history

class. Neither /(So) was my brother. One day we took a test. I got questions 18 and 20
 1.

wrong. My brother did so / too. I didn't spell *Constantinople* correctly, and either / neither
 2.   **3.**

did my brother. The teacher was sure we had cheated. As a result, I got an F on the test,

and so did / got my brother. We tried to convince Mr. Jacobs of our innocence. After all,
 4.

I had sat on the left side of the room, but my brother didn't / hadn't. As always, he sat
 5.

on the right. But Mr. Jacobs just thought we had developed some elaborate way of

sharing answers across the room. Our parents believed we were honest, but Mr. Jacobs

didn't / weren't. The principal didn't either / too. We finally convinced them to give us
 6.   **7.**

another test. This time I got items 3 and 10 wrong. Guess what? Neither / So did my
 8.

brother. Our teacher was astounded, and / but we weren't. We were just amused.
 9.

③ WE HAVE SO MUCH IN COMMON

*Two twins are talking. They agree on everything. Complete their
conversation with responses.*

MARTA: I'm so happy we finally found each other.

CARLA: So _____am I_____. I always felt like something was missing from my life.
 1.

MARTA: So _____. I always knew I had a double somewhere out there.
 2.

CARLA: I can't believe how similar we are.

MARTA: Neither _____. It's like always seeing myself in the mirror.
 3.

CARLA: Not only do we look identical, we like and dislike all the same things.

MARTA: Right. I hate lettuce.

CARLA: I _____. And I detest liver.
 4.

MARTA: So _____. I love pizza, though.
 5.

CARLA: So _____. But only with tomato and cheese. I don't like pepperoni.
 6.

MARTA: Neither _____.
 7.

CARLA: This is amazing! I wonder if our husbands have so much in common.

MARTA: So _____!
8.

4 THE TWO BOBS

Look at this chart about the twins' husbands. Then complete the sentences about them. Add statements with **so, too, neither, not either,** *and* **but.**

	BOB BOWEN	BOB PHILLIPS
Age	42	42
Height	6'2"	5'8"
Weight	180 lb	180 lb
Color hair	blond	blond
Color eyes	blue	brown
Hobbies	tennis	tennis
Favorite food	steak	steak
Military service	yes	no
Education	graduate degree	graduate degree
Languages	English, Spanish	English, French
Job	lawyer	engineer
Brothers or sisters	none	none

1. Bob Bowen is 42, __and so is Bob Phillips. OR and Bob Phillips is too.__

2. Bob Bowen is 6'2", _____

3. Bob Bowen weighs 180 pounds, _____

4. Bob Bowen has blond hair, _____

5. Bob Bowen doesn't have green eyes, _____

6. Bob Bowen plays tennis, _____

7. Bob Bowen likes steak, _____

8. Bob Bowen served in the military, _____

9. Bob Bowen has attended graduate school, _____

10. Bob Bowen doesn't speak French, _____

11. Bob Bowen became a lawyer, _____

12. Bob Bowen doesn't have any brothers or sisters, _____

5 EDITING

Read this student's composition. There are five mistakes in the use of sentence additions. Find and correct them. The first mistake is already corrected.

Name: Ryan Tarver

MY BROTHER AND I

My brother is just a year older than I am. (I'm 18.) We have a lot of things in common. We look

alike. I am 5'10", and so ~~be is~~ *is he*. I have straight black hair and dark brown eyes, and so does he. We

share some of the same interests, too. I love to play soccer, and he too. Both of us swim every day,

but I can't dive, and either can he.

   Although there are a lot of similarities between us, there are also many differences. For example,

he likes eating all kinds of food, but I don't. Give me hamburgers and fries every day! My brother

doesn't want to go to college, but I don't. I believe it's important to get as much education as

possible, but he wants to get real-life experience. Our personalities are quite different. I am quiet

and easygoing, but he not. He has lots of energy and talks a lot. When I think about it, we really

are more different than similar.

6 BROTHERS   Grammar Notes 2–5

Look at Exercise 5. Complete the chart by putting a check in the correct column(s).

	RYAN	RYAN'S BROTHER
1. is 18 years old	☑	☐
2. is 5'10" tall	☐	☐
3. has black hair	☐	☐
4. has dark brown eyes	☐	☐
5. loves soccer	☐	☐
6. swims	☐	☐
7. dives	☐	☐
8. prefers hamburgers and fries	☐	☐
9. wants to go to college	☐	☐
10. prefers "real-life" experience	☐	☐
11. is quiet	☐	☐
12. is easygoing	☐	☐

COMMUNICATION PRACTICE

⑦ LISTENING

A couple is out on a first date. Listen to their conversation. Then listen again and complete the chart by putting a check in the correct column(s).

	Man	Woman		Man	Woman
1. loves Italian food	☑	☑	**6.** enjoys fiction	☐	☐
2. cooks	☐	☐	**7.** plays sports	☐	☐
3. eats out a lot	☐	☐	**8.** watches sports on TV	☐	☐
4. enjoys old movies	☐	☐	**9.** watches news programs	☐	☐
5. reads biographies	☐	☐	**10.** wants to see the documentary	☐	☐

⑧ LET'S EAT OUT

Work in pairs. Look at these two restaurant ads. What do the two restaurants have in common? In what ways are they different? Discuss these questions and agree upon the restaurant you want to go to.

Luigi's
Italian Restaurant

Family-style eating since 1990

Open Tuesday–Sunday, 12:00–9:00

EARLY-BIRD SPECIAL
(full dinner for $10.95 if ordered before 6:00)

No reservations necessary
No credit cards

875 Orange St.

Antonio's
Ristorante Italiano

Established in 1990

Relaxed dining in a romantic atmosphere
open seven days a week—dinner only
reservations suggested

---

all credit cards accepted

1273 Orange Street 453-3285

one free beverage with this ad

EXAMPLE:
A: Luigi's serves Italian food.
B: So does Antonio's.

9 A GOOD MATCH?

Work in pairs. Look at the chart in Exercise 7. Do you think that the man and woman are a good "match"? Discuss your reasons. How important is it for couples to have a lot in common?

EXAMPLE:

The man and woman have a lot in common.

He loves Italian food, and so does she.

10 HOW COMPATIBLE ARE YOU?

Complete these statements. (For 11 and 12, add your own statements). Then read your statements to a classmate. He or she will give you a short response. Check the items the two of you have in common.

EXAMPLE:

A: I like to walk in the rain.

B: So do I. OR Oh, I don't. I like to stay home and watch TV.

	I have these things in common with:	
	(Classmate 1)	(Classmate 2)
1. I like to _____	❏	❏
2. I never _____	❏	❏
3. I get angry when _____	❏	❏
4. I love _____ (name of food)	❏	❏
5. I can't _____	❏	❏
6. I would like to _____	❏	❏
7. I have never _____	❏	❏
8. When I was younger, I didn't _____	❏	❏
9. I will never _____	❏	❏
10. I have to _____	❏	❏
11. _____	❏	❏
12. _____	❏	❏

Now work with another classmate. Count the number of checks for each of the two classmates. Which classmate do you have more in common with?

11 MICHAEL AND MATTHEW

Work with a partner. Look at the pictures of these twins. How many things do they have in common? How many differences can you find? You have eight minutes to write your answers. Then compare your answers with those of another pair.

Michael

Matthew

EXAMPLE:
Michael has a mustache, and so does Matthew.

12 NATURE OR NURTURE?

Reread the article beginning on page 101. Which is more important, nature or nurture? Have a class discussion. Give examples to support your views.

13 WRITING

Do you know any twins? If so, write about them. What do they have in common? What are their differences? If you don't know any twins, write about two people who are close (siblings, cousins, friends, spouses, etc.). Use the composition in Exercise 5 as a model.

PART III

REVIEW OR SELFTEST

I. *Complete these tag questions and negative questions.*

1. Mr. Chen comes from China, _____doesn't he_____?

2. He's been staying with the Carsons, _____?

3. The Carsons haven't been to China yet, _____?

4. _____ they meet Mr. Chen for the first time in school?

5. They hadn't known him before then, _____?

6. The Carsons don't speak Chinese, _____?

7. _____ we having dinner with them next Saturday?

8. We should bring something, _____?

9. _____ we be staying there pretty late?

10. We'll have a lot of questions to ask, _____?

11. _____ it going to be an interesting evening?

II. *Complete the tag questions and negative questions with an appropriate form of the verb in parentheses. Choose between affirmative and negative.*

1. _____Isn't_____ the population of China over a billion?
   (be)

2. Its land area _____ much bigger than the United States, is it?
   (be)

3. China _____ a lot of rice, doesn't it?
   (export)

4. _____ the Yangtze Delta usually _____ 25 percent of China's crop?
   (produce)

5. _____ the Chinese now _____ millions of trees to stop erosion?
   (plant)

6. Beijing _____ always _____ the capital of China, has it?
   (be)

7. Marco Polo _____ Beijing, did he?
   (build)

8. _____ Kublai Khan _____ Beijing *Dadu* a long time ago?
   (name)

114

9. The Chinese language _____ an alphabet, does it?
(use)

10. _____ people _____ different dialects today in China?
(speak)

III. *Circle the letter of the correct response.*

1. John lives in L.A.   Ⓐ **B C D**
   (A) So does Alice.   (C) But Alice does.
   (B) Neither does Alice.   (D) Alice doesn't either.

2. Didn't he use to live in New York?   **A B C D**

   _____ He lived in Boston.
   (A) No, he didn't.   (C) Neither did he.
   (B) Yes, he did.   (D) But he did.

3. Alice got married two years ago.   **A B C D**
   (A) Neither did John.   (C) So did John.
   (B) So does John.   (D) But John did.

4. Alice is going to China, isn't she?   **A B C D**

   _____ She's flying there on Friday.
   (A) No, she isn't.   (C) But she is.
   (B) Yes, she is.   (D) But she isn't.

5. Doesn't John work for A. Linden & Co.?   **A B C D**
   (A) He doesn't either.   (C) Yes, he is.
   (B) Neither does he.   (D) Yes, he does.

6. Alice has been working there for five years.   **A B C D**
   (A) But John hasn't.   (C) So does John.
   (B) John hasn't either.   (D) Neither has John.

7. Alice is looking for a new job.   **A B C D**
   (A) So is John.   (C) John does too.
   (B) But John doesn't.   (D) But John is.

8. John has an interview tomorrow, doesn't he?   **A B C D**
   (A) Yes, he will.   (C) So does he.
   (B) Yes, he does.   (D) Neither does he.

9. John should look at the employment ads.   **A B C D**
   (A) But Alice should.   (C) Alice should too.
   (B) Alice shouldn't either.   (D) Neither should Alice.

10. Wasn't Alice going to speak to her boss?   **A B C D**
   (A) No, she wasn't.   (C) No, she won't.
   (B) So is she.   (D) Neither does she.

IV. *Complete these conversations with responses.*

1. **A:** I've never eaten here before.

   B: I ___haven't either___. But it's supposed to be very good.

2. **A:** I don't like cabbage.

   B: _____ my husband. He never eats the stuff. Maybe they have another

   vegetable.

3. **A:** My dish tastes very salty.

   B: _____ mine. We're going to be really thirsty later.

4. **A:** My mother used to make this dish.

   B: My mother _____. It was always one of my favorites.

5. **A:** I was going to invite Alice to join us.

   B: That's funny. I _____. I'm sorry we didn't.

6. **A:** I'd love some dessert.

   B: _____ I. The chocolate cake looks good.

7. **A:** I'm full.

   B: I _____. I can't eat another bite.

8. **A:** Luigi's doesn't accept credit cards.

   B: This restaurant _____. But don't worry. I have enough cash on me.

9. **A:** I shouldn't have any more coffee.

   B: _____ I. I won't be able to sleep.

10. **A:** I'm glad we did this.

    B: _____ I. It was a lot of fun.

V. *Read this letter. There are seven mistakes in the use of negative questions, tag questions, and sentence additions. Find and correct them. The first mistake is already corrected.*

Dear Stacy,

    I'm a pretty bad letter writer, ~~ain't~~ *aren't* I? How are you? You didn't mention Marta in your last letter. Don't you roommates anymore? My new roommate's name is Rafaella. We have a lot in common. She's 18, and so I am. She used to live in Chicago, and, of course, I did too. We have the same study habits, too. She doesn't stay up late, and neither don't I.

    Luckily, there are some important differences, too. You remember what my room looked like at home, didn't you? Well, I'm not very neat, but Rafaella is. I can't cook, but she can too. So life is improving. You have a break soon, do you? Why don't you come for a visit? I know the three of us would have a good time.

                  Love,

                  Mona

▶ **To check your answers, go to the Answer Key on page 120.**

PART III
FROM GRAMMAR TO WRITING
AVOIDING REPETITION WITH SENTENCE ADDITIONS

When you write, one way to avoid repetition is to use sentence additions.

EXAMPLE:
Brasília is a capital city. Washington, D.C. is a capital city. ⟶
Brasília is a capital city, **and so is Washington, D.C.**

 Read this student's essay comparing and contrasting Brasília and Washington, D.C. Underline once all the additions that express similarity. Underline twice all the additions that express contrast.

BRASÍLIA AND WASHINGTON, D.C.

Citizens of Brasília and citizens of Washington, D.C. live on different continents, but their cities still have a lot in common. Brasília is its nation's capital, <u>and so is Washington</u>. Brasília did not exist before it was planned and built as the national capital. Neither did Washington. Both cities were designed by a single person, and both have a definite shape. However, twentieth century Brasília's shape is modern—that of an airplane—<u><u>but eighteenth century Washington's isn't</u></u>. Its streets form a wheel.

The cities reflect their differences in location and age. Brasília is located in a dry area in the highlands, while Washington was built on a swamp. As a result, Brasília has moderate temperatures all year. But Washington doesn't. It is famous for its cold winters and hot, humid summers. Brasília was built 600 miles from the Atlantic coast in order to attract people to an unpopulated area. Washington, near the Atlantic coast, includes old towns that had already existed. Brasília is home to the national theater and famous museums, and so is Washington. However, as a new city, Brasília has not yet become its nation's real cultural center. Washington hasn't either. Washington is its country's capital, but it is not its country's most popular city. Neither is Brasília. Many residents still prefer the excitement of Rio and New York to their nations' capitals.

2 *Before writing the essay in Exercise 1, the student made a Venn diagram showing the things that Brasília and Washington, D.C. have in common, and the things that are different. Complete the student's diagram.*

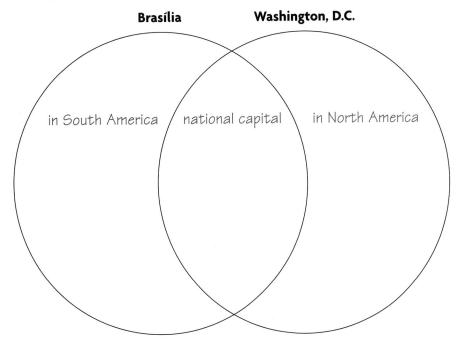

Brasília **Washington, D.C.**

in South America / national capital \ in North America

3 *Before you write . . .*

- Work with a partner. Agree on a topic for an essay of comparison and contrast. For example, you can compare two places, two people, two types of food, or two TV programs.

- Brainstorm ideas and complete a Venn diagram like the one in Exercise 2.

4 *Write an essay of comparison and contrast using your diagram in Exercise 3.*

5 *Exchange essays with a different partner. Underline once all the additions that show similarity. Underline twice the additions that show difference. Write questions marks (?) above the places you think have a problem. Then answer the following questions.*

a. Did the writer use the correct auxiliary verbs in the additions?   Yes / No

b. Did the writer use correct word order?   Yes / No

c. Do the examples show important similarities and differences?   Yes / No

d. List some other details you would like to know about the two things the writer compared. _____

_____

6 *Discuss your editing suggestions with your partner. Then rewrite your essay with any necessary corrections.*

PART III

REVIEW OR SELFTEST
ANSWER KEY

I. **(Unit 7)**

2. hasn't he
3. have they
4. Didn't
5. had they
6. do they
7. Aren't
8. shouldn't we
9. Won't
10. won't we
11. Isn't

II. **(Unit 7)**

2. isn't
3. exports
4. Doesn't . . . produce
5. Aren't . . . planting
6. hasn't . . . been
7. didn't build
8. Didn't . . . name
9. doesn't use
10. Don't . . . speak

III. **(Units 7–8)**

2. A
3. C
4. B
5. D
6. A
7. A
8. B
9. C
10. A

IV. **(Unit 8)**

2. Neither does
3. So does
4. did too
5. was too
6. So would
7. am too
8. doesn't either
9. Neither should
10. So am

V. **(Units 7–8)**

I'm a pretty bad letter writer,
~~amn't~~ *aren't* I? How are you? You didn't
mention Marta in your last letter.
~~Don't~~ *Aren't* you roommates anymore? My
new roommate's name is Rafaella. We
have a lot in common. She's 18, and
so ~~I am~~ *am I*. She used to live in Chicago,
and, of course, I did too. We have the
same study habits, too. She doesn't
stay up late, and neither ~~don't~~ *do* I.

Luckily, there are some important
differences, too. You remember what
my room looked like at home, ~~didn't~~ *don't*
you? Well, I'm not very neat, but
Rafaella is. I can't cook, but she can
~~too~~. So life is improving. You have a
break soon, ~~do~~ *don't* you? Why don't you
come for a visit? I know the three of
us would have a good time.

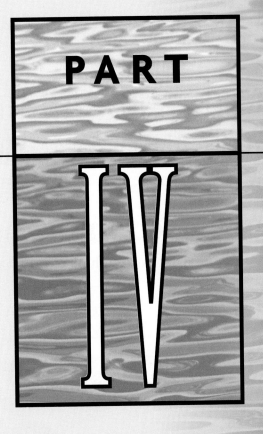

PART

IV

GERUNDS AND INFINITIVES

9 GERUNDS AND INFINITIVES: REVIEW AND EXPANSION

GRAMMAR **IN CONTEXT**

BEFORE YOU READ What do you think of fast-food restaurants like McDonald's?

Read this article about the largest international fast-food restaurant.

McWORLD

BY MICK BERGER

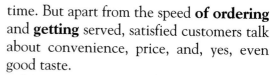

"**I**'ll have a Big Mac, a large fries, and a medium soda." The language may change, but you can **expect to hear** this order in more than 100 countries all over the world. Fast food has become almost synonymous with McDonald's™, the best known of all multinational fast-food restaurant chains. At the moment, Antarctica is the only continent that doesn't (yet!) have a McDonald's. And the numbers **keep growing**. In the United States, alone, most McDonald's customers **need to travel** less than four minutes to arrive at the next golden arch.

Dining on fast food has become a way of life for millions and millions of people from Illinois, U.S.A. (the first McDonald's location) to Colombo, Sri Lanka (a more recent opening). What is it **about eating** on the run that so many people find appealing? Of course, the most obvious answer is that, true to its name, fast food is fast. In today's hectic society, people **don't want to waste**

time. But apart from the speed **of ordering** and **getting** served, satisfied customers talk about convenience, price, and, yes, even good taste.

Many people also like the familiarity and reliability that fast-food chains provide. You can be **sure of getting** the same thing every time, every place. McDonald's **has started to introduce** some local variety, though. For example, in the New England region of the United States, you can get a lobster roll, in Japan you can order a teriyaki McBurger, and in India you can have a Maharaja Mac or a Vegetable Burger. And although most McDonald's restaurants resemble one another, some **try to adjust** to

(continued on next page)

New Delhi, India

foods to other countries and **for underpaying** their workers. Then there is the issue of the environment. Those Big Macs and Quarter Pounders use a lot of disposable packaging and this, in turn, creates a lot of waste. It's a high **price to pay** for convenience.

But like it or not, it's **easy to see** that fast-food restaurants like McDonald's are **here to stay**. From Rovaniemi, Finland, in the north; Invercargill, New Zealand, in the south; Gisborne, New Zealand, in the east; and Western Samoa in the west, the sun never sets on the golden arches.

the surroundings. In Freiburg, Germany, one McDonald's is housed in an historic building more than 700 years old, and in Sweden, there's even a McSki lodge.

Not everyone is **in favor of** fast-food restaurants **spreading** over the globe. In fact, a lot of people are **fed up with seeing** the same restaurants wherever they go. "**Walking** down the Champs Elysées just isn't as romantic as it used to be. When I see McDonald's or Kentucky Fried Chicken everywhere I go, I feel that the world is shrinking too much," complained one traveler. But there are more serious objections.

Nutritionists point to the health consequences **of eating** fast foods since they are generally high in calories, fat, and salt, but low in fiber. In a word, they're unhealthy. Sociologists complain that fast-food restaurants may **prevent** families **from spending** quality time together around the dinner table. Social critics **condemn** fast-food chains **for introducing** unhealthy

Tokyo, Japan

Fast Facts

- The average adult in the U.S. visits a fast food restaurant six times a month.
- Hamburgers are the most popular fast food in the U.S.
- Tacos are the second most popular fast-food choice in the U.S., followed by pizza and chicken.
- Men are more **likely** than women **to order** a hamburger.
- Lunch is the most popular meal at a fast-food restaurant.

GRAMMAR PRESENTATION
GERUNDS AND INFINITIVES

GERUNDS
Eating fast foods is convenient.
They **recommend reducing** fats in the food.
She **started buying** McBreakfast every day.
He **remembered getting** some fruit.
We're **tired of reading** calorie counts for fast foods.
I didn't like **his ordering** fries.

INFINITIVES
It's convenient **to eat** fast foods.
They **plan to reduce** fats in the food.
She **started to buy** McBreakfast every day.
He **remembered to get** some fruit.
We were **surprised to read** the number of calories in fast foods.
I urged **him to order** fries.
It's **time to eat**.

NOTES

1. The **gerund** is often used as the <u>subject</u> of a sentence.

EXAMPLES

- *Eating* fast food can be fun.
- *Not caring* about calories is a mistake.

---

2. The **gerund** is often used after certain verbs as the <u>object</u> of the verb.

You can use a <u>possessive</u> (*Anne's, the boy's, your, his, her, its, our, their*) <u>before the gerund</u>.

USAGE NOTE: In informal spoken English, many people use <u>object pronouns</u> instead of possessives before the gerund.

(See Appendix 3 on page A-2 for a list of verbs that can be followed by the gerund.)

- I **dislike** *eating* fast food every day.
- John **considered** *not eating* fast foods.

- I dislike ***John's eating*** fast foods.
- I dislike ***his eating*** fast foods.

- I dislike ***him eating*** fast foods.

3. Some verbs can be followed by the **infinitive**. These verbs fall into three patterns.

   a. Verbs always followed directly by the <u>infinitive</u>

- They **hope** *to open* a new McDonald's.
- She **chose** *not to give up* on meat.

   b. Verbs always followed by an <u>object + the infinitive</u>

- I **urge** *you to try* that new restaurant.
- She **convinced** *him not to order* fries.

   c. Verbs that can be followed directly by the <u>infinitive</u> or by an <u>object + the infinitive</u>.

- I **want** *to try* that new restaurant.
- I **want** *her to try* it too.

(See Appendices 4 and 5 on page A-3 for lists of these verbs.)

USAGE NOTE: In formal written English, it is considered <u>incorrect to "split" an infinitive</u> by placing a word between *to* and the base form of the verb. However, many people do not follow this rule.

- The community wants **to stop** the spread of fast-food chains immediately. NOT ~~The community wants to immediately stop the spread of fast-food chains.~~

---

4. Some verbs can be followed by either the **gerund or the infinitive**.

(See Appendix 6 on page A-3 for a list of these verbs.)

▶ **BE CAREFUL!** A few verbs (for example, *stop, remember,* and *forget*) can be followed by either a gerund or the infinitive, but the <u>meanings are very different</u>.

- I **started** *bringing* my own lunch.
  OR
- I **started** *to bring* my own lunch.

- She **stopped eating** pizza.
  (She doesn't eat pizza anymore.)
- She **stopped to eat** pizza.
  (She stopped another activity in order to eat pizza.)

- He **remembered buying** milk.
  (First he bought milk. Then he remembered that he did it.)
- He **remembered to buy** milk.
  (First he remembered. Then he bought milk. He didn't forget.)

- They **forgot answering** the letter.
  (They answered it, but afterward they didn't remember the event.)
- They **forgot to answer** the letter.
  (They didn't answer it.)

(continued on next page)

5. The **gerund** is the only verb form that can <u>follow a preposition</u>.

There are many common <u>verb + preposition</u> and <u>adjective + preposition</u> combinations that must be followed by the gerund and not the infinitive.

▶ **BE CAREFUL!** *To* can be part of the infinitive or it can be a preposition. Use the <u>gerund after the preposition *to*</u>.

(See Appendices 7 and 8 on page A-3 for lists of common verb + preposition and adjective + preposition combinations.)

- I read an article **about** *counting* calories.

- I don't **approve of** *eating* fast food.
- We're **interested in** *trying* different types of food.

- We look forward **to** *having* dinner with you.
  NOT ~~We look forward to have dinner with you.~~

---

6. The **infinitive** can often <u>follow an adjective</u>. Many of these adjectives express feelings or attitudes about the action in the infinitive.

(See Appendix 9 on page A-3 for a list of common adjectives that can be followed by the infinitive.)

- They were **eager** *to try* the new taco.
- She was **glad** *to hear* that it was low in calories.
- We're **ready** *to try* something different.

---

7. The **infinitive** can also <u>follow certain nouns</u>.

- It's **time** *to take* a break.
- I have the **right** *to eat* what I want.
- They made a **decision** *to lose* weight.
- It's a high **price** *to pay*.
- He has **permission** *to stay* out late.

---

8. Use the **infinitive** to explain the <u>purpose of an action</u>.

- Doug eats fast food **(in order)** *to save* time.

---

9. To make <u>general statements</u> you can use:
   gerund + verb + adjective
             OR
   it + verb + adjective + **infinitive**

- *Cooking* is fun.
             OR
- **It's** fun *to cook*.

FOCUSED PRACTICE

1 DISCOVER THE GRAMMAR

Read this questionnaire about fast-food restaurants. Underline the gerunds and circle the infinitives.

FAST-FOOD QUESTIONNAIRE

Please take a few minutes (to complete) this questionnaire about fast-food restaurants. Check (✔) all the answers that are appropriate for you.

1. In your opinion, <u>eating</u> fast food is
- ❏ convenient   ❏ fast   ❏ healthy   ❏ cheap   ❏ fun

2. Which meals are you used to eating at a fast-food restaurant?
- ❏ breakfast   ❏ lunch   ❏ dinner   ❏ snacks   ❏ none

3. Which types of fast food do you like to eat?
- ❏ hamburger   ❏ pizza   ❏ fried chicken ❏ tacos   ❏ sushi
- ❏ Other: _____   ❏ None

4. What is the most important issue to you in selecting a fast-food restaurant?
- ❏ menu selection   ❏ quality of food
- ❏ fast service   ❏ low prices
- ❏ Other: _____

5. How often are you likely to eat at a fast-food restaurant?
- ❏ 1–3 times a week   ❏ 4–6 times a week
- ❏ more than 6 times a week ❏ never

6. How much do you enjoy going to fast-food restaurants?
- ❏ I like it very much.   ❏ It's just OK.
- ❏ I don't enjoy it.   ❏ I never go.

7. How do you feel about seeing the same fast-food restaurants all over the world?
- ❏ I like it.   ❏ It doesn't bother me.   ❏ I don't like it.

8. Do you think the government should require fast-food restaurants to include healthy choices?
- ❏ Yes   ❏ No

② FOOD FOR THOUGHT

Grammar Notes 1–3, 5–6

Complete the statements with the correct form of the verbs in parentheses. Use the bar graph to find the number of calories.

Calorie Content of Fast-Food Favorites

Source: Based on information from The Minnesota Attorney General's Office.

1. _____Ordering_____ a Big Mac will "cost" you about _____560_____ calories.
   (Order)

2. _____ a Taco Bell taco is much less fattening. It has only about
   (Have)
   _____ calories.

3. If you want _____ weight, you should probably avoid _____
   (lose)   (eat)
   an Arby's giant roast beef sandwich. It contains around _____ calories.

4. You're likely _____ weight if you eat half of a medium pepperoni pizza. A
   (gain)
   single slice at Pizza Hut has about _____ calories.

5. Stop _____ so many french fries! An order at Wendy's contains about
   (consume)
   _____ calories.

6. Think about _____ an eggroll instead of fries. Leeann Chin's has just a
   (choose)
   little over _____ calories.

7. Nutritionists advise people _____ from fried chicken. A two-piece order at
   (stay away)
   KFC's contains about _____ calories.

3 FOOD EXCHANGES   Grammar Notes 2–4

Complete each summary with the appropriate form of a verb from the box plus the gerund or infinitive form of the verb in parentheses.

| admit | deserve | ~~forget~~ | recommend | remember | stop | try | volunteer |

1. **CUSTOMER:** Uh, didn't I order a large fries too?

   SERVER: That's right, you did. I'll bring them right away.

   SUMMARY: The server ___forgot to bring___ the fries.
   (bring)

2. **DAD:** That Happy Meal isn't enough for you anymore. Have a Big Mac, OK?

   CHILD: OK, but I really wanted the toy in the Happy Meal.

   SUMMARY: The father _____ a Big Mac.
   (order)

3. **MOM:** This car is a mess! Somebody throw out all those fast-food containers!

   STAN: I'll do it, Mom.

   SUMMARY: Stan _____ the fast-food containers.
   (throw out)

4. **PAT:** Hi, Renee. Want to go to Pizza Hut with us?

   RENEE: Thanks, but I can't eat fast food now. I'm training for the swim team.

   SUMMARY: Renee _____ fast food.
   (eat)

5. **EMPLOYEE:** Thanks for the raise. I can really use it.

   MANAGER: You've earned it. You're our best drive-through server.

   SUMMARY: The employee _____ a raise.
   (receive)

6. **VIJAY:** I think you should quit that fast-food job. Your grades are suffering.

   CAROL: It's hard to decide. I need to save for college, but if my grades are bad . . .

   SUMMARY: Carol _____ whether to keep her job.
   (decide)

7. **MOM:** You're not eating dinner. You had some fast food today, didn't you?

   CHRIS: Well . . . Actually, I stopped at Arby's, but I only had a large fries.

   SUMMARY: Chris _____ at Arby's after school.
   (stop)

8. **TIM:** I used to stay in the McDonald's playground for hours when I was little.

   WANG: Yeah, me too. My mother couldn't get me to leave.

   SUMMARY: The boys _____ in the playground when they were younger.
   (play)

❹ CHOICES

Use the words in parentheses to complete these letters to the editor of a school newspaper.

📫 Mailbag

8

To the Editor,

Yesterday, my roommate Andre <u>persuaded me to have</u> lunch with him in the
　　　　　　　　　　　　　　1. (persuade / I / have)

dining hall. I wondered about _____ there because last year he
　　　　　　　　　　　　　　　2. (Andre / want / go)

_____ the dining hall completely. But when we went in, I
3. (stop / use)

understood. Instead of _____ greasy fries and mystery meat, I was
　　　　　　　　　　　　4. (find)

_____ the colorful Taco Bell sombrero. In my opinion, _____
5. (delighted / see)　　　　　　　　　　　　　　　　　　　　　　　　　　　6. (switch)

to fast foods is the way _____. The administration made a great choice.
　　　　　　　　　　　　7. (go)

I _____ fast food, and I _____ me
　8. (support / they / offer)　　　　　　　　9. (appreciate / my friend / persuade)

to give campus food another try.

M. Rodriguez

To the Editor,

I'm writing this letter _____ my anger at _____
　　　　　　　　　　　10. (express)　　　　　　　　　　　　11. (have)

fast-food chains in the dining halls. When a classmate and I went to eat yesterday,

I _____ the usual healthy choices of vegetables and salads. I
　12. (expect / we / find)

_____ a fast-food court. In my opinion, it was outrageous
13. (not count on / see)

_____ fast food into the college dining hall. As a commuter, I
14. (bring)

_____ a healthy meal every evening before class, so I
15. (need / have)

_____ away from fast foods. I _____
16. (attempt / stay)　　　　　　　　　17. (urge / the administration / set up)

a salad bar so that students like me can _____ meals on campus.
　　　　　　　　　　　　　　　　　　　18. (keep on / buy)

B. Chen

5 EDITING

Read these postings to an international on-line discussion group. Find and correct fifteen mistakes in the use of the gerund and infinitive. The first mistake is already corrected.

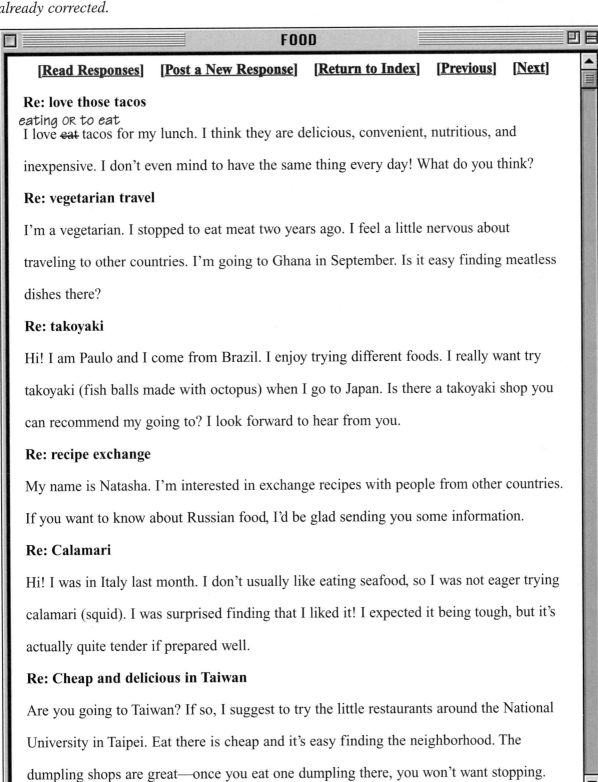

FOOD

[**Read Responses**]   [**Post a New Response**]   [**Return to Index**]   [**Previous**]   [**Next**]

Re: love those tacos

eating OR *to eat*
I love ~~eat~~ tacos for my lunch. I think they are delicious, convenient, nutritious, and inexpensive. I don't even mind to have the same thing every day! What do you think?

Re: vegetarian travel

I'm a vegetarian. I stopped to eat meat two years ago. I feel a little nervous about traveling to other countries. I'm going to Ghana in September. Is it easy finding meatless dishes there?

Re: takoyaki

Hi! I am Paulo and I come from Brazil. I enjoy trying different foods. I really want try takoyaki (fish balls made with octopus) when I go to Japan. Is there a takoyaki shop you can recommend my going to? I look forward to hear from you.

Re: recipe exchange

My name is Natasha. I'm interested in exchange recipes with people from other countries. If you want to know about Russian food, I'd be glad sending you some information.

Re: Calamari

Hi! I was in Italy last month. I don't usually like eating seafood, so I was not eager trying calamari (squid). I was surprised finding that I liked it! I expected it being tough, but it's actually quite tender if prepared well.

Re: Cheap and delicious in Taiwan

Are you going to Taiwan? If so, I suggest to try the little restaurants around the National University in Taipei. Eat there is cheap and it's easy finding the neighborhood. The dumpling shops are great—once you eat one dumpling there, you won't want stopping.

COMMUNICATION PRACTICE

6 LISTENING

Listen to two college students discuss their responses to a Food Services survey. Listen again and check the suggestions that each student agrees with.

School Food Services Survey

We're changing and you can help! Please complete the survey by checking (✓) the changes you want to see.

		Lily	Viktor
1. Introducing Burger Queen fast foods	☐	☐	☑
2. Showing fat and calorie content of each serving	☐	☐	☐
3. Providing more healthy choices	☐	☐	☐
4. Lowering prices	☐	☐	☐
5. Improving food quality	☐	☐	☐
6. Offering Chinese food	☐	☐	☐
7. Starting breakfast at 6:30 A.M.	☐	☐	☐

7 QUESTIONNAIRE

Look again at the questionnaire on page 127. Answer the questions. Discuss your answers with your classmates. Then tally the results.

EXAMPLE:
Fifteen students agree that eating fast food is convenient and cheap.

8 FOODS FROM AROUND THE WORLD

Imagine that you are planning an international food festival. Which foods from your country would you like to see there? Which foods from other countries would you enjoy trying? Make a list. Compare your list with other groups' lists.

EXAMPLE:
I'd like people to try takoyaki. For myself, I'm interested in trying Turkish food.

❾ INFORMATION GAP: THE RIGHT JOB?

Work in pairs (A and B). Student B, go to page 135 and follow the instructions there. Student A, ask Student B questions in order to complete the quiz below. Answer Student B's questions.

EXAMPLE:

A: What does Jennifer enjoy doing?

B: She enjoys working with others.
What does Jennifer expect to do?

A: She expects to make a lot of money.

JOB / PERSONALITY QUIZ

Before you start looking at job ads, take this quiz to find out about your job preferences. Complete the statements with information about yourself.

Name: ___Jennifer Johnson___

1. I enjoy ___working with others___.
2. I expect ___to make a lot of money___.
3. I'm good at _____.
4. I dislike ___working inside___.
5. I don't mind _____.
6. I'm willing ___to learn new skills___.
7. I never complain about _____.
8. I'm eager ___to meet new people___.
9. I plan _____ next year.
10. I dream about ___owning my own business___ one day.
11. I can't stand _____.
12. I expect people ___to be friendly___.

JOB CENTER

Word Processor
in busy 2-person office
~ 3 days/week
~ must type 60 wpm
~ must meet deadlines
~ $10/hr

Volunteering can lead to a high-paying job
Be a Park Volunteer!
Learn about plants and wildlife
Lead tours through park

Athletic Department
Office Assistant
– answer phones
– assist students during registration
– file papers
– $6/hr

BURGER QUEEN
Server Wanted
evenings
$6/hr

Now compare quizzes. Are they the same? Look at the job notices to the right of the quiz. Which jobs do you think would be good for Jennifer? Which jobs wouldn't be good for her? Explain your choices.

🔟 TROUBLESHOOTING

Work in small groups. For each of the problems below, brainstorm as many solutions as you can in five minutes. Then compare your answers with those of another group. You can use some of the following expressions.

I'm in favor of . . .	I'm opposed to . . .
I support . . .	I'm against . . .
I suggest . . .	What about . . .
I go along with . . .	We need . . .
I advise . . .	I recommend . . .
We should start / stop . . .	I urge . . .

1. In the United States, more than half the population is overweight. What can people do about this problem?

   EXAMPLE:

   A: How about improving physical education programs in schools?

   B: I'm in favor of offering healthier meals in schools.

   C: We need to educate people about the role of exercise.

2. Heavy traffic is a big problem in both cities and suburbs. What can we do about it?

3. Many adults can't read or write well enough to function in society. What can be done about this problem?

4. There are millions of homeless people living in the streets and parks. How can we help solve this problem?

5. Other social problems: _____

⓫ WRITING

Write a short editorial about a social problem. You can use one of the topics in Exercise 10 or choose your own. Express your opinions and give reasons for your ideas.

   EXAMPLE:

   I'm in favor of requiring people to take a road test every time they renew their license. By polishing their skills and knowledge every few years, people will become better drivers. . . .

Exchange editorials with a classmate. After you read your classmate's editorial, write a letter to the editor explaining why you agree or disagree with your classmate's viewpoint.

   EXAMPLE:

   To the Editor:

   I go along with requiring additional road tests for drivers. People's eyesight and reflexes can change a lot in five years. . . .

INFORMATION GAP FOR STUDENT B

Student B, answer Student A's questions. Then ask questions in order to complete the quiz below.

EXAMPLE:

A: What does Jennifer enjoy doing?

B: She enjoys working with others.
What does Jennifer expect to do?

A: She expects to make a lot of money.

JOB/PERSONALITY QUIZ

Before you start looking at job ads, take this quiz to find out about your job preferences. Complete the statements with information about yourself.

Name: ___Jennifer Johnson___

1. I enjoy ___working with others___.

2. I expect ___to make a lot of money___.

3. I'm good at ___talking to people___.

4. I dislike _____.

5. I don't mind ___working nights___.

6. I'm willing _____.

7. I never complain about ___following orders___.

8. I'm eager _____.

9. I plan ___to major in business___ next year.

10. I dream about _____ one day.

11. I can't stand ___rushing___.

12. I expect people _____.

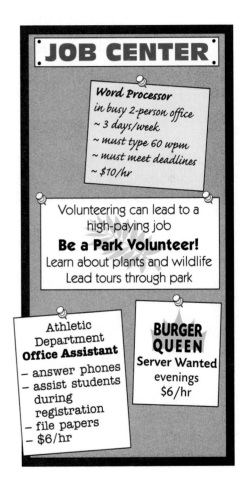

JOB CENTER

Word Processor
in busy 2-person office
~ 3 days/week
~ must type 60 wpm
~ must meet deadlines
~ $10/hr

Volunteering can lead to a high-paying job
Be a Park Volunteer!
Learn about plants and wildlife
Lead tours through park

Athletic Department
Office Assistant
– answer phones
– assist students during registration
– file papers
– $6/hr

BURGER QUEEN
Server Wanted
evenings
$6/hr

Now compare quizzes. Are they the same? Look at the job notices to the right of the quiz. Which jobs do you think would be good for Jennifer? Which jobs wouldn't be good for her? Explain your choices.

MAKE, HAVE, LET, HELP, AND GET

GRAMMAR **IN CONTEXT**

BEFORE YOU READ   Look at the pictures of two classrooms. Talk about some of the differences between them.

 Read part of an article on teaching.

Two Teaching Styles

All teachers want to **help *their students* learn**. There are, however, different teaching approaches. Teachers who use a "student-centered" approach **let *students* choose** the tasks they perform and sometimes even the material they learn. Teachers who use a "teacher-centered" approach plan what to teach and how to teach it, usually with an assigned textbook.

Dan Quintana, a writing teacher at Dudley Community College, follows a teacher-centered approach. If you walk into his class at 8:05 A.M., you will see his students sitting quietly at their desks facing the blackboard. Dan is easy to spot—he's standing in the front taking attendance. Right after the bell rings, he **has *everyone* turn** to page 51 of their textbook, an introduction to paragraph development. He **gets *students* to read** passages aloud from the book, and he **makes**

them **stop** several times while he explains a point. After this presentation, he **gets *students* to answer** questions. One student can't answer, so he **has *her* go back** and find the answer in the textbook. At the end of the class, he assigns an essay topic and announces a test for the following Wednesday. He will correct both the homework and test, and both grades will count toward the students' final grades.

(continued on next page)

Two Teaching Styles (continued)

If most of your learning has been teacher-centered, you will be surprised when you walk down the hall to visit Sandra Jacobson's writing class. For one thing, Sandra usually **has *her students* work** in groups or pairs, and often they are all talking at once. For another, it's hard to find the teacher, since Sandra is usually sitting with one of the groups.

The classroom reflects Sandra's student-centered approach. She doesn't assign writing topics. Instead, she **has *her students* keep** journals, and she **gets *them* to select** their own topics from interests they express in their journal writing. She doesn't correct students' papers, either. Instead, she **has *her students* help *each other* edit** their work. As writing problems emerge,

she does mini-lessons and holds individual conferences. At the end of the semester, Sandra evaluates a portfolio of each student's writing. She **lets *her students* choose** which essays to put into their portfolios.

Both these teaching approaches have many followers, but it is unclear which approach **makes *students* learn** more effectively. Of course, a totally teacher-centered or student-centered class is rare. Many traditional teachers **have *students* work** in groups. Many student-centered teachers structure their courses with a textbook. Students and situations differ, and there is probably no single correct way that fits everyone everywhere.

CARMEN DIEGO

137

GRAMMAR **PRESENTATION**
MAKE, HAVE, LET, HELP, AND *GET*

MAKE, HAVE, LET, HELP					
SUBJECT	**MAKE / HAVE / LET / HELP**		**OBJECT**	**BASE FORM**	
They	(don't)	make have let help*	us students	do	homework.

*Help can also be followed by the infinitive.

GET				
SUBJECT	**GET**	**OBJECT**	**INFINITIVE**	
They	(don't) get	us students	to do	homework.

NOTES	EXAMPLES
1. Use *make, have,* and *let* followed by <u>object + base form</u> of the verb to talk about things that someone can **require, cause, or permit another person to do.***	• They **make *their students* do** homework every night. *(They require them to do homework.)* • They **have *them* take** responsibility for their own learning. *(They cause them to take responsibility.)* • They **let *them* choose** their own curriculum. *(They permit them to choose their own curriculum.)*
You can also use *make* to mean *cause to*.	• This will **make *you* become** a better student. *(This will cause you to become a better student.)*
2. *Help* can be followed either by: <u>object + base form</u> of the verb OR <u>object + infinitive</u> The meaning is the same. USAGE NOTE: *Help* + base form of the verb is more common.	• She **helped *me* understand** the homework. OR • She **helped *me* to understand** the homework.
3. *Get* has a similar meaning to *make* and *have*, but it is followed by <u>object + infinitive</u>, not the base form of the verb.	• The teacher **got *us* to stay** a little later. NOT ~~The teacher got us stay a little later.~~ *(After some effort the teacher succeeded in persuading us to stay.)*

* *Make, have,* and *get* are causative verbs. In this unit they are grouped together with *let* and *help* because all five verbs are related in meaning and structure.

FOCUSED PRACTICE

① DISCOVER THE GRAMMAR

*Read each numbered statement. Then choose the sentence (**a** or **b**) that best describes the situation.*

1. My teacher made me rewrite the report.
   ⓐ I wrote the report again.
   b. I didn't write the report again.

2. Ms. Trager let us use our dictionaries during the test.
   a. We were allowed to use our dictionaries.
   b. We had to use our dictionaries.

3. Mr. Goldberg had us translate a short story.
   a. Mr. Goldberg translated a short story for us.
   b. We translated a short story.

4. Paulo helped Meng do her homework.
   a. Paulo did Meng's homework for her.
   b. Both Paulo and Meng worked on her homework.

5. Ms. Bates got the director to arrange a class trip.
   a. Ms. Bates arranged a class trip.
   b. The director arranged a class trip.

6. Professor Washington let us choose our own topic for our term paper.
   a. We chose our own topic.
   b. We didn't choose our own topic.

② WHO'S THE BOSS?   Grammar Notes 1–2

Students in an English conversation class are talking about their experiences with authority figures. Complete the sentences by circling the correct underlined verbs. Then match each situation with the person in authority.

Situation	Authority Figure
_g_ **1.** I didn't really want to work overtime this week, but she (made)/ let me work late because some of my coworkers were sick.	**a.** my teacher
_____ **2.** I forgot to turn on my headlights before I left the parking lot a few nights ago. She made / let me pull over to the side of the road and asked to see my license.	**b.** my doctor
_____ **3.** At first, we didn't really want to write in our journals. He explained that it would help us. Finally, he had / got us to try it.	**c.** my father

Situation	Authority Figure
_____ **4.** My check was delayed in the mail. I told him what had happened, and he <u>had / let</u> me pay the rent two weeks late.	**d.** a police officer
_____ **5.** I needed to get a blood test for my school physical. He <u>got / had</u> me roll up my sleeve and make a fist.	**e.** the judge
_____ **6.** We're a big family, and we all have our own chores. While she washed the dishes, she <u>helped / had</u> me dry. My brother swept.	**f.** my landlord
_____ **7.** I'm an only child, and when I was young I felt lonely. He <u>let / got</u> me sleep over at my friend's house.	**g.** my boss
_____ **8.** I wasn't paying attention, and I hit a parked car. He <u>let / made</u> me tell the court what happened.	**h.** my mother

③ IN CLASS   Grammar Notes 1–3

Read these short conversations that take place in Ms. Allen's English class. Complete the summary sentences, using the correct form of the verbs in parentheses. Choose between affirmative and negative forms.

1.   **PABLO:** Ms. Allen, do I have to rewrite this composition?

MS. ALLEN: Only if you want to.

SUMMARY: She __didn't make him rewrite__ his composition.
                          (make / rewrite)

2. MS. ALLEN: OK, now. Please get into groups of six.

ANA: I really prefer working alone.

MS. ALLEN: You need to work in a group today.

SUMMARY: She _____ in a group.
                     (make / work)

3. **MASAMI:** Can we use our dictionaries during the test?

MS. ALLEN: No. You should be able to guess the meaning of the words from the context.

SUMMARY: She _____ their dictionaries.
                     (let / use)

4. MS. ALLEN: Fernando, could you do me a favor and clean the board before you leave?

FERNANDO: Sure.

MS. ALLEN: Thank you.

SUMMARY: She _____ the board.
                     (have / clean)

(continued on next page)

5. **YASUKO:** Can I leave the room?

MS. ALLEN: Of course. The key to the ladies' room is hanging next to the door.

SUMMARY: She _____ the room.
(let / leave)

6. **MS. ALLEN:** OK. Now repeat after me: "thorn."

URI: "Torn."

MS. ALLEN: Try putting the tip of your tongue between your teeth like this: "th, thorn."

URI: "Thorn."

MS. ALLEN: That's it! Great!

SUMMARY: She _____ an English *th*.
(get / pronounce)

7. **HECTOR:** What does *intractable* mean?

MS. ALLEN: Why don't you see if one of your classmates can explain it to you?

SUMMARY: She _____ his classmates for help.
(have / ask)

8. **AN-LING:** Do you mind if we record the class?

MS. ALLEN: Not at all. In fact, I think it's an excellent idea.

SUMMARY: She _____ the class.
(let / record)

9. **GRETA:** *Bitte, was bedeudet* telecommute? *Ich kann das Wort nicht verstehen.*

MS. ALLEN: In English, please, Greta!

GRETA: Sorry. What does *telecommute* mean?

SUMMARY: She _____ in German.
(let / speak)

10. **JEAN-PAUL:** Ms. Allen, can you recommend a video in English for us to watch?

MS. ALLEN: Sure. I have a list of recommended ones right here.

SUMMARY: She _____ an appropriate video to rent.
(help / find)

11. **TAMARA:** I can't think of anything to write about.

MS. ALLEN: Just pick a topic that interests you. A hobby, perhaps.

TAMARA: Oh! I know. I could write about ice-skating.

SUMMARY: She _____ her own topic.
(get / choose)

④ EDITING

Read this student's composition. Find and correct six mistakes in the use of **make**, **have**, **get**, **let**, *and* **help**. *The first mistake is already corrected.*

Name: _____Justin Pemberton_____   Class: _____Writing 101_____

All Work and No Play

When I was a teenager, my parents were very strict with me. They never let me ~~to~~ play until I had finished all my homework. They even made me helping my brothers and sisters with their homework before I could have any fun.

On the one hand, I believe their discipline was good for me. By being so demanding, they certainly got me to learn a lot more. As a result, I always got good grades in school. But I wish they had let me to have a little more fun. I was much too serious. I think parents should help their children learn to enjoy life. There is plenty of time for adult responsibility later on.

If I become a parent, I hope to find a good balance between discipline and permissiveness. I would want to have my child learns responsibility, but also I would want to let he or she have fun. I agree with Ben Franklin, who said that all work and no play makes Jack to become a dull boy. I want to avoid that mistake.

COMMUNICATION PRACTICE

5 LISTENING

Listen to a student talking to his teacher about a writing assignment. Then listen again and write **True (T)** *or* **False (F)** *next to each statement.*

__T__ **1.** Ms. Jacobson let Simon choose his own topic.

_____ **2.** She let him change the topic of his essay.

_____ **3.** She got him to talk about his uncle.

_____ **4.** She had him remove some details from his second paragraph.

_____ **5.** She helped him correct a grammar mistake.

_____ **6.** Simon got Ms. Jacobson to correct the gerunds in his essay.

_____ **7.** Ms. Jacobson made Simon look for the gerunds in his essay.

_____ **8.** She let Simon make an appointment for another conference.

6 TEXTBOOK SURVEY

Complete this survey. Then work in small groups. Compare answers. Do you and your classmates have the same perception of your textbook?

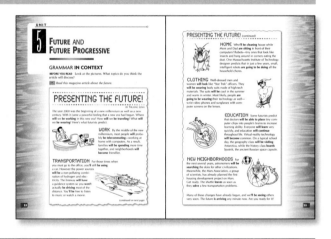

Does this textbook . . .	Always	Often	Sometimes	Rarely	Never
1. make you think?	☐	☐	☐	☐	☐
2. help you learn?	☐	☐	☐	☐	☐
3. have you work in pairs and groups?	☐	☐	☐	☐	☐
4. get students to speak in class?	☐	☐	☐	☐	☐
5. get you to practice outside of class?	☐	☐	☐	☐	☐
6. let you find and correct mistakes?	☐	☐	☐	☐	☐
7. help you to speak accurately?	☐	☐	☐	☐	☐
8. make learning fun?	☐	☐	☐	☐	☐
9. let you test your own progress?	☐	☐	☐	☐	☐
10. let you choose your own topics for discussion?	☐	☐	☐	☐	☐

7 BRINGING UP TEENAGERS

*Look at this list. Check the things you think are important to make and let a
teenager do. Compare and discuss your list with a partner.*

- ☐ stay out until midnight on weekends
- ☐ stay over at a friend's house
- ☐ travel alone to a foreign country
- ☐ get a part-time job
- ☐ dye his or her hair another color
- ☐ smoke
- ☐ drink alcohol

- ☐ take care of younger children
- ☐ learn to drive
- ☐ study every day, including weekends
- ☐ exercise
- ☐ go to the dentist every year
- ☐ learn another language
- ☐ pay part of the bills

> **EXAMPLE:**
>
> **A:** I think it's important to make your kids come home before midnight—even on weekends.
>
> **B:** I'm not so sure. I think parents should let their children stay out late one night a week. It gives them a sense of responsibility. . . .

8 ROLE PLAY

*Work with a partner. Read about the following problems. Role-play your
discussion about how to solve each one. Begin with **I (don't) think you should
let / make / have / help / get** . . .*

1. You are a parent. Your twelve-year-old daughter asks permission to go to a school dance with a boy from her class who you do not know. She wants to buy a new dress and wear makeup. Role-play the discussion between the parent and the daughter.

   > **EXAMPLE:**
   >
   > **A:** All my friends are going. You never let me have any fun.
   >
   > **B:** You can go, but have your date's parents call me before.

2. You are married. Your husband or wife wants to buy a very expensive watch. You don't think a new watch is necessary. In addition, you are saving money for a car that you both need very badly. Role-play the discussion between the husband and wife.

3. You have been dating someone for a year. Your boyfriend or girlfriend now wants to go out with other people but still continue to see you. You were hoping to marry this person. Role-play the discussion between the boyfriend and girlfriend.

9 WRITING

*Write about someone who helped you learn something (for example, a parent,
other relative, teacher, friend). What did the person get you to do that you never
did before? How did this person help you? Did he or she let you make mistakes in
order to learn?*

REVIEW OR SELFTEST

I. *Circle the letter of the correct word or words to complete each sentence.*

1. Sue has always wanted _____ her own restaurant.   A Ⓑ C D
   (A) opening   (C) open
   (B) to open   (D) she opens

2. She took accounting courses _____ for her business.   A B C D
   (A) prepare   (C) to prepare
   (B) prepared   (D) for preparing

3. Last year, she succeeded in _____ a loan from   A B C D
   the bank.
   (A) getting   (C) her getting
   (B) got   (D) to get

4. We all celebrated _____ opening Sue's Kitchen.   A B C D
   (A) she   (C) she was
   (B) hers   (D) her

5. When she first opened, she avoided _____ people to   A B C D
   help her.
   (A) asked   (C) asking
   (B) to ask   (D) their asking

6. She was tired, but we couldn't _____ her accept   A B C D
   our help.
   (A) made   (C) making
   (B) to make   (D) make

7. At first she was terrible at _____ the place.   A B C D
   (A) she managed   (C) managed
   (B) managing   (D) to manage

8. _____ experience is important, so we all told her to   A B C D
   keep trying.
   (A) Getting   (C) She's getting
   (B) To get   (D) She was getting

9. After a few weeks, she let _____ help her cook.   A B C D
   (A) my   (C) I
   (B) mine   (D) me

10. I think she appreciated _____ giving her a hand.   A B C D
    (A) I was   (C) my
    (B) I am   (D) mine

11. Recently, she's been having me _____ entire meals.   **A B C D**

   (A) preparing   (C) to prepare

   (B) prepare   (D) prepared

12. Now she's finally thinking _____ hiring someone to help.   **A B C D**

   (A) on   (C) for

   (B) about   (D) to

13. A lot of people are afraid of _____ a business, but Sue isn't.   **A B C D**

   (A) they own   (C) owning

   (B) to own   (D) they're owning

14. We're proud of her for _____ such a big decision.   **A B C D**

   (A) made   (C) makes

   (B) to make   (D) making

15. Now we have to make _____ take a vacation.   **A B C D**

   (A) her   (C) hers

   (B) to   (D) she

II. *Complete this letter to the editor of a newspaper. Use the correct form of the verbs in parentheses.*

Dear Editor:

   Cars are essential in today's society. We need them _____*to get*_____ from place to

place. However, _____ is a privilege, not a right. I'm in favor of
                       2. (drive)

_____ licenses for serious moving violations. Furthermore, if someone has his
    3. (suspend)

or her license suspended more than once, that person should not be permitted

_____ at all.
   4. (drive)

   I learned _____ when I was sixteen. I remember _____ very
           5. (drive)   **6. (be)**

happy when I first got my license. In fact, my friends and family even celebrated my

_____ the road test. But my parents cautioned me _____ this
   7. (pass)   **8. (not take)**

new responsibility lightly. In order _____ in me a sense of responsibility, they
                      9. (instill)

made me _____ my own car insurance from the start. They expected me
      10. (pay)

_____ a cautious and courteous driver at all times. They insisted on my
   11. (be)

_____ all rules and regulations.
   12. (obey)

   Some of my friends objected to _____ wear seatbelts. They couldn't stand
                          13. (have to)

_____ "confined." Seatbelts save lives and help _____ serious
   14. (feel)   **15. (prevent)**

(continued on next page)

injuries. It's irresponsible _____ them, and if my friends refused
16. (not use)

_____, I didn't even let them _____ with me.
17. (buckle up)   18. (ride)

I believe that too many people consider _____ a sport. Stricter laws, and
19. (drive)

the enforcement of those laws, will make people _____ more carefully on the
20. (behave)

road, and that, in turn, will result in _____ lives. It's time _____
21. (save)   22. (make)

our roads safer.

Sally McKay

Detroit

III. *Each sentence has four underlined words or phrases. The four underlined parts of the sentences are marked A, B, C, or D. Circle the letter of the <u>one</u> underlined word or phrase that is NOT CORRECT.*

1. When I <u>was</u> sixteen, my parents <u>started</u> <u>to let</u> <u>I eat</u> whatever   **A   B   C   Ⓓ**
      A   B   C   D
   I wanted.

2. They stopped <u>to try</u> <u>to make</u> <u>me</u> <u>eat</u> healthy foods.   **A   B   C   D**
               A   B   C   D

3. I <u>had begun</u> <u>working</u>, so I <u>could</u> afford <u>buying</u> fast food.   **A   B   C   D**
       A   B   C   D

4. <u>Keeping</u> my weight down had never been a problem, so I   **A   B   C   D**
    A

   <u>couldn't understand</u> <u>I</u> suddenly <u>gaining</u> fifteen pounds.
        B   C   D

5. <u>Jogging</u> and <u>ride my bike</u> didn't help <u>me lose</u> weight, so I asked   **A   B   C   D**
    A   B   C

   <u>to see</u> my doctor.
    D

6. The doctor <u>had me</u> <u>to write down</u> everything I ate for a week, and she   **A   B   C   D**
            A   B

   <u>made me</u> <u>calculate</u> the fat grams.
    C   D

7. I was amazed <u>to find out</u> how much fat fast food <u>contains</u>, and I   **A   B   C   D**
            A   B

   <u>couldn't stand</u> <u>eat</u> it anymore.
    C   D

8. By <u>they let</u> me <u>make</u> mistakes, my parents got <u>me</u> <u>to learn</u> a lesson.   **A   B   C   D**
      A   B   C   D

IV. *Complete these sentences, using the correct form of the words in parentheses.*

1. My daughter's teacher _____wants her to work_____ harder.
   (want / she / work)

2. She _____ questions when she doesn't understand.
   (urge / Alicia / ask)

3. The teacher always _____ after class to ask questions.
   (let / students / stay)

4. She _____ the class.
   (not mind / my daughter / tape)

5. Alicia _____ patient.
   (appreciate / the teacher / be)

6. All the students _____ a lot from them.
   (be used to / Ms. Allen / demand)

7. She _____ responsibility for their own learning.
   (make / they / take)

8. She often _____ each other.
   (get / they / help)

9. She really _____ well.
   (want / they / do)

10. The students _____.
    (be happy with / she / teach)

V. *Read these conversations. Write a summary statement using the appropriate form of the verbs in the box.*

afford	deny	invite	let	make
offer	persuade	~~postpone~~	quit	suggest

1. **CARYN:** It's raining. Maybe we shouldn't take the class on the field trip today.

   JASON: You're right. Let's wait for a nicer day.

   SUMMARY: Caryn and Jason just ____postponed taking the class on____ the field trip.

2. **CARYN:** Can I use the new car tomorrow? I'm driving students on a field trip, and

   my seatbelts aren't in good shape.

   DAN: OK. But please be sure to bring it back by five.

   SUMMARY: Dan _____ the new car tomorrow.

3. **DAN:** Why didn't you buy that van? I thought you liked it.

   CARYN: I do like it. But it's too expensive. I don't have the money for it now.

   SUMMARY: Caryn can't _____ the van.

(continued on next page)

4. **JASON:** You need a break. You're working too hard.

   CARYN: I really have to finish this report.

   JASON: You'll feel better if you take a break.

   CARYN: Oh, all right. I suppose you're right.

   SUMMARY: Jason _____ a break.

5. **DAN:** Would you like to join us? We're going to Monticello, and it's supposed to be a beautiful day.

   JASON: Thanks. It would be nice to get out of the city.

   SUMMARY: Dan _____ them.

6. **JASON:** Oh, no. I forgot to bring my lunch.

   CARYN: Why don't you share ours? We have fruit and some cheese sandwiches.

   JASON: Oh, thanks a lot. I'll just have some fruit. I don't eat cheese anymore. I'm trying to lower my fat intake.

   SUMMARY: Jason _____ cheese.

7. **CARYN:** I can't lift the cooler into the van. Can you give me a hand?

   JASON: Sure. Just leave it. I'll do it.

   SUMMARY: Jason _____ the cooler.

8. **CARYN:** It's hot in here.

   DAN: I know. Why don't we turn on the air conditioner?

   SUMMARY: Dan _____ the air conditioner.

9. **OFFICER:** Your license, sir.

   DAN: Here it is, officer. What's the problem?

   SUMMARY: The officer _____ his license.

10. **CARYN:** Did you call me last night at 11:00 P.M.?

   JASON: No, I wouldn't call you that late. Besides, I was tired from our trip. I fell asleep at eight.

   SUMMARY: Jason _____ at eleven.

▶ *To check your answers, go to the Answer Key on page 154.*

From Grammar to Writing Parallelism of Gerunds and Infinitives

Parallelism means that all items in a list should have the same form. If a list starts with a gerund, all items in that list should be gerunds. If it starts with an infinitive, all items in the list should be infinitives. You should not mix gerunds and infinitives in the same list.

> **EXAMPLE:**
> Homer loved hunting, fishing, and to hike. ⟶
> Homer loved **hunting**, **fishing**, **and hiking**.
> OR
> Homer loved **to hunt**, **fish**, **and hike**.

Note that in a list of infinitives it is usually not necessary to repeat *to*.

---

1 *Read this movie summary. Correct any gerunds or infinitives that are not parallel.*

> **OCTOBER SKY**
>
> Directed by Joe Johnston
>
> It's October 1957, and the Soviet Union has just launched Sputnik. A teenage boy watches the satellite fly over his poor coal-mining town in West Virginia and dreams of building and ~~to launch~~ his own rocket. He teams up with three friends, and "The Rocket Boys" start to put together and firing their homemade missiles. The boys' goal is to win the regional science fair. First prize will bring college scholarships and a way out of Coalville. The school science teacher, Miss Riley, encourages him, but Homer's father is angry about the boys' project. He wants Homer to follow in his footsteps and working at the mine. Nevertheless, the boys continue launching rockets, failing in different ways, and to learn with each failure. People begin changing their minds and to admire the Rocket Boys. Some even help them.

(continued on next page)

151

However, success does not come easily in Coalville. When a forest fire starts nearby, a rocket is blamed, and the boys must give up their project. Then Homer's father is injured, and Homer quits school to support his family as a miner. His father is proud of him, but Homer can't stand giving up his dream and to work underground. He uses mathematics to prove a rocket did not start the fire. Then he tells his father he plans to leave the mine and returning to school.

The Rocket Boys win first prize at the science fair, and all of them receive scholarships. The whole town celebrates, and Homer wins another valuable prize— his father attends and launches the rocket. It's clear that the two men will try to make peace and respecting each other.

2 *Complete the story map. Use information from Exercise 1.*

MOVIE TITLE: _____

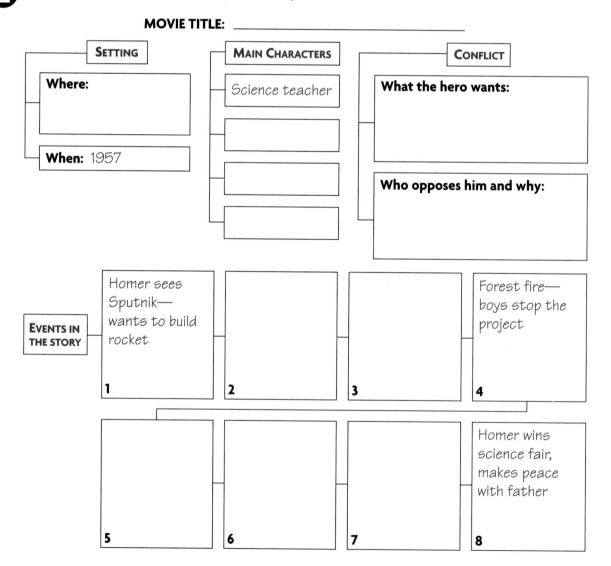

SETTING	MAIN CHARACTERS	CONFLICT
Where:	Science teacher	**What the hero wants:**
When: 1957		**Who opposes him and why:**

EVENTS IN THE STORY

1. Homer sees Sputnik— wants to build rocket
2.
3.
4. Forest fire— boys stop the project
5.
6.
7.
8. Homer wins science fair, makes peace with father

3 *Before you write . . .*

Work with a partner. Choose a movie or TV show that you have both
seen and create a story map.

4 *Write about the movie or TV show you chose in Exercise 3. Use your story map for
information. Use gerunds and infinitives.*

5 *Exchange your writing with a different partner. Answer the following
questions. Put a question mark (?) over anything that appears incorrect in
your partner's summary.*

a. Did the writer use gerunds and infinitives?	Yes / No
b. Did the writer use gerunds and infinitives correctly?	Yes / No
c. Are gerunds and infinitives parallel when they are in a list?	Yes / No
d. Did you understand the story?	Yes / No

6 *Rewrite your movie summary. Make any necessary corrections.*

REVIEW OR SELFTEST
ANSWER KEY

I. (Units 9–10)

2. C
3. A
4. D
5. C
6. D
7. B
8. A
9. D
10. C
11. B
12. B
13. C
14. D
15. A

II. (Units 9–10)

2. driving
3. suspending
4. to drive
5. to drive
6. being
7. passing
8. not to take
9. to instill
10. pay
11. to be
12. obeying
13. having to
14. feeling
15. to prevent (OR prevent)
16. not to use
17. to buckle up
18. ride
19. driving
20. behave
21. saving
22. to make

III. (Units 9–10)

2. A
3. D
4. C
5. B
6. B
7. D
8. A

IV. (Units 9–10)

2. urges Alicia to ask
3. lets students stay
4. doesn't mind my daughter's OR daughter taping
5. appreciates the teacher's OR teacher being
6. are used to Ms. Allen's OR Allen demanding
7. makes them take
8. gets them to help
9. wants them to do
10. are happy with her teaching

V. (Units 9–10)

2. is letting OR is going to let OR will let Caryn use
3. afford to buy
4. persuaded Caryn to take
5. invited Jason to join
6. quit eating
7. offered to lift
8. suggested turning on
9. made Dan show him OR her
10. denied calling Caryn

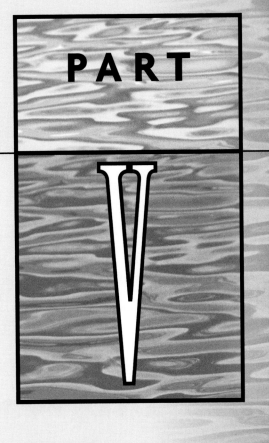

PART

V

PHRASAL VERBS

PHRASAL VERBS: REVIEW

GRAMMAR IN CONTEXT

BEFORE YOU READ Look at the picture. How does this room make you feel? Why? Can your environment affect your mood or your life?

 Read this article about the ancient Chinese art of feng shui.

Wind and Water

Ho Da-ming couldn't **figure out** why his restaurant was failing. He had **set it up** on a busy street. His chef was famous. He had **laid out** a fortune for interior design. But customers rarely **came back**. Why? Mr. Ho **called in** a *feng shui* consultant to **find out**. Feng shui (meaning "wind and water" and pronounced FUNG SHWAY) is the ancient Chinese art of placing things in the environment. According to this art, the arrangement of furniture, doors, and windows affects our health, wealth, and happiness.

The consultant told Mr. Ho that the restaurant entrance **was letting** prosperity **out**. The desperate owner **tore down** the old entrance and **put up** a new one. His action **paid off**. Soon business **picked up**, and Mr. Ho became rich.

Feng shui **has caught on** with modern architects and homeowners everywhere. Although the complex charts of feng shui are hard to **work out**, the theory is simple: We are part of nature, and we must adjust to its natural energies. To be healthy and prosperous, we must **lay out** our homes and work-places to allow *chi* (good energy) to circulate gently and to **cut off** *sha* (harmful energy).

Try this activity **out** in your home or dorm room. First **sit down** and think about how you feel in this room. Now look around. Try to **pick out** the things that make you feel good or bad. To **find out** more, go to your library or bookstore and **pick up** a book on basic feng shui. You'll be surprised at what you learn.

GRAMMAR **PRESENTATION**
PHRASAL VERBS: REVIEW

SEPARABLE TRANSITIVE PHRASAL VERBS

NOT SEPARATED			
SUBJECT	**VERB**	**PARTICLE**	**DIRECT OBJECT**
She	**called**	**in**	a consultant.
He	**figured**	**out**	the problem.

SEPARATED			
SUBJECT	**VERB**	**DIRECT OBJECT**	**PARTICLE**
She	**called**	a consultant him	**in**.
He	**figured**	the problem it	**out**.

INTRANSITIVE PHRASAL VERBS

NOT SEPARATED			
SUBJECT	**VERB**	**PARTICLE**	
They	**came**	**back**	quickly.
It	**caught**	**on**	everywhere.

NOTES

1. A **phrasal verb** (also called a two-part or two-word verb) consists of a <u>verb + particle</u>.

Verb + Particle = Phrasal Verb

Particles and prepositions look the same. However, particles are <u>part of the verb phrase</u>, and they often <u>change the meaning</u> of the verb.

EXAMPLES

- verb + particle
Let's **figure out** this problem now.

- verb + particle
Ho **called in** a consultant.

- verb + preposition
She's **looking up** at the roof.
(*She's looking in the direction of the roof.*)

- verb + particle
She's **looking up** the word.
(*She's searching for the word in the dictionary.*)

(continued on next page)

2. The verb and particle are usually common words, but their separate meanings may not help you guess the **meaning of the phrasal verb**.

PHRASAL VERB	MEANING
set up	*establish*
catch on	*become popular*
put up	*erect*

USAGE NOTE: Phrasal verbs are much more common in everyday speech than their one–word equivalents.

▶ **BE CAREFUL!** Like other verbs, phrasal verbs often have more than one meaning.

- They **set up** a business last year.
- It **didn't catch on** right away.
- They **put up** a new entrance.

- We're **putting up** signs for our business.
  NOT ~~We're erecting signs~~ . . .

- Please **turn down** the radio. The music is too loud.
  (Please lower the volume.)

- Bill didn't get the job. They **turned down** his application.
  (They rejected his application.)

3. Many phrasal verbs are **transitive**. (They take direct objects.)

PHRASAL VERB	MEANING
pick out something	*select*
call up someone	*phone*
lay out something	*spend*

(See Appendix 15 on pages A-5–A-6 for a list of transitive phrasal verbs.)

phrasal verb + object
- **Pick out** *the chair* you like best.

phrasal verb + object
- **Call up** *the consultant*.

phrasal verb + object
- Mr. Ho **laid out** *a fortune*.

4. Most transitive phrasal verbs are **separable**. This means that a <u>noun object</u> can go . . .

a. <u>after</u> the particle

OR

b. <u>between</u> the verb and the particle.

Notice that when the noun object is <u>part of a long phrase</u>, we <u>do not separate</u> the phrasal verb.

▶ **BE CAREFUL!** If the direct object is a <u>pronoun</u>, it must go <u>between the verb and the particle</u>.

(See Unit 12 for information about transitive verbs that are inseparable.)

verb + particle + object
* They **tore down** *the entrance*.

verb + object   +   particle
* They **tore** *the entrance* **down**.

* Ho **tried out** the complex theories of feng shui.
NOT ~~Ho tried the complex theories of feng shui out.~~

* I didn't understand the word so I **looked** *it* **up** in the dictionary.
NOT ~~I looked up it.~~

---

5. Some phrasal verbs are **intransitive**. (They do not take an object.)

PHRASAL VERB	MEANING
catch on	*become popular*
sit down	*take a seat*

(See Appendix 16 on pages A-6–A-7 for a list of intransitive phrasal verbs.)

* Feng shui has **caught on** all over.

* **Sit down** over there.

FOCUSED PRACTICE

1 DISCOVER THE GRAMMAR

Read this article about feng shui. Underline the phrasal verbs and circle the direct objects of the transitive phrasal verbs.

Everyday Feng Shui

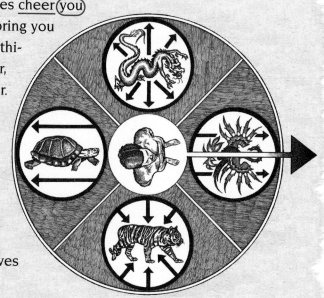

Have you noticed that some spaces cheer you up and give you energy, while others bring you down? This feng shui diagram uses mythical animals to explain why. Look it over, and then imagine yourself in the center. A phoenix takes off in front of you and gives you inspiration. Behind you, a tortoise guards you from things you cannot see. On your left and right, a dragon and a tiger balance each other. The dragon floats above the floor and helps you take in the big picture, not just small details. The tiger's energy gives you courage.

These symbols can be important in setting up a work environment. Dana, for example, needed ideas and energy in order to get ahead. Unfortunately, her undecorated, windowless cubicle took away most of her powers. After she hung up a scenic poster in the phoenix area in front of her desk, she began to feel more inspired. She gave her tiger some power by picking out plants to put on the file cabinet to her right, and she hung a cheerful mobile from the top of her left cubicle wall for her dragon. Try these ideas out in your own workplace and see what happens!

*Read these sentences and decide if they are **True (T)** or **False (F)**.*

___T___ **1.** Your environment can bring about changes in your mood.

_____ **2.** The phoenix remains sitting in the space ahead of you.

_____ **3.** The dragon's energy helps you understand an overall plan.

_____ **4.** Dana wanted a promotion.

_____ **5.** From the beginning, Dana's work area inspired her.

_____ **6.** She removed a poster from the area in front of her desk.

_____ **7.** There were no plants in her cubicle at first.

2 FENG SHUI Q AND A

Circle the correct particles to complete these questions and answers from an online feng-shui message board.

Q: I just moved into a furnished apartment. I've been having a lot of trouble sleeping. My

bed faces north. Is that OK?

A: Turn it (around)/ up so that your head is to the north, and your feet to the south. It's
1.

also important to be able to see the entrance to the bedroom from the bed.

Q: We used to have a nice park in front of our building, but the building owner has cut

down / up all the trees. Now we hear that he is going to put on / up a tall building
2.   3.

there! This is going to block away / out our light, ruin our view, and destroy our
4.

privacy. Is there anything we can do?

A: I don't know if you can work this problem off / out. You may need to think about
5.

moving.

Q: I am opening a new restaurant and would like to have a feng shui consultant come

and look it over / up to see if the energy is positive. Could you recommend a good
6.

practitioner in the Los Angeles area?

A: Sorry. We don't give out / up names online, but if you call me off / up, I would be glad
7.   8.

to make a recommendation.

Q: I just finished redecorating my bedroom. I'm very happy with the current arrangement,

but I read your advice about seeing the entrance to the bedroom from the bed. I can't.

How can I solve this problem without having to do the whole thing over / up?
9.

A: If it's not possible to change the position of the bed, try hanging over / up a mirror
10.

somewhere in your bedroom, so that you can see the entrance in the reflection.

Q: I don't know much about feng shui. How can I find after / out more about it?
11.

A: There are hundreds of books about feng shui. Go to your local library and take some

out / up. Or look after / up *feng shui* on an online bookstore website to get a list
12.   13.

of titles.

3 I.M. PEI

Read about one of the most famous architects of the twentieth century. Complete the information with the correct form of the appropriate phrasal verbs in the boxes.

| ~~grow up~~ | pick out | put up | turn out |

Born in 1917, Ieoh Ming Pei (better known as I.M. Pei) _____grew up_____ in
1.
Canton, China. As a child, he watched workers _____ large new
2.
buildings. When he was seventeen, he went to the United States to learn about building. He considered becoming an engineer or an architect. In fact, he didn't

I.M. Pei in front of the Louvre pyramid.

_____ his career until after he enrolled in college. As it _____,
3.   4.
Pei became one of the most famous architects of the twentieth century.

| figure out | go up | let in | put on | tear down |

Pei is famous for his strong geometric forms made of steel, glass, concrete, and stone. One of his most controversial projects was his glass pyramid at the Louvre in Paris. The old museum was dark, confusing, and crowded. No one wanted to

_____ the old structure, so Pei had to _____ a solution to
5.   6.
the Louvre's problems and still be sensitive to the famous old building and its surroundings. When he proposed his 71-foot-high glass pyramid as a new entrance to the museum, many Parisians were shocked and _____ buttons asking
7.
"Why the pyramid?" The glass pyramid _____ anyway, blending with the
8.
environment, reflecting the sky, and _____ the sunlight. Today, many
9.
people say that it is a good example of the principles of feng shui.

draw together	give up	go back	keep on	set up

Meanwhile, Pei _____ in spite of harsh criticism. He continued building
                         10.
structures that reflected their environment—from the seventy-floor Bank of China

skyscraper in Hong Kong to the Rock 'n' Roll Hall of Fame in Cleveland, Ohio. He has

received many prizes for his work. He used the money from one of these prizes to

_____ a scholarship fund for Chinese students to study architecture in
            11.
the United States and then to _____ to China to work as architects.
                                          12.
Pei is both creative and perfectionistic. He is also persistent. Throughout his

career he has faced a lot of opposition to his work, but he always manages to

_____ different viewpoints. The result, many people believe, are
          13.
structures that are in harmony with their surroundings. It hasn't always been easy, but Pei strongly believes that "you have to identify the important things and press for them, and not _____."
                                       14.

Inside the Louvre pyramid.

4 IN THE DORM
Grammar Notes 3 and 4

Complete each conversation with the correct form of the phrasal verb and a pronoun object.

1. A: Could I borrow your truck? I need to pick up some new furniture this week.

   B: Sure. When are you _going to pick it up?_____

2. A: Hey! Who took down my feng shui posters?

   B: Sorry. I _____. I thought you didn't like them anymore.

(continued on next page)

3. A: I need to cheer up my roommate. He just flunked a big test.

   B: Why don't you straighten up the room? That will _____.

4. A: This room is depressing. Let's try out some of these feng shui ideas.

   B: I agree. Let's _____ this weekend.

5. A: We need something to light up that corner. It's awfully dark.

   B: I have an extra lamp. This will _____ nicely.

6. A: Can someone touch up the paint in my dorm room? It's cracked in several places.

   B: Sure. We'll send someone to _____ next week.

5 EDITING

Read this student's journal entry. Find and correct ten mistakes in the use of phrasal verbs. The first mistake is already corrected.

I just finished reading an article about feng shui. At the end, the author suggests sitting ~~up~~ down in your home and thinking about how your environment makes you feel. I decided to try out it.

The thing I like best about my apartment is that it is bright and sunny. This cheers me out. At night, it's very dark, but I've figured up what to do about it. I'm going to buy another lamp to light the apartment at night up. I'll leave it on when I go out at night, so I can see light as soon as I come in. I also like the light green walls in my bedroom, but the chipped paint has been bringing down me. I'm going to touch it over as soon as possible.

My apartment is too small, but I can't tear up the walls. I think it will look more spacious if I just straighten it up. I'll try to put books back after I take them off the shelves, and hang away my clothes at night. With just a few small changes, I'll end up feeling happier in my home. It's certainly worth trying on.

COMMUNICATION PRACTICE

6 LISTENING

Listen to these short conversations. Circle the words that you hear. Then listen again and check your answers.

1. **AMY:** How's the temperature in here?

   BEN: It's a little too cold for me. Would you mind if I turn the air-conditioner (down)/ off?
   1.

2. **AMY:** What did you think about that information on feng shui?

   BEN: I haven't had the chance to look it <u>over / up</u> yet.
   2.

3. **AMY:** Have you finished redecorating your office?

   BEN: Almost. I'm going to Conran's today to pick <u>out / up</u> a new couch.
   3.

4. **AMY:** The living room is a mess. Your books are all over the place.

   BEN: Don't worry. I'll put them <u>away / back</u> as soon as I'm done with my homework.
   4.

5. **AMY:** I really don't like those new curtains.

   BEN: Neither do I. I'm going to take them <u>back / down</u> tomorrow.
   5.

6. **AMY:** This mattress isn't as comfortable as it used to be.

   BEN: I know. I think we need to turn it <u>around / over</u>.
   6.

7. **AMY:** What color should we paint the kitchen?

   BEN: I don't know. Let's discuss it when we get <u>back / up</u>.
   7.

Now look at your completed sentences. Decide if the statements below are **True (T)** *or* **False (F)**.

__F__ **8.** Ben doesn't want to have any air-conditioning on.

_____ **9.** He is going to look in a book for information about feng shui.

_____ **10.** He hasn't selected a couch yet.

_____ **11.** He is going to return the books to their original place.

_____ **12.** He is going to return the curtains to the store tomorrow.

_____ **13.** He thinks they should change the position of the mattress so that the underside is now on top.

_____ **14.** Amy and Ben are going somewhere.

7 REDECORATING

Work in small groups. How would you like to change the appearance of your classroom or your school? What would you like to remain the same? Try to use some of these phrasal verbs in your discussion.

cover up	light up	put away	throw away
do over	make up	put up	touch up
hang up	move around	straighten up	turn around
leave on	pick out	tear down	turn on / off

EXAMPLE:

A: I think we should hang up some posters.

B: It would be nice to hang some photographs up, too.

8 WHAT'S DIFFERENT?

*Work with a partner. Look at these **Before** and **After** pictures of Lisa's room for two minutes. Write down all the differences you can find. Then compare your list with another pair's list.*

BEFORE   AFTER

EXAMPLE:
She took the curtains down.

9 WRITING

Write about how you feel in your home, office, or classroom. What makes you feel good? What makes you feel bad? What would you like to change? You can use the journal entry in Exercise 5 as a model.

PHRASAL VERBS: SEPARABLE AND INSEPARABLE

GRAMMAR **IN CONTEXT**

BEFORE YOU READ Look at the cartoons. What do you think the article is about?

 Read this magazine article.

Burr

Who **put together** the first personal computer? You may think that it was scientists working in a lab. In fact, two college dropouts working in a garage **came up with** this invention that changed the world. Inventors are often elementary schoolchildren, homemakers, or the guy next door working on his car. They **dream up** ideas in classrooms, kitchens, and home workshops.

How do inventors **come up with** new ideas? What is the key to invention if it isn't education, age, or a laboratory? It's creativity, and everyone has it. This ability to **think up** something new seems like magic to many people, but in fact, anyone can develop the qualities that **go along with** creativity.

Curiosity comes first. Inventors are people who want to **find out** why things happen the way they do. For example, when George de Mestral, a Swiss inventor, took his dog for walks in the mountains, burrs would get stuck in the dog's coat. De Mestral wondered why they were so hard to remove. Acting on his curiosity, he examined the burrs through a microscope. When he saw the many

(continued on next page)

Eureka! (continued)

tiny hooks on each burr, he realized that he was looking at the perfect fastener. Years later, de Mestral developed this idea into Velcro®, now used to fasten everything from sneakers to space suits.

Imagination is also crucial for an inventor. This quality helps inventors **put** things **together** in a new way. One U.S. sixth grader invented a solar-powered bicycle light by combining solar cells and his bicycle. When he rides his bike during the day, the sunlight **charges up** two batteries. Then at night, when he needs the light, he **switches** it **on**. Imagination can also mean seeing a new use for a common object. The original Frisbee® was a pie pan that two truck drivers were tossing to each other in a parking lot. As he watched the two men **playing around**, Walter Morrison **came up with** his idea for a new toy that became popular all over the world.

Inventors are often problem solvers. When fifteen-year-old Chester Greenwood's ears got frostbitten during Maine's bitter winters, he **didn't give up** and stay indoors. Instead, he attached fur cups to the ends of a piece of wire, and wrapped the wire around his head. His friends made fun of him at first, but soon the idea **caught on**, and they wanted earmuffs too. The Greenwood family had to work hard to **keep up with** the orders. Chester patented his invention when he was only nineteen.

After an inventor says "Eureka!" (Greek for "I've found it!") there's still a lot of work to do. Another quality found in successful inventors is tenacity—the ability to **stick with** a project until it is completed. This usually involves **looking up** information related to the idea. George Eastman, inventor of the Kodak® camera and film, spent years researching chemicals and photography. Tenacity also involves **trying out** different materials and designs. De Mestral experimented with many kinds of materials before he perfected Velcro®.

Finally, inventors need a lot of self-confidence. They have to believe in their ideas and be willing to learn from failures. Gail Borden developed a process for condensing and canning milk, but the government **turned down** his first application for a patent. He **kept on** trying to perfect his method and after years he finally succeeded. His invention probably saved many lives at a time when there was no way to refrigerate milk. Borden's motto is engraved on his tombstone: "I tried and failed; I tried again and again and succeeded."

GRAMMAR **PRESENTATION**
PHRASAL VERBS: SEPARABLE AND INSEPARABLE

SEPARABLE TRANSITIVE			
SUBJECT	VERB	PARTICLE	DIRECT OBJECT
She	**turned**	**on**	the TV.

SEPARABLE TRANSITIVE			
SUBJECT	VERB	DIRECT OBJECT	PARTICLE
She	**turned**	the TV it	**on**.

INSEPARABLE TRANSITIVE			
SUBJECT	VERB	PARTICLE	DIRECT OBJECT
He	**ran**	**into**	his teacher. her.

INTRANSITIVE		
SUBJECT	VERB	PARTICLE
They	**sat**	**down**.

NOTES

1. As you learned in Unit 11, most transitive phrasal verbs are **separable**. This means that <u>noun objects</u> can go <u>after</u> the particle <u>or between</u> the verb and the particle.

(See Appendix 15 on pages A-5–A-6 for a list of common separable phrasal verbs.)

▶ **BE CAREFUL!**

a. If the direct object is a <u>pronoun</u>, it must go <u>between</u> the verb and the particle.

b. When the noun object is <u>part of a long phrase</u>, it goes <u>after</u> the particle.

EXAMPLES

verb + particle + object
- I just **dreamed up** *a new idea*.

OR

verb + object + particle
- I just **dreamed** *a new idea* **up**.

- I **dreamed** *it* **up**.
  NOT I dreamed up it.

- She **tried out** an unusually complicated new device.
  NOT She tried an unusually complicated new device out.

(continued on next page)

2. Some transitive phrasal verbs are **inseparable**. This means that both <u>noun and pronoun objects</u> always go <u>after</u> the particle. You cannot separate the verb from its particle.

(See Appendix 15 on pages A-5–A-6 for a list of common inseparable transitive phrasal verbs.)

- She **ran into** *her science teacher* in the library.
  NOT ~~She ran her science teacher into the library.~~
- She **ran into** *her*.
  NOT ~~She ran her into.~~

3. A small group of phrasal verbs **must be separated**.

PHRASAL VERB	MEANING
keep something **on**	*not remove*
talk someone **into**	*persuade*

(See Appendix 15 on page A-5–A-6 for a list of common phrasal verbs that must be separated.)

- **Keep** *your earmuffs* **on**.
  NOT ~~Keep on your earmuffs.~~
- She **talked** *them* **into** a raise.
  NOT ~~She talked into them a raise.~~

4. Some transitive phrasal verbs are used in combination with certain prepositions. A **phrasal verb + preposition** combination (also called a <u>three-part</u> or <u>three-word verb</u>) is usually **inseparable**.

PHRASAL VERB	MEANING
come up with something	*imagine*
drop out of something	*quit*
keep up with something /someone	*go as fast as*

(See Appendix 7 on page A-3 for a list of common phrasal verb + preposition combinations.)

- She **came up with** *a brilliant idea*.
- I **dropped out of** *school* and got a job.
- I couldn't **keep up with** *the class*. It went too quickly for me.

5. As you learned in Unit 11, phrasal verbs can also be **intransitive**. This means that they do not take an object.

(See Appendix 16 on pages A-6–A-7 for a list of common intransitive phrasal verbs.)

- His earmuffs **caught on**. Everyone wanted a pair.
- Don't **give up**. Keep trying.

FOCUSED PRACTICE

1 DISCOVER THE GRAMMAR

Underline the phrasal verbs in this article about a recent invention that has changed the world.

If you are looking at a modern laptop computer, it's hard to believe that computers were once huge devices available only to government or big businesses. Today's computers are often not much bigger than a typewriter and we take them for granted in homes, schools, and offices. Technological advances made the small personal computer possible, but two electronic whiz kids working in a garage actually <u>brought</u> it <u>about</u>.

Steven Jobs and Stephen Wozniak first met at Hewlett-Packard, an electronics firm in California. Jobs was a high-school student when William Hewlett, the president, took him on as a summer employee. Wozniak, a college dropout, was also working there, and the two got along right away.

Jobs and Wozniak went separate ways in 1972. When they got together again in 1974, Wozniak was spending a lot of time with a local computer club, and he talked Jobs into joining the group. Jobs immediately saw the potential for a small computer. He teamed up with Wozniak, a brilliant engineer, to build one.

The two designed the Apple I computer in Jobs's bedroom, and they put the prototype together in his garage. With $1,300 in capital raised by selling Jobs's car and Wozniak's scientific calculator, they set up their first production line.

Apple I, which they brought out in 1976, had sales of $600, a promising beginning. By 1980, Apple Computers, which had started four years earlier as a project in a garage, had a market value of $1.2 billion.

Now write down each phrasal verb from the article next to its meaning.

Phrasal Verb	Meaning
1. _____	started
2. _____	started working (with)
3. _____	introduced
4. _____	met
5. _____ brought about _____	made happen
6. _____	hired
7. _____	assembled
8. _____	related well
9. _____	persuaded

2 EDISON, THOMAS ALVA (1847–1931)   Grammar Notes 1–5

*Read about one of the greatest inventors in history. Complete the information
with the correct form of the appropriate phrasal verbs in the boxes.*

> drop out of   grow up   think back on   ~~try out~~

Thomas Alva Edison was born on February 11, 1847.

Being curious, he _____tried out_____ almost
                              1.
anything he had read about or seen. His parents liked to

_____ the time they found young
            2.
Thomas sitting on a number of eggs. He had recently

seen a goose hatch eggs and wanted to see if it would

work for him, too.

   Edison _____ in the midwestern
                      3.
part of the United States. When he was seven, his family

moved from Ohio to Michigan. He was a poor student and _____ school
                                                                        4.
after just a few months. From then on, he received his education from his mother. An avid

reader, he read—and remembered—everything he could get his hands on.

> break out   carry out   fill up   keep away   set up

   When he was twelve, he started to work, selling newspapers, candy, and sandwiches on

trains. With the money he saved, he _____ a laboratory in the basement
                                                    5.
of his home. He had collected hundreds of bottles from junk heaps and

_____ them _____ with chemicals he needed to
                                            6.
_____ his experiments. He labeled all his bottles "poison" to
          7.
_____ his family _____ from them. Soon, Edison
                                                8.
moved his lab to the baggage car of the train. As the result of an overturned bottle of

chemicals, a fire _____ in the car, putting an end to his career on the rails.
                            9.

| break down | bring about | carry on | find out | pay back | set up |

At the age of fifteen, he saved the life of a child who had been playing on the railroad tracks. The grateful father, a telegraph operator, _____ Edison

_____ by teaching him the skill of telegraphy. For the next five years,
10.
Edison earned money as a telegraph operator working in various cities in the United States and Canada. He worked nights so that he could _____ his
11.
experiments. In 1868, he built his first patented invention, a vote recorder. No one wanted it. From that point on, he never worked on a project before _____ first if
12.
there was a need for it.

In 1869, he went to New York City. Trying to find work, he walked into a company which supplied quotations on gold prices by wire. The electrical device for sending the prices to brokers had just _____. Edison repaired it and was hired on the
13.
spot. This incident _____ his first useful invention—the stock ticker—for
14.
which he received $40,000. With the money, he _____ a workshop in
15.
Newark, New Jersey, and began his career as a professional inventor. He was just twenty-two.

| carry out | come up with | give up | keep on |

During the next sixty years, Edison patented over a thousand inventions, among them the electric lightbulb, the record player, the storage battery, the movie camera and projector, and the telephone transmitter. He worked tirelessly—often more than eighteen hours a day. He frequently had to be reminded to eat and sleep. Whenever he

_____ a new idea he read everything he could about it. Then he
16.
_____ test after test. He never _____ or became
17.   **18.**
discouraged. If an experiment failed, he _____ trying new approaches
19.
until he found the one that worked. Ten thousand tests were required before he succeeded in developing the storage battery. Edison once said, "Genius is one percent inspiration and ninety-nine percent perspiration."

Source: Based on information from *The World Book Encyclopedia*

❸ IN THE LAB

Complete these conversations that take place in a school lab. Use phrasal verbs and pronouns.

1. A: Please put on your lab coats.

B: Do we really have to _____put them on_____? It's hot in here.

A: Sorry. You know the rules. I'll open a window if you'd like.

2. A: I can't figure out this problem.

B: I know what you mean. I can't _____ either.

3. A: Remember to fill out these forms.

B: Can we _____ at home, or do we have to do it right now?

4. A: Are you going to hand out the next assignment today?

B: I _____ a few minutes ago. Weren't you here?

5. A: I can't get this to work. I think we'd better do the whole procedure over again.

B: We don't have time to _____. Class is over in ten minutes.

6. A: Please remember to turn off your Bunsen burner before you leave the lab.

B: I've already _____.

7. A: Are we supposed to turn in our lab reports today?

B: No. Please _____ next week.

8. A: You left your safety goggles on.

B: Thanks. I _____ last week too. I couldn't figure out why everyone on the bus was staring at me.

❹ CREATIVITY

Complete this article about creativity with the phrasal verbs and objects in parentheses. Place the object between the verb and the particle whenever possible.

There are three parts to creativity: _____dreaming an idea up_____,
1. (dream up / an idea)
_____, and marketing it. Remember, anyone can
2. (follow through / it)
invent new things. Here are some ways to get started.

GETTING AN IDEA

Practice creativity. Make a list of common everyday objects.

_____ and have a brainstorming session with another
　　　　3. (Pick out / one)

person. _____. Give yourself five minutes and don't
　　　　4. (Think up / uses for the object)

_____ . _____ and
5. (throw away / any ideas)　　　　　　6. (Write down / them)

_____ with the other person.
7. (talk over / them)

Ask around. Another way to get ideas is to talk to people about things that they use

every day. _____ someone has with a common, everyday
　　　　8. (Find out about / a problem)

object, and then _____. If you succeed in
　　　　9. (work out / a solution)

_____ , then you'll have something that people
10. (come up with / one)

really need.

DEVELOPING THE IDEA

After you get your idea, _____. Learn all you can
　　　　　　11. (stick with / it)

about everything related to your invention. Write to manufacturers or

_____ in a library. _____
12. (look up / information)　　　　　　　13. (Try out / different materials)

until you find the best ones. You will _____ every failure.
　　　　　　14. (get out of / something)

Remember Edison's words: "Results! Why, man, I have plenty of results. I know a

thousand things that won't work."

MARKETING YOUR INVENTION

Your new gizmo is now perfect, and it's time to _____.
　　　　　　　15. (go after / customers)

A Web page is always a good idea. As you _____ ,
　　　　　　16. (put together / it)

find ways to show people why your product stands out. Good photos will

help you _____ to your audience. Never
17. (get across / this)

_____ to _____. Take
18. (pass up / an opportunity)　　　　19. (show off / your product)

it to trade shows and fairs. If it's inexpensive, it might be a good idea

_____ . _____ and
20. (give away / samples)　　　　　　21. (Stick to / your plan)

don't give up!

⑤ EDITING

Read an inventor's notes. Find and correct seven mistakes in the use of phrasal verbs. The first mistake is already corrected.

> May 3, 1999. Today, I came up a good idea ~~with~~—a jar of paint with an
>
> applicator like the kind used for shoe polish. It can be used to paint dirty spots
>
> or nicks on a wall after a paint job, when people don't want to do a whole room.
>
> Market: Homeowners, renters, anyone who paints a home or apartment.
>
> Idea for product design:
>
> Jar
>
> Applicator
>
> Touch Up It!
>
> *Dan Borgel* 5/10/99   *Fern Aster* 5/10/99
>
> May 10. I went to five paint stores today and asked the owners about my
>
> idea. I found out that nothing like this is on the market right now. They
>
> seemed to be excited by this idea. I asked two of them to sign my notebook.
>
> That way I can prove that the idea was actually mine.
>
> May 12. I found a manufacturer of applicators. I called up him and ordered
>
> several types.
>
> June 10. The applicators finally arrived. I tried in several and found one that
>
> worked well. I'm going to have about two dozen samples made.
>
> August 4. I filled down an application for a patent and mailed it yesterday.
>
> I'll be able to set a strong and convincing demonstration of the product up soon.
>
> August 30. I demonstrated the product at a decorator's exhibition yesterday.
>
> I wanted to point out that it's very neat and easy to use, so I put white gloves
>
> and evening clothes for the demonstration. It went over very well.

COMMUNICATION PRACTICE

6 LISTENING

 *Listen to a teacher explain how to make a simple camera. Then listen again and in the boxes number the pictures to show the correct order. Listen a third time and complete each caption with the correct phrasal verb.*

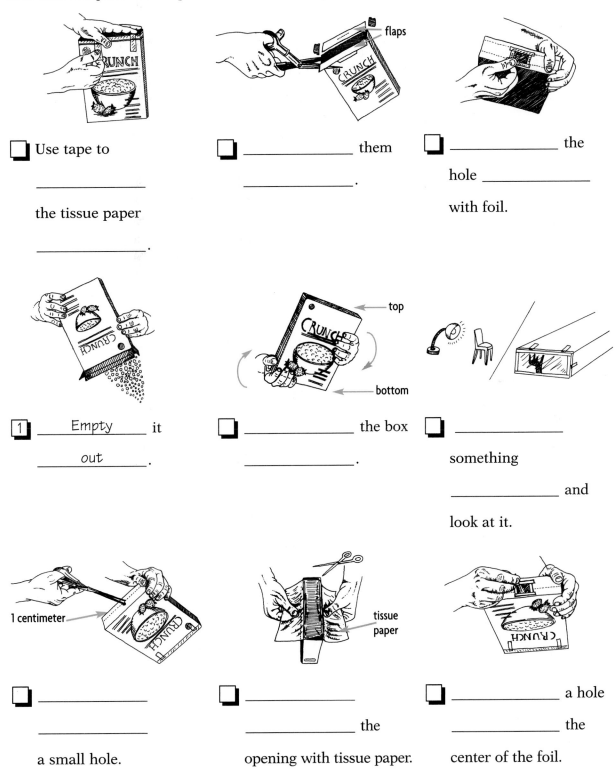

☐ Use tape to _____ the tissue paper _____.

☐ _____ them _____.

☐ _____ the hole _____ with foil.

1 ___Empty___ it ___out___ .

☐ _____ the box _____.

☐ _____ something _____ and look at it.

☐ _____ _____ a small hole.

☐ _____ _____ the opening with tissue paper.

☐ _____ a hole _____ the center of the foil.

7 MATCHING SETS

Work with a partner. Read each set of words. Decide on a phrasal verb that can be used with every word in the set. Then compare your answers with those of your classmates. There may be more than one right answer!

1. balloon   photograph   dynamite   firecracker

> **EXAMPLE:**
> **A:** You can blow up a balloon. And dynamite and firecrackers blow up. But what about a photograph?
> **B:** When you enlarge a photograph it's called blowing it up.

2. car	plane	bus	boat
3. tax	problem	puzzle	bill
4. answer	word	phone number	address
5. lipstick	glasses	shoes	clothes
6. light	CD player	oven	TV

Can you make up your own sets? Use the lists of phrasal verbs in Appendices 15 and 16 on pages A-5–A-7 for help. Then see if your classmates can come up with the answer.

7. _____   _____   _____   _____

8. _____   _____   _____   _____

9. _____   _____   _____   _____

10. _____   _____   _____   _____

11. _____   _____   _____   _____

12. _____   _____   _____   _____

8 CRAZY INVENTIONS

Rube Goldberg was a cartoonist who became famous in the early twentieth century for his cartoons of crazy inventions. His drawings became so popular that people now use the term "a Rube Goldberg machine" to describe any gadget that performs a simple task in a very complicated way.

Prepare to invent your own Rube Goldberg machine. Work with a partner to do the following puzzle. Look at one of Goldberg's inventions. Complete the description of how the machine works with the appropriate phrasal verbs in the box.

Simple Way to Open an Egg

RUBE GOLDBERG™ and © of Rube Goldberg, Inc. Distributed by United Media.

come off
end up
get out
go off
jump up
~~pick up~~
push up
set off

1. When you _____pick up_____ your morning paper (A), the string (B) opens the door of the birdcage (C).

2. The bird (D) can now _____ of the cage.

3. The bird follows the bird seed (E) up the platform (F).

4. The bird falls over the edge of the platform and _____ in the pitcher of water (G).

5. The water splashes on the flower (H).

6. The flower grows and _____ the rod (I).

7. The rod causes the string (J) to _____ the pistol (K).

8. The pistol _____ and scares the monkey (L).

9. The monkey _____, hitting its head against the bumper (M).

10. The bumper forces the razor (N) into the egg (O).

11. The broken shell _____ and falls into the saucer (P).

Now make up a crazy invention to perform a simple task. Use the following ideas or one of your own.

swat a fly	open a window	scratch your back
water the flowers	shut a door	put a stamp on a letter

9 WHAT THE WORLD NEEDS NOW

Work in small groups. Brainstorm ideas for inventions that you would like to see. Choose your top three ideas and share them with the rest of the class.

> **EXAMPLE:**
> I think we need a solar-powered car. It wouldn't use up resources, and it wouldn't pollute the atmosphere.

10 QUOTABLE QUOTES

Work in small groups. Read what people have said about imagination, inventiveness, and discovery. Discuss the quotes. What do they mean? Which do you agree with?

Genius is one percent inspiration and ninety-nine percent perspiration.
   —*Thomas Alva Edison (U.S. inventor, 1847–1931)*

> **EXAMPLE:**
> I think this means that it's easier to come up with an idea than to carry it out. But I don't know if I agree with it. I think Edison was just being modest.

Necessity is the mother of invention.
   —*Latin saying*

Invention breeds invention.
   —*Ralph Waldo Emerson (U.S. writer, 1803–1882)*

Name the greatest of all inventors: Accident.
   —*Mark Twain (U.S. writer, 1835–1910)*

Discovery consists of seeing what everybody has seen and thinking what nobody has thought.
   —*Albert Szent-Gyorgyi (U.S. chemist, 1893–1986)*

11 WRITING

Imagine that while you are sailing, you are shipwrecked on an island. There are large trees and a cave next to a stream. There are fish and shellfish near the seashore. You have sails, a compass, a saw, some paper, and some string. You are going to be there for some time, so you need to come up with shelter, food, ways to cook and make clothing, and some entertainment. How will you do it? What will you use? What will you do first, second, and third? Write your plans. Use phrasal verbs.

> **EXAMPLE:**
> First, I'll cut down some trees with the saw in order to . . .

REVIEW OR SELFTEST

PART

V

I. *Circle the words to complete these classroom guidelines.*

1. Fill (out)/ up the school questionnaire completely.

2. Answer all the questions. Don't leave anything off / out.

3. Clear away / up any problems you have about your homework assignment before you begin.

4. If you make a lot of mistakes, do the assignment over / up.

5. Look over / up your homework before submitting it.

6. Please hand out / in all your homework on time.

7. You must come up with / to an idea for your science project by March 2.

8. Next week, I will pass out / up a list of suggested topics for your project.

9. Pick out / up one of the suggested topics or choose your own.

10. If you have an idea for a topic, please talk it into / over with me.

11. If you are having trouble with your project, don't give up / away. Come speak to me.

12. If I turn down / off your project topic, I will help you think back on / up another one.

13. If you don't know how to spell a word, look it over / up in the dictionary. Spelling counts!

14. All projects must be turned in / up on time. There will be no extensions!

15. If you are having trouble keeping away from / up with the class, let me know. Additional help can be arranged for you.

16. There are extra handouts in the back of the room. Supplies are limited. Please take one before they run out / over.

17. All tests will be graded and given back / up on the next day of class.

18. The final exam is scheduled for May 15 and cannot be put away / off.

(continued on next page)

19. If you get <u>over / through with</u> the exam early, you may leave.

20. Please put <u>away / off</u> all test tubes and chemicals after class.

21. Please shut <u>away / off</u> all lights and equipment before leaving the room.

22. Straighten <u>over / up</u> your desks before the break so we have a neat room to come <u>off / back</u> to.

II. *Circle the letter of the words closest in meaning to the underlined words.*

1. A question <u>arose</u> while we were talking about the science project.　A　B　Ⓒ　D
(A) set up　　　　(C) came up
(B) brought up　　(D) looked up

2. Jiang wants to <u>redecorate</u> her office.　A　B　C　D
(A) set up　　　　(C) work out
(B) do over　　　 (D) hang up

3. Do you think feng shui will ever <u>become popular</u> here?　A　B　C　D
(A) straighten up　(C) catch on
(B) touch up　　　(D) try out

4. What a great idea! Who <u>invented it</u>?　A　B　C　D
(A) thought it up　(C) let it in
(B) charged it up　(D) let it out

5. This paint is scratched. Let's <u>improve it</u> a little.　A　B　C　D
(A) fill it up　　　(C) make it up
(B) touch it up　　(D) bring it up

6. Mark works so hard that he's sure to <u>succeed</u>.　A　B　C　D
(A) give up　　　　(C) turn over
(B) work off　　　 (D) get ahead

7. When did the company <u>hire them</u>?　A　B　C　D
(A) take them off　(C) work them out
(B) take them on　(D) bring them up

8. My student days were great. I <u>remember them</u> often.　A　B　C　D
(A) leave them on　 (C) think back on them
(B) see them through (D) look them up

9. Kevin's going to <u>return</u> from vacation tomorrow.　A　B　C　D
(A) call back　　　(C) get back
(B) give back　　　(D) get along

10. A lamp will <u>illuminate</u> this corner nicely.　A　B　C　D
(A) turn on　　　　(C) put up
(B) blow up　　　　(D) light up

11. Instead of arguing about the problem, let's <u>discuss it</u>. **A B C D**
    (A) look it over   (C) take it away
    (B) charge it up   (D) talk it over

12. Carla <u>got</u> some interesting ideas from the Internet. **A B C D**
    (A) picked out   (C) picked up
    (B) pointed out   (D) called up

13. Jason wanted to be an artist, but he <u>unexpectedly went</u> to medical **A B C D**
school.
    (A) ended up going   (C) figured out going
    (B) dreamt up going   (D) brought about going

14. Be careful with those chemicals. They could <u>explode</u>. **A B C D**
    (A) break down   (C) come off
    (B) blow up   (D) take down

15. Can someone <u>indicate</u> the mistake in that equation? **A B C D**
    (A) touch up   (C) give out
    (B) show off   (D) point out

III. *Complete these conversations. Use phrasal verbs and pronouns.*

1. A: I'm thinking over a possible topic for my project.

   B: Well, don't _____think it over_____ too long. It's almost the end of the semester.

2. A: I heard that they called off the last class.

   B: Really? Why did they _____?

3. A: Today we're going to carry out an experiment.

   B: What materials do we need to _____?

4. A: Could you switch on the light?

   B: I've already _____.

5. A: Do you get along with John?

   B: Sure. I _____. Why do you ask?

6. A: Keep away from those chemicals! They're dangerous.

   B: Don't worry! I'll _____.

7. A: Could you put back that book when you're done?

   B: Sure. I'll _____.

(continued on next page)

8. A: You can take off your safety goggles now.

    B: We've already _____.

9. A: Will someone please wake up Alice? She's fallen asleep again.

    B: I'll _____.

10. A: We have three problems to work out before our next class.

    B: When are you going to _____?

IV. *Each sentence has four underlined words or phrases. The four underlined parts of the sentences are marked A, B, C, or D. Circle the letter of the <u>one</u> underlined word or phrase that is NOT CORRECT.*

1. You <u>ought to</u> <u>look over</u> your notes for the test, so don't <u>throw</u>
      A   B   C
   <u>away them</u>.
     D
               A   B   C Ⓓ

2. The teacher <u>turned off</u> my idea, so I <u>have to</u> <u>think</u> up a new one.
              A   B   C D
               A   B   C D

3. We've <u>looked</u> <u>up</u> a lot of information, and now we're <u>trying</u> to draw
          A   B   C
   <u>together it</u> for our report.
      D
               A   B   C D

4. Put <u>the new white lab coat I bought you on</u> before <u>you</u> <u>set up</u>
                      A   B   C
   <u>the experiment</u>.
      D
               A   B   C D

5. You really <u>let</u> <u>me down</u> when you stopped <u>handing</u> <u>up</u> your
            A   B   C   D
   homework.
               A   B   C D

6. I couldn't <u>work</u> <u>out</u> the charts in Chapter 6, and I just <u>gave</u> <u>down</u>.
            A   B   C   D
               A   B   C D

7. Please <u>call off</u> <u>for an appointment</u>. Don't just <u>show</u> <u>up</u> without one.
         A   B   C   D
               A   B   C D

8. <u>Go after</u> your goals aggressively, and you'll <u>be sure</u> to <u>get</u> <u>over</u>.
     A   B   C D
               A   B   C D

9. Today I have to <u>pick</u> <u>up Nilda</u> at school and <u>drop</u> <u>off her</u> at the library.
               A   B   C   D
               A   B   C D

10. We <u>came up</u> <u>the answer with</u> while we were <u>fooling</u> <u>around</u> on the
         A   B   C   D
    computer.
                A   B   C D

11. The school <u>laid</u> <u>out a fortune</u> for the new microscope. Have you tried
            A   B
    <u>it</u> <u>on</u> yet?
     C D
                A   B   C D

V. *Rewrite the sentences that have underlined words. Use appropriate phrasal verbs in the box to replace the underlined words.*

blow up	turn down	leave out	turn in	let down
point out	~~come up~~	show up	give up	throw away

1. A question <u>arose</u> about the science project.

   A question came up about the science project.

2. Keep all your old notes. Please don't <u>discard</u> them.

3. The teacher <u>rejected</u> my topic proposal.

4. All forms must be <u>submitted</u> by April 8.

5. Be very careful when working with these chemicals. They could <u>explode</u>.

6. Don't <u>abandon</u> hope. Keep trying.

7. What happened to the last problem? You <u>omitted</u> it.

8. The test grades were very high. The students didn't <u>disappoint</u> me.

9. There's something wrong with that equation. Can someone <u>indicate</u> what the mistake is?

10. Please make an appointment to see me. Don't just <u>appear</u> without one.

▶ *To check your answers, go to the Answer Key on page 188.*

FROM GRAMMAR TO WRITING USING THE APPROPRIATE DEGREE OF FORMALITY

Phrasal verbs are more common in informal writing than their one-word synonyms.

> **EXAMPLE:**
> **FORMAL:** What time do you **board** the bus? ⟶
> **INFORMAL:** What time do you *get on* the bus?

1 *Read this letter to a friend. Make it more informal by replacing the underlined words with phrasal verbs. Use Appendices 15 and 16, pages A-5–A-7, for help. Remember to put pronouns in the correct place. You may also have to change some verb forms.*

Dear Van,

Sorry I haven't written sooner, but I've been really busy. I just moved into a new

apartment. Here's what a typical day looks like for me. I ~~arise~~ *get up* early, usually at 6:30. After

running two miles, showering, and having breakfast, I <u>board</u> the bus and go to my 9:00

English class. In addition to English, I'm taking statistics this semester. I'm finding it really

hard, but I'm going to <u>persevere with</u> it. I'll need it later for business school.

After classes I have just enough time for a quick lunch with some friends before

getting to McDonald's at 1:00 for my four-hour shift. On the way home, I've been

<u>purchasing</u> some things for my apartment. Today, for example, I bought a computer work

station which I'm going to <u>assemble</u> this weekend. (By the way, thanks for telling me about

feng shui! I've been using it to decorate my apartment.)

When I get home, I prepare a quick dinner, and then spend several hours on my

homework. I'm also writing a report for my statistics class. I can't believe how much paper

(and time) this project <u>consumes</u>! It's interesting, but I'll be glad when it's over. Then at

least I'll be able to <u>recline</u> on the couch that I just bought and watch some TV before going

to bed. These days I go straight to bed as soon as I finish my homework. By the time I

<u>extinguish</u> the lights, it's 11:00 P.M. and I'm absolutely exhausted.

Well, that's enough about me and my life. I don't think I've <u>omitted</u> anything important. How are you? What have you been doing? I'd love to see you. Is there any chance that I could <u>persuade you to come</u> for a visit during your semester break? The weekend of the 12th I'll be going to visit Tania, but I'm sure it would be OK for you to <u>accompany</u> me. Let me know!

Looking forward to hearing from you,

Marta

P.S. I think I <u>discarded</u> Victor's e-mail address before copying it into my electronic address book. Do you have it?

---

2 *Work with a partner. Use information from the letter in Exercise 1 to complete Marta's schedule.*

Time	To Do
6:30 A.M.	get up
6:45	run two miles
7:30	
7:45	breakfast
8:15	
	English class
11:00	statistics class

Time	To Do
12:00 noon	
P.M.	McDonald's
5:30–6:00	
6:30	dinner
7:00–10:30	
	go to bed

---

3 *Before you write . . .*

Make a schedule like the one in Exercise 2 of a typical day in your life.

---

4 *Write an informal letter to a friend or relative about your current activities. Use information from your schedule in Exercise 3. Include phrasal verbs.*

---

5 *Exchange letters with a different partner. Underline the phrasal verbs in your partner's letter. Then answer the following questions. Put a question mark (?) in the letter where something seems wrong or missing.*

a. Did your partner use phrasal verbs correctly? Yes / No

b. Are there other places where your partner could use phrasal verbs? Yes / No

c. If there are phrasal verbs with pronouns, are the pronouns in the correct location? Yes / No

---

6 *Discuss your editing suggestions with your partner. Then rewrite your own paragraph. Make any necessary corrections.*

PART

V

REVIEW OR SelfTest
ANSWER KEY

I. (Units 11–12)

2. out
3. up
4. over
5. over
6. in
7. with
8. out
9. out
10. over
11. up
12. down, up
13. up
14. in
15. up with
16. out
17. back
18. off
19. through with
20. away
21. off
22. up, back

II. (Units 11–12)

2. B
3. C
4. A
5. B
6. D
7. B
8. C
9. C
10. D
11. D
12. C
13. A
14. B
15. D

III. (Units 11–12)

2. call it off
3. carry it out
4. switched it on
5. get along with him
6. keep away from them
7. put it back
8. taken them off
9. wake her up
10. work them out

IV. (Units 11–12)

2. A
3. D
4. A
5. D
6. D
7. A
8. D
9. D
10. B
11. D

V. (Units 11–12)

2. Please don't throw them away.
3. The teacher turned down my topic proposal (OR turned my topic proposal down).
4. All forms must be turned in by April 8.
5. They could blow up.
6. Don't give up hope.
7. You left it out.
8. The students didn't let me down.
9. Can someone point out what the mistake is?
10. Don't just show up without one.

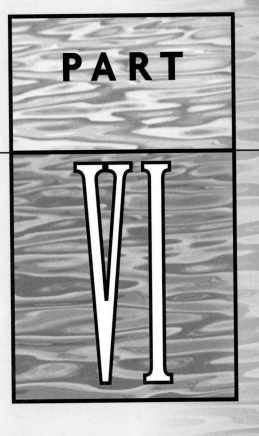

PART

VI

ADJECTIVE CLAUSES

ADJECTIVE CLAUSES WITH SUBJECT RELATIVE PRONOUNS

GRAMMAR **IN CONTEXT**

BEFORE YOU READ   Look at the pictures. How do you think the people feel about each other? What is your definition of a friend?

Read this article about friendship.

Section 5   October, 2001   **LIFESTYLES**   Page 15

A Word with Many Meanings

Almost everyone has friends, but ideas about friendship vary from person to person. For some, a friend is someone **who chats with you on the Internet.** For others, a friend is someone **who has known you all your life**—someone **whose family knows you, too.** Others only use the term for someone **who knows your innermost secrets.** What one person defines as a friend, another calls an acquaintance, and vice versa.

If definitions of friendship can vary so much within a single culture, imagine the differences between cultures. Surprisingly, there are only a few studies about friendship in different cultures. In one study, anthropologist Margaret Mead compared notions of friendship in some Western countries. She says:

"For the French, friendship is a one-to-one relationship **that demands keen awareness of the other person's intellect, temperament, and particular interests.** A friend is someone **who brings out your own best qualities.**"

For French friends, **who enjoy arguing about intellectual issues,** disagreement is "the breath of life." However, Mead notes, ". . . for Germans, **whose friendships are based on mutuality of feeling,** deep disagreement on any subject **that matters to both** is . . . a tragedy."

(continued on next page)

A Word with Many Meanings *(continued)*

Germans form friendships early in life, and friends usually become part of each other's family life. As a result, Mead reports, young Germans **who come to the United States** often have difficulty making friends with Americans, **whose friendships are less permanent**. American friendships fade "as people move, change their jobs, marry, or discover new interests."

British friendships, **which usually remain outside the family**, follow yet another pattern. According to Mead, shared activity is the basis for friendship among the British. British friends may not be as deeply attached to each other as German friends, but their relationships can survive a long separation.

Americans **who have made British friends** comment that, even years later, "you can take up just where you left off." Meeting after a long interval, friends are like a couple **who begin to dance again** when the orchestra strikes up after a pause.

Studies of American friendships indicate that, like the French and British, people in the United States often form friendships around interests. They have friends **who enjoy sports**, friends **who go shopping with them**, friends **who share a hobby**. And, like the Germans, they also form long-lasting friendships **which are based on feelings**. In fact, the variety of relationships that Americans call friendships can confuse people from other cultures, especially when Americans say things like, "I just made a new friend yesterday."

Nevertheless, the term does not seem to confuse Americans, **who know very well the difference between friends and acquaintances**. According to a survey in *Psychology Today*, those **who answered the survey** "find it easy to distinguish between close and casual friends and reported they have more close friends than casual ones."

Although different people and cultures emphasize different aspects of friendship, there is one element **which is always present**, and that is the element of choice. We may not be able to select our families, our co-workers, or even the people **that ride the bus with us**, but we can pick our friends. As Mead puts it, "a friend is someone **who chooses and is chosen**." It is this freedom of choice **that makes friendship such a special and unique relationship**.

Sources: Margaret Mead and Rhoda Metraux, *A Way of Seeing* (New York: McCall, 1970); *Psychology Today*, October, 1979.

GRAMMAR **PRESENTATION**
ADJECTIVE CLAUSES WITH SUBJECT RELATIVE PRONOUNS

ADJECTIVE CLAUSES AFTER THE MAIN CLAUSE

MAIN CLAUSE			ADJECTIVE CLAUSE		
SUBJECT	**VERB**	**PREDICATE NOUN / PRONOUN**	**SUBJECT RELATIVE PRONOUN**	**VERB**	
I	read	a book	*that*	discusses	friends.
A friend	is	someone	*who*	knows	you well.

			WHOSE + NOUN		
I	have	a friend	*whose* home	is	in Boston.

ADJECTIVE CLAUSES INSIDE THE MAIN CLAUSE

MAIN CLAUSE	ADJECTIVE CLAUSE			MAIN CLAUSE (cont.)	
SUBJECT NOUN / PRONOUN	**SUBJECT RELATIVE PRONOUN**	**VERB**		**VERB**	
The book	*that*	discusses	friends	is	by Ruben.
Someone	*who*	knows	you	can give	you advice.

	WHOSE + NOUN				
My friend	*whose* sister	writes	books	lives	in Boston.

NOTES	EXAMPLES
1. Use **adjective clauses** (also called relative clauses) <u>to identify or give additional information about nouns</u> (people, places, or things).	• I know the woman **who lives across the street**. *(The clause* who lives across the street *identifies the woman we are talking about.)* • Boston, **which is my hometown**, is still my favorite city. *(The clause* which is my hometown *gives additional information about Boston.)*
Adjective clauses can also identify or describe <u>indefinite pronouns</u> such as ***someone, somebody, something, another***, and ***other(s)***.	• I'd like to meet *someone* **who speaks Spanish**.
In most cases the adjective clause <u>directly follows the noun</u> (or pronoun) it is identifying or describing.	
2. Sentences with adjective clauses can be seen as a <u>combination of two sentences</u>.	*I have a friend. + She loves to shop. =* • I have a friend **who loves to shop**. *Tom calls often. + He lives in Rome. =* • Tom, **who lives in Rome**, calls often. *Lea has a son. + His name is Max. =* • Lea has a son **whose name is Max**.

(continued on next page)

3. Adjective clauses are introduced by **relative pronouns**. Relative pronouns that can be the <u>subject of the clause</u> are *who*, *that*, *which*, and *whose*.

a. Use *who* or *that* to refer to <u>people</u>.

- I have a **friend *who*** lives in Mexico.

  subj.

  OR

- I have a **friend *that*** lives in Mexico.

  subj.

b. Use *which* or *that* to refer to <u>places or things</u>.

USAGE NOTE: *That* is less formal than *who* and *which*.

- New York is a **city *which*** attracts a lot of tourists.

  subj.

  OR

- New York is a **city *that*** attracts a lot of tourists.

  subj.

c. Use *whose* to refer to <u>people's possessions</u>.

- He's the **man *whose* dog** barks at night.

  subj.

▶ **BE CAREFUL!** Do not use a subject pronoun (*I, you, he, she, it, we, they*) and a subject relative pronoun in the same adjective clause.

- Scott is someone *who* **never forgets** a friend's birthday.
  NOT Scott is someone ~~who he never forgets~~ a friend's birthday.

4. Relative pronouns have the <u>same form</u> whether they refer to singular or plural nouns or to masculine or feminine nouns.

- That's the **man *who*** lives next door.
- That's the **woman *who*** lives next door.
- Those are the **people *who*** live next door.

5. The **verb in the adjective clause** is singular if the subject relative pronoun refers to a singular noun. It is plural if it refers to a plural noun.

- Ben is my **friend *who lives*** in Boston.
- Al and Ed are my **friends *who live*** in Boston.

▶ **BE CAREFUL!** When *whose* + **noun** is the subject of an adjective clause, the verb agrees with the subject of the adjective clause.

- Maria is a person **whose friends *are*** important to her.
  NOT Maria is a person ~~whose friends is~~ important to her.

6. There are two kinds of adjective clauses, **identifying** and **nonidentifying**.

a. Use an **identifying adjective clause** (also called a restrictive or defining clause) to <u>identify which member of a group</u> the sentence talks about.

- I have a lot of friends. My friend **who lives in Chicago** visits me once a year. *(The adjective clause is necessary to identify which friend is meant.)*

b. Use a **nonidentifying adjective clause** (also called a nonrestrictive or nondefining clause) to <u>give additional information</u> about the noun it refers to. The information is not necessary to identify the noun.

Notice that commas are used to separate a nonidentifying clause from the rest of the sentence.

- I have a lot of friends. My best friend**, who lives in Chicago,** visits me once a year. *(The friend has already been identified as the speaker's best friend. The adjective clause gives additional information, but it isn't needed to identify the friend.)*

▶ **BE CAREFUL!** Do not use *that* to introduce <u>nonidentifying adjective clauses</u>. Use *who* for people and *which* for places and things.

- **Marielle,** *who* introduced us at the party, called me last night.
  NOT Marielle, ~~that introduced us at the party~~, called me last night.

- **Miami,** *which* reminds me of home, is my favorite vacation spot.
  NOT Miami, ~~that reminds me of home~~, is my favorite vacation spot.

7. In <u>writing</u>, a nonidentifying adjective clause is separated from the rest of the sentence by **commas**.

nonidentifying adjective clause
- My sister, **who lives in Seattle,** came to visit me this year.

In <u>speaking</u>, a nonidentifying adjective clause is separated from the rest of the sentence by brief **pauses**.

- My sister *(pause)* **who lives in Seattle** *(pause)* came to visit me this year. *(I have only one sister. She lives in Seattle.)*

identifying adjective clause
Without commas or pauses the same sentence has a very <u>different meaning</u>.
- My sister **who lives in Seattle** came to visit me this year. *(I have several sisters. This one lives in Seattle.)*

FOCUSED PRACTICE

 DISCOVER THE GRAMMAR

Read the article about different types of friends. First circle the relative pronouns and underline the adjective clauses. Then draw an arrow from the relative pronoun to the noun or pronoun that it describes.

Not Just Friends
BY BUD E. FREUND

Most of us have very few "best friends" throughout our lives. These are friends who stand by us through thick and thin. They are people who accept us completely (warts and all) and who know our most secret thoughts. But our lives crisscross with many others whose relationships with us may be less deep but are still important. What would our lives be without these acquaintances, buddies, and dear old friends?

ACQUAINTANCES. These are people whose paths often cross ours. We attend the same school committee meetings or share a car pool with them. Acquaintances may exchange favors easily. The neighbor who borrows your chairs for a big party or the colleague who waters your plants while you're on vacation fits this category. But we usually don't get too intimate with them. One woman commented, "Our next-door neighbor, who car pools with us, is very nice. But we don't have anything in common. We never get together for anything but car pool."

BUDDIES. A lot of people have a friend who shares a particular activity or interest. These usually aren't close relationships, but they're important ones that keep us connected to our interests and hobbies. Because they're based on activities rather than feelings, it's relatively easy to make a new buddy. One foreign-exchange student reported, "For the first two months, I didn't have any real friends. My table-tennis partner, who's from Beijing, was my only social contact. We couldn't communicate in English very well, but we had a good time anyway. Without him, I would have been completely isolated."

OLD FRIENDS. "Delores knew me when I worked in the mailroom," recalls an advertising executive. "I'll never forget this day. The vice president who promoted me called me for an interview. I didn't have the right clothes, and Delores was the one who came with me to buy my first business suit." We all have old friends who knew us "back when." They keep us in touch with parts of ourselves which are easy to lose as we move through life. "Whenever I go home, I always visit Delores," recalls the executive. "We look through old albums and talk about experiences that have helped form us. She always reminds me how shy I used to be. I agree with George Herbert, who said that the best mirror is an old friend."

Now read these sentences from the article. Each one is followed by a statement.
Decide if the statement is **True (T)** *or* **False (F)**.

1. The colleague who waters your plants while you're on vacation is your acquaintance.

___T___ The writer believes that you have more than one colleague.

2. Our next-door neighbor, who car pools with us, is very nice.

_____ The speaker may have only one next-door neighbor.

3. My table-tennis partner, who was from Beijing, was my only social contact.

_____ The speaker probably had only one table-tennis partner.

4. The vice president who promoted me called me for an interview.

_____ The company has only one vice president.

2 DEFINITIONS Grammar Note 3

First, match the words on the left with the descriptions on the right.

Word	Description
__e__ **1.** acquaintance	**a.** This person is married to you.
_____ **2.** album	**b.** This event brings people together after a long separation.
_____ **3.** soul mate	**c.** This relationship exists between friends.
_____ **4.** colleague	**d.** This person is a relative.
_____ **5.** confidant	**e.** This person knows you but is not a close friend.
_____ **6.** empathy	**f.** This feeling lets you experience another person's feelings.
_____ **7.** friendship	**g.** This person is very similar to you in thought and feeling.
_____ **8.** kin	**h.** This book has pages for saving photos.
_____ **9.** reunion	**i.** This person listens to your private feelings and thoughts.
_____ **10.** spouse	**j.** This person has the same job or profession as you.

Now, write definitions for the words on the left. Use the correct description on the right and appropriate relative pronouns.

1. ___An acquaintance is a person who knows you but is not a close friend.___

2. _____

3. _____

4. _____

(continued on next page)

5. _____

6. _____

7. _____

8. _____

9. _____

10. _____

❸ SURVEY RESULTS

Grammar Notes 3–6

A U.S. magazine, Psychology Today, *conducted a national survey on friendship.
Below are some of the results. Complete the sentences with an appropriate relative
pronoun and the correct form of the verbs in parentheses.*

1. People ____who____ ____have____ moved a lot have fewer casual friends.

(have)

2. People _____ _____ lived in the same place have more casual friends.

(have)

3. The qualities _____ _____ most important in a friend are loyalty,

(be)
   warmth, and the ability to keep secrets.

4. People _____ _____ a crisis turn first to their friends for help, not to

(face)
   their families.

5. Betrayal is the cause _____ _____ most responsible for ending a

(be)
   friendship.

6. Most people can maintain friendships with friends _____ _____

(have)
   become more successful than they are.

7. Many people have friends _____ social or religious backgrounds
   _____ different from theirs.

(be)

8. Most people _____ friends _____ members of the opposite sex say

(include)
   that these relationships are different from relationships with the same sex.

9. This survey, _____ _____ in *Psychology Today,* was completed by

(appear)
   typical readers of this magazine.

10. Someone _____ _____ *Psychology Today* might have different ideas

(not read)
    about friendship.

4 **BETWEEN FRIENDS**

Read these conversations between friends. Then use the first sentence in each conversation to help you write a summary. Use adjective clauses. Remember to use commas where necessary.

1.　　**A:** This article is really interesting.
　　　B: What's it about?
　　　A: It discusses the different types of friendship.

　　SUMMARY:　This article, which discusses the different types of friendship, is really interesting.

2.　　**A:** So, they'll meet us at the restaurant, OK?
　　　B: Which restaurant?
　　　A: You know the one. It's across the street from the library.

　　SUMMARY: _____

3.　　**A:** The navy blue suit looked the best.
　　　B: Which navy blue suit?
　　　A: The one on sale.

　　SUMMARY: _____

4.　　**A:** Bill and Sue aren't close friends with the Swabodas, are they?
　　　B: Well, the Swabodas' interests are very different from theirs.

　　SUMMARY: _____

5.　　**A:** The neighbors came by while you were gone.
　　　B: Do you know what they wanted?
　　　A: They wanted to borrow some folding chairs.

　　SUMMARY: _____

6.　　**A:** I was just laughing at an old picture of Jason.
　　　B: Which one? You have hundreds.
　　　A: You know the one—it's in his high school yearbook.

　　SUMMARY: _____

7.　　**A:** My boyfriend left me a lot of plants to water.
　　　B: How come?
　　　A: He took a group of students to Venezuela for two weeks.

　　SUMMARY: _____

5 **EDITING**

Read this student's essay about a friend. Find and correct ten mistakes in the use of adjective clauses. Each incorrectly punctuated clause counts as one mistake. The first mistake is already corrected.

Good Friends

A writer once said that friends are born, not made. I think he meant that friendship is like love at first sight—we become friends immediately with people who ~~they~~ are compatible with us. I don't agree with this writer. Last summer I made friends with some people who's completely different from me.

In July, I went to Mexico City to study Spanish for a month. In our group, there were five adults, which were all language teachers from our school. Two teachers stayed with friends in Mexico City, and we only saw those teachers during the day. But we saw the teachers, who stayed with us in the dormitory, both day and night. They were the ones who they helped us when we had problems. Bob Taylor who is much older than I am became a really good friend. In my first week, I had a problem that was getting me down. Mexico City, that is a very exciting place, was too distracting. I went out all the time, and I stopped going to my classes. Bob, who have studied abroad a lot, helped me get back into my studies. After the trip I kept writing to Bob, who's letters are always interesting and encouraging. Next summer, he's leading another trip what sounds interesting. It's a three-week trip to Spain, a place he knows a lot about. I hope I can go.

COMMUNICATION PRACTICE

6 LISTENING

Some friends are at a high school reunion. They haven't seen one another for twenty-five years. Listen to the friends talk about the people at the table. Then listen again and label the people with their correct names.

Ann   Asha   ~~Bob~~   Kado   Pat   Pete

7 A FRIEND IS SOMEONE WHO . . .

Complete the questionnaire. Check all the items that you believe are true.

A friend is someone who . . .

- **1.** always tells you the truth.
- **2.** has known you for a very long time.
- **3.** cries with you.
- **4.** lends you money.

(continued on next page)

☐ **5.** talks to you every day.

☐ **6.** helps you when you are in trouble.

☐ **7.** listens to your problems.

☐ **8.** does things with you.

☐ **9.** respects you.

☐ **10.** accepts you the way you are.

☐ **11.** understands you.

☐ **12.** gives you advice.

☐ **13.** keeps your secrets.

☐ **14.** cares about you.

Other: _____

Now, work with a partner and compare questionnaires. Discuss the reasons for your choices.

EXAMPLE:
A: I think a friend is someone who always tells you the truth.
B: I don't agree. Sometimes the truth can hurt you.

After your discussion, tally the results of the whole class.

8 WHAT'S THE DIFFERENCE?

Work in small groups. Discuss the differences between these terms:

a friend and an acquaintance

a friend and a best friend

a friend and a colleague

a friend and a buddy

Now discuss these questions:

What is the word for *friend* in your first language? Is it used the same as the English word?

Can men and women be friends? What about people of different ages?

Can people from different religious, social, or economic backgrounds be friends?

9 QUOTABLE QUOTES

Work with a group and choose five of these quotations. Talk about what the quotations mean. Give examples from your own experience to support your ideas.

Chance makes our relatives, but choice makes our friends.
—Jacques Delille (French poet, 1738–1813)

EXAMPLE:
A: I think this means that we can't choose our families, but we can choose our friends.
B: I agree. When I was in high school my best friend was someone who was completely different from my family. . . .

The best mirror is an old friend.
—*George Herbert (English poet and novelist, 1593–1633)*

Friendship is a plant which we must often water.
—*German proverb*

A good man finds all the world friendly.
—*Hindustan proverb*

He is wise who can make a friend of a foe.
—*Scottish proverb*

Show me a friend who will weep with me; those who will laugh with me I can find myself.
—*Yugoslav proverb*

A friend in need is a friend indeed.
—*English proverb*

Very few people can congratulate without envy a friend who has succeeded.
—*Aeschylus (Greek playwright, 525–456 B.C.)*

[A friend is] another I.
—*Zeno (Greek philosopher, 335–263 B.C.)*

Wherever you are it is your own friends who make your world.
—*Ralph Barton Perry (U.S. philosopher, 1876–1957)*

One friend in a lifetime is much; two are many; three are hardly possible.
Friends are born, not made.
—*Henry Brooks Adams (U.S. writer and historian, 1838–1918)*

Have no friends not equal to yourself.
—*Confucius (Chinese philosopher, 551–479 B.C.)*

A true friend is somebody who can make us do what we can.
—*Ralph Waldo Emerson (U.S. writer, 1803–1882)*

🔟 WRITING

Write an essay of two paragraphs about a friend. You may want to begin your essay with one of the quotations from Exercise 9. You can use the student's essay in Exercise 5 as a model.

14 ADJECTIVE CLAUSES WITH OBJECT RELATIVE PRONOUNS OR *WHEN* AND *WHERE*

GRAMMAR **IN CONTEXT**

BEFORE YOU READ What is an autobiography? Look at the title of the book review below. What do you think the books are about?

🎞 *Read a review of two autobiographies.*

Torn Between Two Worlds

"I'm filled to the brim with what I'm about to lose—images of Cracow, **which I loved as one loves a person**, of the sun-baked villages **where we had taken summer vacations**, of the hours **I spent** poring over passages of music with my music teacher, of conversations and escapades with friends."

So writes Eva Hoffman, author of *Lost in Translation: A Life in a New Language* (New York: Penguin, 1989). Hoffman, whose early childhood was spent in Cracow, Poland, moved with her family to Vancouver, Canada when she was thirteen. Her autobiography relates her experiences as she is uprooted from her beloved Cracow and as she struggles to understand her surroundings and herself in a new language.

In spite of poverty, a small, crowded apartment, and her parents' wartime memories, Ewa Wydra (Hoffman's Polish name) loved her native Cracow. It was a city of "shimmering light and shadow," a place **where life was lived intensely**. As a child, she had visited its cafés with her father, **who she watched in**

(continued on next page)

Torn Between Two Worlds

(continued)

lively conversations with his friends. Hoffman remembers neighbors, "People **between whose apartments there's constant movement with kids, sugar, eggs, and tea time visits**." Her friendship with Marek, **whose apartment she visited almost daily**, deepened, and the two grew up assuming that they would be married.

Pani Witeszcak, Ewa's piano teacher, was the last person **Ewa said goodbye to** before she left Poland. "What do you think you'll miss most?" her teacher asked. "Everything. Cracow. The School. . . . You. Everything. . . ."

At her new school in Vancouver, Ewa is given her English name, Eva, **which her teachers find easier to pronounce**. Eva, however, feels no connection to the name, or to the English name of anything **that she feels is important**. All her memories and feelings are still in her first language, Polish. The story of Eva as she grows up and comes to terms with her new identity and language is fascinating and moving.

Also recommended is *The Rice Room*, by Ben Fong-Torres (New York: Hyperion, 1994). Unlike Hoffman, a first-generation immigrant, Fong-Torres was born in the United States of parents who had emigrated from China. Many of the problems **that he faces**, however, are similar to Hoffman's. Fong-Torres must try to reconcile his family's culture with his new culture. To do this, he must struggle with a language barrier. A successful radio announcer and journalist, Fong-Torres describes the frustration of trying to communicate

with his parents, **for whom English is still a foreign language**.

"Over the years, I've talked with my parents many times, but we've never really communicated. . . . When we talk, it sounds like baby talk—at least my half of it. . . . I don't know half the words **I need**; I either never learned them, or I heard but forgot them." Fong-Torres continues to describe the language barrier that stands between his parents and him ". . . through countless moments **when we needed to talk with each other**, about the things **parents and children usually discuss**; jobs and careers; marriage and divorce; health and finances; history, the present, and the future. This is one of the great sadnesses of my life. How ironic. . . . I'm a journalist and a broadcaster—my job is to communicate—and I can't with the two people **with whom I want to most**."

Whether first- or second-generation immigrant—the issues remain the same. These two books eloquently describe the lives of people trying to bridge the gap between the worlds that were left behind and the worlds **that they now call home**.

GRAMMAR **PRESENTATION**
ADJECTIVE CLAUSES WITH OBJECT RELATIVE PRONOUNS OR *WHEN* AND *WHERE*

ADJECTIVE CLAUSES AFTER THE MAIN CLAUSE

MAIN CLAUSE			ADJECTIVE CLAUSE		
SUBJECT	**VERB**	**PREDICATE NOUN / PRONOUN**	**(OBJECT RELATIVE PRONOUN)**	**SUBJECT**	**VERB**
He	read	the book	*(that)*	she	wrote.
She	is	someone	*(who[m])*	I	respect.

			WHOSE + NOUN		
That	is	the author	*whose* book	I	read.

			WHERE / *(WHEN)*		
She	loves	the city	*where*	she	grew up.
They	cried	the day	*(when)*	they	left.

ADJECTIVE CLAUSES INSIDE THE MAIN CLAUSE

MAIN CLAUSE	ADJECTIVE CLAUSE			MAIN CLAUSE (cont.)	
SUBJECT	**(OBJECT RELATIVE PRONOUN)**	**SUBJECT**	**VERB**	**VERB**	
The book	*(that)*	I	read	is	great.
Someone	*(who[m])*	you	know	was	there.

	WHOSE + NOUN				
The man	*whose* sister	you	know	writes	books.

MAIN CLAUSE	ADJECTIVE CLAUSE			MAIN CLAUSE (cont.)	
SUBJECT	WHERE / (WHEN)	SUBJECT	VERB	VERB	
The library	**where**	**I**	**work**	has	videos.
The summer	**(when)**	**she**	**left**	passed	slowly.

NOTES

EXAMPLES

1. In Unit 13, you learned about adjective clauses in which the **relative pronoun** was the <u>subject of the adjective clause</u>.

Relative pronouns can also be the **object of an adjective clause**. Notice that:

a. The **object relative pronoun** comes <u>at the beginning</u> of the adjective clause.

b. Relative pronouns (subject or object) have the <u>same form</u> whether they refer to singular or plural nouns, or to masculine or feminine nouns.

c. The **verb in the adjective clause** <u>agrees with the subject</u> of the adjective clause. It does not agree with the relative pronoun or the noun that the relative pronoun refers to.

▶ **BE CAREFUL!** Do not use an object pronoun (*me, you, him, her, it, us, them*) together with an object relative pronoun in an adjective clause.

REMEMBER: There are two kinds of adjective clauses, identifying and nonidentifying. (*See Unit 13, page 195.*)

subj.
Eva is a writer. + **She** *was born in Poland.* =

subj.
- Eva, ***who was born in Poland***, is a writer.

obj.
Eva is a writer. + *I saw* **her** *on TV.* =

obj.
- Eva, ***who(m)*** **I saw on TV**, is a writer.

- That's the **man *who(m)*** I met.
- That's the **woman *who(m)*** I met.
- Those are the **people *who(m)*** I met.

subj. verb
- I like the **columns which he *writes*.**
- I like the **column which they *write*.**

- She is the writer ***who*** I saw on TV.
  NOT She is the writer ~~who I saw her on TV.~~

(continued on next page)

2. Relative pronouns that can be the <u>object of the adjective clause</u> are **who(m)**, **that**, **which**, and **whose**.

a. Use **whom**, **who**, or **that** to refer to <u>people</u>. Note that in this case, you can also leave out the relative pronoun.

USAGE NOTE: **Whom** is very formal. Most speakers do not use *whom* in everyday speech. **That** is less formal than **who**. The most common spoken form is the one with no relative pronoun.

- She's the writer **whom** I met.
  OR
- She's the writer **who** I met.
  OR
- She's the writer **that** I met.
  OR
- She's the writer I met.

More

Less

b. Use **which** or **that** to refer to <u>things</u>. You can also leave out the relative pronoun.

USAGE NOTE: Again, **that** is less formal than **which**. The most common spoken form is the one with no relative pronoun.

- I read the book **which** she wrote.
  OR
- I read the book **that** she wrote.
  OR
- I read the book she wrote.

More

Less

c. Use **whose** to refer to <u>people's possessions</u>. You cannot leave out *whose*.

- That's the author **whose** book I read.

▶ **BE CAREFUL!** You can only leave out relative pronouns in identifying adjective clauses. You <u>cannot leave out the relative pronoun in a nonidentifying</u> adjective clause.

- She remembers Marek, **who** she visited often.
  NOT She remembers Marek ~~she visited often~~.

3. The relative pronouns *who(m)*, *that*, *which*, and *whose* can be the <u>object of a preposition</u>.

Note that they can all (except for *whose*) be left out.

*He's the writer. + I work **for him**. =*

FORMALITY

More

- He's the writer *whom* I work **for**.
  OR
- He's the writer *who* I work **for**.
  OR
- He's the writer *that* I work **for**.
  OR
- He's the writer I work **for**.

Less

*He's the writer. + I work **for his wife**. =*

- He's the writer *whose* wife I work **for**.

USAGE NOTE: In everyday **spoken English** and in **informal writing**, we place the <u>preposition at the end</u> of the clause.

- He's the writer *who* I work **for**.
- That's the book *that* I told you **about**.

In **formal English**, we put the <u>preposition at the beginning</u> of the clause. Also, we use only *whom* (not *who* or *that*) to refer to <u>people</u>, and *which* (not *that*) to refer to <u>things</u>.

- He's the writer **for** *whom* I work.
- That's the book **about** *which* I told you.

4. *When* and *where* can also be used to introduce adjective clauses.

a. *Where* refers to a <u>place</u>.

*That's the library. + She works **there**. =*
- That's the library *where* she works.

b. *When* or *that* refer to a <u>time</u>.
Note that you can leave out *when* and *that* in identifying adjective clauses.

*I remember the day. + I met him **then**. =*
- I remember the day *when* I met him.
  OR
- I remember the day *that* I met him.
  OR
- I remember the day I met him.

FOCUSED PRACTICE

1 DISCOVER THE GRAMMAR

The excerpt below comes from Eva Hoffman's book, Lost in Translation. *It describes Hoffman's home in Cracow, Poland. First circle all the words that introduce adjective clauses (relative pronouns,* **when,** *and* **where***) and underline the adjective clauses. Then draw a line from the relative pronoun to the noun or pronoun that it refers to.*

> The kitchen is usually steamy with large pots of soup cooking on the wood stove for hours, or laundry being boiled in vats for greater whiteness; behind the kitchen, there's a tiny balcony, barely big enough to hold two people, on (which) we sometimes go out to exchange neighborly gossip with people peeling vegetables, beating carpets, or just standing around on adjoining balconies. Looking down, you see a paved courtyard, in which I spend many hours bouncing a ball against the wall with other kids, and a bit of garden, where I go to smell the few violets that come up each spring and climb the apple tree, and where my sister gathers the snails that live under the boysenberry bushes, to bring them proudly into the house by the bucketful. . . .
>
> . . . Across the hall from us are the Twardowskis, who come to our apartment regularly. . . . I particularly like the Twardowskis' daughter, Basia, who is several years older than I and who has the prettiest long braids, which she sometimes coils around her head. . . .

Now read this excerpt about Hoffman's music school. There are four adjective clauses in which the relative pronouns have been omitted. Find the other clauses and underline them. The first one is already underlined.

> Pani Konek teaches at the Cracow Music School, which I've been attending for two years—ever since it has been decided that I should be trained as a professional pianist. I've always liked going to school. At the beginning of the year, I like buying smooth navy blue fabric from which our dressmaker will make my school uniform—an anonymous overdress <u>we are required to wear</u> over our regular clothes in order to erase economic and class distinctions; I like the feel of the crisp, untouched notebook . . . and dipping my pen into the deep inkwell in my desk, and learning how to make oblique letters. It's fun to make up stories about the eccentric characters I know, or about the shapes icicles make on the winter windows, and to try to outwit the teacher when I don't know something, and to give dramatic recitations of poems we've memorized. . . .

Source: Eva Hoffman, *Lost in Translation: A Life in a New Language* (New York: Penguin, 1989).

2 **FIRST IMPRESSIONS**   Grammar Notes 1–4

Complete this interview from a school newspaper. Use a relative pronoun, **when**,
or **where** *and the correct form of the verbs in parentheses.*

The Grover	September 10, 2001	page 3

Meet Your Classmates

Maniya, _____ who _____ a lot of our readers already _____ know _____,
                                                              1. (know)

has been at Grover High for three years now. We interviewed Maniya

about her experiences coming to the United States.

INTERVIEWER: How did your family choose Atlanta, Maniya?

MANIYA: My cousin, _____ we _____ with at
                                              2. (stay)

first, lives here.

INTERVIEWER: What were your first impressions?

MANIYA: At first it was fun. We got here in the summer, _____ there

_____ no school, so I didn't feel much pressure to speak English.
3. (be)

INTERVIEWER: What was the most difficult thing about going to school?

MANIYA: Of course, the class in _____ I _____ the biggest problems
                                                    4. (have)

at first was English. It was so hard for me to write compositions or to say the

things _____ I _____ to say. Now it's much easier.
                       5. (want)

INTERVIEWER: What was the biggest change for you when you got here?

MANIYA: We used to live in a big house, _____ there _____ always
                                                              6. (be)

a lot of people. Here I live with my parents and sister, _____

I _____ after school.
      7. (take care of)

INTERVIEWER: How did you learn English so quickly?

MANIYA: At night, I write words and idioms on a piece of paper, _____ I

_____ in my shirt pocket. Then I study them at school whenever
8. (put)
I have a chance.

INTERVIEWER: Is there anything you still have trouble with?

MANIYA: One thing _____ I still _____ hard to do is make jokes in
                                        9. (find)

English. Some things are funny in Tagalog but not in English.

3 MEMORIES

Combine the pairs of sentences, using adjective clauses. Make any other necessary changes.

1. That's the house. I grew up in the house.

That's the house that I grew up in.

2. I lived with my parents and my siblings. You've met my parents.

3. I had two sisters and an older brother. I got along well with my sisters.

4. My sisters and I shared a room. We spent nights talking there.

5. My brother slept on the living room couch. I hardly ever saw him.

6. It was a large old couch. My father had made the couch himself.

7. My best friend lived across the hall. I saw her every day.

8. We went to the same school. We both studied English there.

9. Mr. Robinson was our English teacher. Everyone was a little afraid of Mr. Robinson.

10. After school I worked in a bakery. My aunt and uncle owned it.

11. They sold delicious bread and cake. People stood in line for hours to buy the bread and cake.

12. I took piano lessons from a woman. The woman's sister worked in the bakery.

13. I remember one summer. The whole family went to the lake then.

_____

14. It was a great summer. I'll never forget that summer.

_____

15. My brother and sisters live far away now. I miss them.

_____

16. When we get together we like to reminisce about the old days. We were all together then.

_____

4 EDITING

Read this student's essay. First put commas where necessary. (Remember: Nonidentifying adjective clauses need commas.) Then delete the relative pronouns where possible.

Tai Dong, where I grew up, is a small city on the southeast coast of Taiwan. My family moved there from Taipei the summer ~~when~~ I was born. I don't remember our first house which we rented from a relative, but when I was two, we moved to the house that I grew up in. This house where my parents still live is on a main street in Tai Dong. To me, this was the best place in the world. My mother had a food stand in our front courtyard where she sold omelettes early in the morning. All her customers whom I always chatted with were very friendly to me. On the first floor, my father conducted his tea business in the front room. After school, I always went straight to the corner where he sat drinking tea with his customers. In the back was our huge kitchen with its stone floor and brick oven. I loved dinnertime because the kitchen was always full of relatives and the customers that my father had invited to dinner. It was a fun and noisy place to be. Next to the kitchen, there was one small bedroom. My oldest cousin whose father wanted him to learn the tea business slept there. Our living room and bedrooms were upstairs. My two sisters slept in one bedroom, and my older brother and I slept in the other. My younger sister shared a room with my grandmother who took care of her a lot of the time.

COMMUNICATION PRACTICE

5 LISTENING

Listen to a woman describe her childhood room. Then listen again and choose the correct picture.

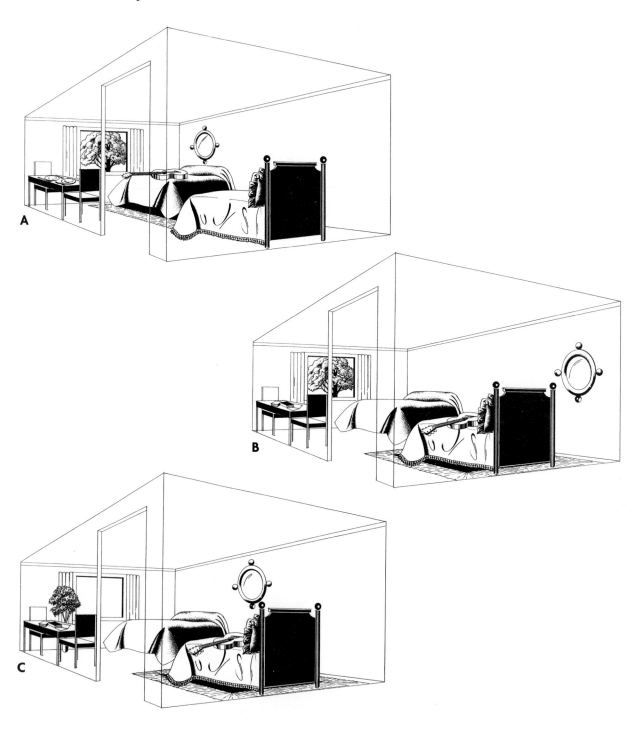

A

B

C

Listen again. Decide if the description is in formal or informal English.

6 INFORMATION GAP: BIOGRAPHY

Work in pairs (A and B). You are each going to read some biographical information about Ben Fong-Torres, author of The Rice Room. *Each of your biographies is missing some information. Your task is to get the missing information from your partner.*

Student B, look at the Information Gap on page 217 and follow the instructions there.

Student A, read the biographical data about Ben Fong-Torres below. Then ask Student B questions about him in order to fill in the missing information. Answer Student B's questions.

EXAMPLE:

A: When was the Exclusion Act still in effect?

B: In 1929.
Where did his father obtain a birth certificate?

A: In the Philippines.

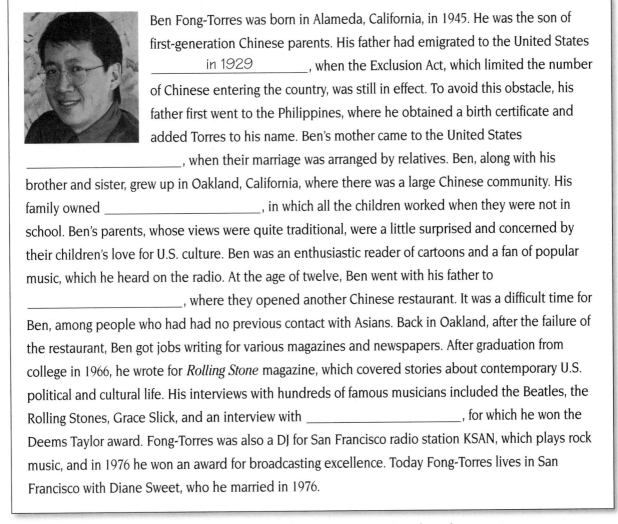

Ben Fong-Torres was born in Alameda, California, in 1945. He was the son of first-generation Chinese parents. His father had emigrated to the United States _____ in 1929 _____, when the Exclusion Act, which limited the number of Chinese entering the country, was still in effect. To avoid this obstacle, his father first went to the Philippines, where he obtained a birth certificate and added Torres to his name. Ben's mother came to the United States _____, when their marriage was arranged by relatives. Ben, along with his brother and sister, grew up in Oakland, California, where there was a large Chinese community. His family owned _____, in which all the children worked when they were not in school. Ben's parents, whose views were quite traditional, were a little surprised and concerned by their children's love for U.S. culture. Ben was an enthusiastic reader of cartoons and a fan of popular music, which he heard on the radio. At the age of twelve, Ben went with his father to _____, where they opened another Chinese restaurant. It was a difficult time for Ben, among people who had had no previous contact with Asians. Back in Oakland, after the failure of the restaurant, Ben got jobs writing for various magazines and newspapers. After graduation from college in 1966, he wrote for *Rolling Stone* magazine, which covered stories about contemporary U.S. political and cultural life. His interviews with hundreds of famous musicians included the Beatles, the Rolling Stones, Grace Slick, and an interview with _____, for which he won the Deems Taylor award. Fong-Torres was also a DJ for San Francisco radio station KSAN, which plays rock music, and in 1976 he won an award for broadcasting excellence. Today Fong-Torres lives in San Francisco with Diane Sweet, who he married in 1976.

When you have finished, compare texts with your partner. Are they the same?

7 PEOPLE AND PLACES

Bring in some family photographs to share with your classmates. They can be recent photographs or ones taken some time ago. Work in small groups. Explain the people and places in your photographs.

EXAMPLE:

A: This is the street where we lived before we moved here.

B: Is that the house you grew up in?

A: Yes, it is. I lived there until I was ten.

8 QUOTABLE QUOTES

Work in groups and choose three of the quotations to discuss. Talk about what the quotations mean. Give examples from your own experience to support your ideas.

Where we love is home,
Home that our feet may leave, but not our hearts.
　　—*Oliver Wendell Holmes, Sr. (U.S. doctor and author, 1809–1894)*

Home is not where you live but where they understand you.
　　—*Christian Morgenstern (German poet, 1871–1914)*

You can't go home again.
　　—*Thomas Wolfe (U.S. novelist, 1900–1938)*

Home is the place where, when you have to go there, they have to take you in.
　　—*Robert Frost (U.S. poet, 1874–1963)*

'Mid pleasures and palaces though we may roam,
Be it ever so humble, there's no place like home.
　　—*John Howard Payne (U.S. actor, 1791–1852)*

What is more agreeable than one's home?
　　—*Marcus Tullius Cicero (Roman statesman, 106–43 B.C.)*

9 WRITING

Write about a place you remember from your childhood. Use adjective clauses to help you explain where things were and why they were important. Use Exercise 4 as a model.

INFORMATION GAP FOR STUDENT B

Read the biographical data about Ben Fong-Torres. Then ask Student A questions about him in order to fill in the missing information. Answer Student A's questions.

EXAMPLE:

A: When was the Exclusion Act still in effect?

B: In 1929.
Where did his father obtain a birth certificate?

A: In the Philippines.

Ben Fong-Torres was born in Alameda, California, in 1945. He was the son of first-generation Chinese parents. His father had emigrated to the United States in 1929, when the Exclusion Act, which limited the number of Chinese entering the country, was still in effect. To avoid this obstacle, his father first went to _____the Philippines_____, where he obtained a birth certificate and added Torres to his name. Ben's mother came to the United States ten years later, when their marriage was arranged by relatives. Ben, along with his brother and sister, grew up in _____, where there was a large Chinese community. His family owned a Chinese restaurant, in which all the children worked when they were not in school. Ben's parents, whose views were quite traditional, were a little surprised and concerned by their children's love for U.S. culture. Ben was an enthusiastic reader of cartoons and a fan of _____, which he heard on the radio. At the age of twelve, Ben went with his father to Texas, where they opened another Chinese restaurant. It was a difficult time for Ben, among people who had had no previous contact with Asians. Back in Oakland, after the failure of the restaurant, Ben got jobs writing for various magazines and newspapers. After graduation from college in 1966, he wrote for _____, which covered stories about contemporary U.S. political and cultural life. His interviews with hundreds of famous musicians included the Beatles, the Rolling Stones, Grace Slick, and an interview with Ray Charles, for which he won the Deems Taylor award. Fong-Torres was also a DJ for San Francisco radio station KSAN, which plays rock music, and in 1976 he won an award for broadcasting excellence. Today Fong-Torres lives in San Francisco with _____, who he married in 1976.

When you are finished, compare texts with your partner. Are they the same?

REVIEW OR SELFTEST

I. *Complete the sentences by circling the correct words.*

1. The neighborhood (that)/ who I grew up in was very friendly.

2. There were a lot of people who / which liked to do things together.

3. Mrs. Morris, that / who lived across the street, was one of my mother's closest friends.

4. She lived in a large old house, where / which I spent many happy hours.

5. I played there every day with her daughter, which / whose name was Katy.

6. Katy had a little dog to which / that I was very attached.

7. We took the dog for walks in the park where / which was down the block.

8. There we met other children who / whose we knew from school.

9. The classmate that / which I remember best was Rosa.

10. She had beautiful long hair, that / which she wore in braids.

11. I remember the summer when / which the whole community had a big picnic in the park.

12. I like to think back on the "good old days" when / which people seemed to have more time for one another.

II. *Combine these pairs of sentences, using adjective clauses. Use a relative pronoun,* **when***, or* **where***. Make any other necessary changes.*

1. That's my neighbor. I water her plants.

   That's my neighbor whose plants I water.

2. She lives in the house. The house is across the street.

   _____

3. This is the time of the year. She always goes away now.

   _____

4. She travels with her older sister. Her sister lives in Connecticut.

_____

5. This year they're taking a trip with the car. She just bought the car.

_____

6. They're going to Miami. They grew up there.

_____

7. They have a lot of relatives in Florida. They haven't seen them in years.

_____

8. The family is going to have a reunion. They've been planning the reunion all year.

_____

9. They'll be staying with their Aunt Sonya. Her house is right on a canal.

_____

10. They really need this vacation. They've been looking forward to it all year.

_____

III. *Each sentence has four underlined words or phrases. The four underlined parts of the sentences are marked A, B, C, or D. Circle the letter of the <u>one</u> underlined word or phrase that is NOT CORRECT.*

1. After a week, <u>we</u> finally got to <u>Miami,</u> <u>where</u> my aunt <u>live</u>.   **A   B   C   Ⓓ**
                A   B   C   D

2. My aunt's new <u>house</u> is next to a beautiful <u>canal</u> <u>in where</u> we <u>go</u>   **A   B   C   D**
                  A   B   C   D

swimming every day.

3. Our cousins, <u>who</u> <u>are</u> five and <u>seven</u> <u>are</u> great.   **A   B   C   D**
                A   B   C   D

4. <u>They</u> love the <u>T-shirts</u> <u>what</u> you <u>helped me</u> pick out.   **A   B   C   D**
    A   B   C   D

5. The <u>hotel</u> at <u>that</u> the family reunion <u>is taking</u> place <u>is</u> gorgeous.   **A   B   C   D**
         A   B   C   D

6. The hotel is right on the <u>beach</u> where I used to play <u>on</u> <u>when</u>   **A   B   C   D**
                           A   B   C

I <u>was</u> a kid.
  D

7. My favorite uncle, <u>which</u> <u>lives</u> in <u>Texas,</u> <u>arrived</u> last night.   **A   B   C   D**
                    A   B   C   D

8. I'll never forget <u>the day</u> <u>where</u> he <u>took</u> <u>me</u> horseback riding.   **A   B   C   D**
                A   B   C   D

9. The horse <u>that</u> he let me ride <u>was</u> the most beautiful animal <u>who</u>   **A   B   C   D**
              A   B   C

I <u>had ever seen</u>.
   D

(continued on next page)

10. My <u>niece</u> and nephew, <u>who</u> <u>lives</u> in England, <u>are arriving</u> tomorrow.   A B C D
    A   B C   D

11. Please remember to water my <u>plants</u>, especially the one <u>that</u> <u>have</u> the   A B C D
    A   B C

    purple <u>flowers</u>.
    D

IV. *Circle the letter of the correct word(s) to complete each sentence. Choose Ø when no word is needed.*

1. Bring in the roll of film _____ Uncle Pete took at the reunion.   A B Ⓒ D
   (A) what   (C) Ø
   (B) with which   (D) whom

2. Send some copies to the reporter who _____ to write an article.   A B C D
   (A) want   (C) will
   (B) Ø   (D) wants

3. Pay all the bills _____ are due this week.   A B C D
   (A) Ø   (C) when
   (B) that   (D) they

4. Call the women _____ I met at lunch.   A B C D
   (A) which   (C) Ø
   (B) whose   (D) those

5. Please write to Mr. Coppel, _____ I met at the pool.   A B C D
   (A) that   (C) Ø
   (B) who   (D) where

6. I'm looking for the books Mr. Jay _____.   A B C D
   (A) recommend   (C) recommends
   (B) recommends them   (D) recommend them

7. The neighbor _____ children watered our plants lives across   A B C D
   the street.
   (A) their   (C) Ø
   (B) whom   (D) whose

8. Annie found the souvenirs that _____ wanted at the gift shop.   A B C D
   (A) Ø   (C) she
   (B) where   (D) which

9. Have you sent thank-you notes to the relatives from _____ you   A B C D
   received gifts?
   (A) which   (C) them
   (B) whom   (D) that

10. Let's try to agree on a time _____ we can all get together.   A B C D
    (A) which   (C) Ø
    (B) where   (D) at

V. *Read this student essay. There are seven mistakes in the use of adjective clauses. Find and correct them. The first mistake is already corrected.*

There is an old German proverb that says "Friendship is a
plant ~~that~~ *which* we must often water." This means that we have to
nurture our relationships to make them grow and flourish. A
relationship that you neglect will wilt and die.

When I was ten, my family moved from Germany to the United
States. There I had a "friend" (whom I will call Jack) who he
never invited me to do things with him. Jack lived in a house
where I never got to see even though it was just a few blocks
away from mine. He had family and friends whom I never met.
Of course, today I realize that Jack really wasn't a friend at all.
He was what in Germany is called a *Bekannter*—someone who you
knows, an acquaintance. And for an acquaintance, his behavior
was fine. I got confused on the day where Jack referred to me as
his friend.

"Friend" is a word that has a different set of expectations for
me. In Germany, that word is reserved for people with that one is
really close. I learned through the experience with Jack that
although you can translate a word from one language to another,
the meaning can still be different. Today I have friends from
many countries. I also have many acquaintances who friendships
I have learned to value, too.

▶ *To check your answers, go to the Answer Key on page 224.*

FROM GRAMMAR TO WRITING
ADDING DETAILS WITH
ADJECTIVE CLAUSES

Details help your reader understand what you are writing about. One way to add details is with adjective clauses that answer questions such as *Who . . .?*, *What . . .?*, *Which . . .?*, *Whose . . .?*, *Where . . .?*, and *When . . .?*.

> **EXAMPLE:**
> She was born in Chile. ⟶
> She was born in Chile, **where her parents had emigrated after the Spanish Civil War**.

---

1 *Read this student essay about a famous person. Underline the adjective clauses.*

Octavio Paz is considered one of the greatest writers that the Spanish-speaking world has produced. He was born in Mexico in 1914. As a child, he was exposed to writing by his grandfather and father. His childhood was hard because of his father's political activities, which forced his family into exile and poverty.

Paz began writing early. He published his first poem at 16. He attended law school in Mexico City, where he joined a Marxist student group. Around the same time, he married his first wife, Elena Garro. Paz's literary career received a boost in his early twenties, when he sent a manuscript to the Chilean poet Pablo Neruda. Neruda was impressed, and he encouraged Paz to go to Spain to attend a writing conference. Paz remained there and joined the forces that were fighting against General Franco in the Spanish Civil War. Later, he went on to become a diplomat, representing his country in France, Japan, the U.S., and India.

Paz wrote both poetry and prose. He is most famous for *The Labyrinth of Solitude*, a collection of essays that deal with the character of the Mexican people. He also founded *Vuelta*. In 1990 he received the Nobel Prize for Literature. He died eight years later.

2 *The student added details in a second draft. Read the student's notes below. Then find places in the essay to add the information. Rewrite the sentences with adjective clauses. Remember to use commas when necessary.*

> Additional Information:
>
> Both his grandfather and father were political journalists.
>
> Elena Garro was also a writer.
>
> Pablo Neruda was already famous in Spain and Latin America.
>
> Vuelta was one of Latin America's most famous literary magazines.

1. As a child, he was exposed to writing by his father and grandfather, who were both political journalists.

2. _____

3. _____

4. _____

3 *Before you write . . .*

- Choose a famous person to write about. Find out about your topic. Take notes about the main events in this person's life.
- Exchange notes with a partner. Put question marks (?) next to items you would like your partner to add more details about.

4 *Write your essay. Try to answer your partner's questions using adjective clauses to add details.*

5 *Exchange essays with a new partner. Underline the adjective clauses. Then complete the following questions. Put question marks (?) where you would like more information.*

a. Did the writer use adjective clauses?	Yes / No
b. Did the writer use the correct relative pronoun for each adjective clause?	Yes / No
c. Did the writer punctuate the adjective clauses correctly?	Yes / No
d. Did the writer give enough details?	Yes / No

6 *Discuss any problems with your partner. Then rewrite your essay with the necessary corrections.*

REVIEW OR SELFTEST
ANSWER KEY

I. (Units 13–14)

2. who	**8.** who
3. who	**9.** that
4. where	**10.** which
5. whose	**11.** when
6. which	**12.** when
7. which	

II. (Units 13–14)

2. She lives in the house which (OR that) is across the street.

3. This is the time of year when (OR that) she always goes away.

4. She travels with her older sister, who lives in Connecticut.

5. This year they're taking a trip with the car that (OR which) she just bought.

6. They're going to Miami, where they grew up.

7. They have a lot of relatives in Florida, who(m) they haven't seen in years.

8. The family is going to have a reunion, which they've been planning all year.

9. They'll be staying with their Aunt Sonya, whose house is right on a canal.

10. They really need this vacation, which they've been looking forward to all year.

III. (Units 13–14)

2. C	**7.** A
3. D	**8.** B
4. C	**9.** C
5. B	**10.** C
6. B	**11.** C

IV. (Units 13–14)

2. D	**7.** D
3. B	**8.** C
4. C	**9.** B
5. B	**10.** C
6. C	

V.

There is an old German proverb that says, "Friendship is a plant ~~what~~ *which OR that OR Ø* we must often water." This means that we have to nurture our relationships to make them grow and flourish. A relationship that you neglect will wilt and die.

When I was ten, my family moved from Germany to the United States. There I had a "friend" (whom I will call Jack) who ~~he~~ never invited me to do things with him. Jack lived in a house ~~where~~ *that OR Ø* I never got to see even though it was just a few blocks away from mine. He had family and friends whom I never met. Of course, today I realize that Jack really wasn't a friend at all. He was what in Germany is called a *Bekannter*—someone who you ~~knows~~ *know*, an acquaintance. And for an acquaintance, his behavior was fine. I got confused on the day ~~where~~ *when OR Ø* Jack referred to me as his friend.

"Friend" is a word that has a different set of expectations for me. In Germany, that word is reserved for people with ~~that~~ *whom* one is really close. I learned through the experience with Jack that although you can translate a word from one language to another, the meaning can still be different. Today I have friends from many countries. I also have many acquaintances ~~who~~ *whose* friendships I have learned to value, too.

APPENDICES

1 Irregular Verbs

BASE FORM	SIMPLE PAST	PAST PARTICIPLE	BASE FORM	SIMPLE PAST	PAST PARTICIPLE
arise	arose	arisen	grind	ground	ground
awake	awoke	awoken	grow	grew	grown
be	was/were	been	hang	hung	hung
beat	beat	beaten	have	had	had
become	became	become	hear	heard	heard
begin	began	begun	hide	hid	hidden
bend	bent	bent	hit	hit	hit
bet	bet	bet	hold	held	held
bite	bit	bitten	hurt	hurt	hurt
bleed	bled	bled	keep	kept	kept
blow	blew	blown	kneel	knelt	knelt
break	broke	broken	knit	knit/knitted	knit/knitted
bring	brought	brought	know	knew	known
build	built	built	lay	laid	laid
burn	burned/burnt	burned/burnt	lead	led	led
burst	burst	burst	leap	leapt	leapt
buy	bought	bought	leave	left	left
catch	caught	caught	lend	lent	lent
choose	chose	chosen	let	let	let
cling	clung	clung	lie (lie down)	lay	lain
come	came	come	light	lit/lighted	lit/lighted
cost	cost	cost	lose	lost	lost
creep	crept	crept	make	made	made
cut	cut	cut	mean	meant	meant
deal	dealt	dealt	meet	met	met
dig	dug	dug	pay	paid	paid
dive	dived/dove	dived	prove	proved	proved/proven
do	did	done	put	put	put
draw	drew	drawn	quit	quit	quit
dream	dreamed/dreamt	dreamed/dreamt	read /rid/	read /rɛd/	read /rɛd/
drink	drank	drunk	ride	rode	ridden
drive	drove	driven	ring	rang	rung
eat	ate	eaten	rise	rose	risen
fall	fell	fallen	run	ran	run
feed	fed	fed	say	said	said
feel	felt	felt	see	saw	seen
fight	fought	fought	seek	sought	sought
find	found	found	sell	sold	sold
fit	fit	fit	send	sent	sent
flee	fled	fled	set	set	set
fling	flung	flung	sew	sewed	sewn/sewed
fly	flew	flown	shake	shook	shaken
forbid	forbade/forbad	forbidden	shave	shaved	shaved/shaven
forget	forgot	forgotten	shine	shone	shone
forgive	forgave	forgiven	shoot	shot	shot
freeze	froze	frozen	show	showed	shown
get	got	gotten/got	shrink	shrank/shrunk	shrunk/shrunken
give	gave	given	shut	shut	shut
go	went	gone	sing	sang	sung

(continued on next page)

BASE FORM	SIMPLE PAST	PAST PARTICIPLE	BASE FORM	SIMPLE PAST	PAST PARTICIPLE
sink	sank	sunk	sweep	swept	swept
sit	sat	sat	swim	swam	swum
sleep	slept	slept	swing	swung	swung
slide	slid	slid	take	took	taken
speak	spoke	spoken	teach	taught	taught
speed	sped	sped	tear	tore	torn
spend	spent	spent	tell	told	told
spill	spilled/spilt	spilled/spilt	think	thought	thought
spin	spun	spun	throw	threw	thrown
spit	spit/spat	spat	understand	understood	understood
split	split	split	upset	upset	upset
spread	spread	spread	wake	woke	woken
spring	sprang	sprung	wear	wore	worn
stand	stood	stood	weave	wove	woven
steal	stole	stolen	weep	wept	wept
stick	stuck	stuck	win	won	won
sting	stung	stung	wind	wound	wound
stink	stank/stunk	stunk	withdraw	withdrew	withdrawn
strike	struck	struck	wring	wrung	wrung
swear	swore	sworn	write	wrote	written

② Common Non-action (Stative) Verbs

EMOTIONS	MENTAL STATES		WANTS AND PREFERENCES	APPEARANCE AND VALUE	POSSESSION AND RELATIONSHIP
admire	agree	know	desire	appear	belong
adore	assume	mean	need	be	contain
appreciate	believe	mind	prefer	cost	have
care	consider	presume	want	equal	own
detest	disagree	realize	wish	feel	possess
dislike	disbelieve	recognize		look	
doubt	estimate	remember	**PERCEPTION**	matter	
envy	expect	see (*understand*)	**AND THE SENSES**	represent	
fear	feel (*believe*)	suppose	feel	resemble	
hate	find	suspect	hear	seem	
hope	guess	think (*believe*)	notice	signify	
like	hesitate	understand	observe	smell	
love	hope	wonder	perceive	sound	
regret	imagine		see	taste	
respect			smell	weigh	
trust			taste		

③ Common Verbs Followed by the Gerund (Base Form of Verb + -*ing*)

acknowledge	consider	endure	give up (*stop*)	miss	quit	resist
admit	delay	enjoy	imagine	postpone	recall	risk
advise	deny	escape	justify	practice	recommend	suggest
appreciate	detest	explain	keep (*continue*)	prevent	regret	support
avoid	discontinue	feel like	mention	prohibit	report	tolerate
can't help	discuss	finish	mind (*object to*)	propose	resent	understand
celebrate	dislike	forgive				

❹ Common Verbs Followed by the Infinitive (*To* + Base Form of Verb)

afford	can('t) afford	expect	hurry	neglect	promise	volunteer
agree	can('t) wait	fail	intend	offer	refuse	wait
appear	choose	grow	learn	pay	request	want
arrange	consent	help	manage	plan	seem	wish
ask	decide	hesitate	mean	prepare	struggle	would like
attempt	deserve	hope	need	pretend	swear	yearn

❺ Verbs Followed by Objects and the Infinitive

advise	challenge	encourage	get	need*	persuade	require	want*
allow	choose*	expect*	help*	order	promise*	teach	warn
ask*	convince	forbid	hire	pay*	remind	tell	wish*
cause	enable	force	invite	permit	request	urge	would like*

*These verbs can also be followed by the infinitive without an object (example: *ask to leave* or *ask someone to leave*).

❻ Common Verbs Followed by the Gerund or the Infinitive

begin	continue	hate	love	remember*	stop*
can't stand	forget*	like	prefer	start	try

*These verbs can be followed by either the gerund or the infinitive but there is a big difference in meaning.

❼ Common Verb + Preposition Combinations

admit to	believe in	count on	insist on	rely on	talk about
advise against	choose between/	deal with	look forward to	resort to	think about
apologize for	among	dream about/of	object to	succeed in	wonder about
approve of	complain about	feel like/about	plan on		

❽ Common Adjective + Preposition Expressions

be accustomed to	be capable of	be fed up with	be pleased about	be slow at
be afraid of	be careful of	be fond of	be ready for	be sorry for/about
be amazed at/by	be concerned about	be glad about	be responsible for	be surprised at/
be angry at	be content with	be good at	be sad about	about/by
be ashamed of	be curious about	be happy about	be safe from	be terrible at
be aware of	be different from	be interested in	be satisfied with	be tired of
be awful at	be excited about	be nervous about	be shocked at/by	be used to
be bad at	be famous for	be opposed to	be sick of	be worried about
be bored with/by				

❾ Common Adjectives that Can Be Followed by the Infinitive*

afraid	anxious	depressed	disturbed	encouraged	happy	pleased	reluctant	surprised
alarmed	ashamed	determined	eager	excited	hesitant	proud	sad	touched
amazed	curious	disappointed	easy	fortunate	likely	ready	shocked	upset
angry	delighted	distressed	embarrassed	glad	lucky	relieved	sorry	willing

*Example: *I'm happy to hear that.*

Irregular Comparisons of Adjectives, Adverbs, and Quantifiers

ADJECTIVE	ADVERB	COMPARATIVE	SUPERLATIVE
bad	badly	worse	worst
far	far	farther/further	farthest/furthest
good	well	better	best
little	little	less	least
many/a lot of	—	more	most
much*/a lot of	much*/a lot	more	most

*Much is usually only used in questions and negative statements.

 Common Participial Adjectives

-ed	-ing	-ed	-ing	-ed	-ing
alarmed	alarming	disturbed	disturbing	moved	moving
amazed	amazing	embarrassed	embarrassing	paralyzed	paralyzing
amused	amusing	entertained	entertaining	pleased	pleasing
annoyed	annoying	excited	exciting	relaxed	relaxing
astonished	astonishing	exhausted	exhausting	satisfied	satisfying
bored	boring	fascinated	fascinating	shocked	shocking
confused	confusing	frightened	frightening	surprised	surprising
depressed	depressing	horrified	horrifying	terrified	terrifying
disappointed	disappointing	inspired	inspiring	tired	tiring
disgusted	disgusting	interested	interesting	touched	touching
distressed	distressing	irritated	irritating	troubled	troubling

 Some Adjectives that Form the Comparative and Superlative in Two Ways

ADJECTIVE	COMPARATIVE	SUPERLATIVE
common	commoner / more common	commonest / most common
cruel	crueler / more cruel	cruelest / most cruel
deadly	deadlier / more deadly	deadliest / most deadly
friendly	friendlier / more friendly	friendliest / most friendly
handsome	handsomer / more handsome	handsomest / most handsome
happy	happier / more happy	happiest / most happy
likely	likelier / more likely	likeliest / most likely
lively	livelier / more lively	liveliest / most lively
lonely	lonelier / more lonely	loneliest / most lonely
lovely	lovelier / more lovely	loveliest / most lovely
narrow	narrower / more narrow	narrowest / most narrow
pleasant	pleasanter / more pleasant	pleasantest / most pleasant
polite	politer / more polite	politest / most polite
quiet	quieter / more quiet	quietest / most quiet
shallow	shallower / more shallow	shallowest / most shallow
sincere	sincerer / more sincere	sincerest / most sincere
stupid	stupider / more stupid	stupidest / most stupid
true	truer / more true	truest / most true

13 Common Reporting Verbs

STATEMENTS

acknowledge	claim	indicate	reply
add	complain	maintain	report
admit	conclude	mean	say
announce	confess	note	state
answer	declare	observe	suggest
argue	deny	promise	tell
assert	exclaim	remark	warn
believe	explain	repeat	write

INSTRUCTIONS, COMMANDS REQUESTS, AND INVITATIONS

advise	invite
ask	order
caution	say
command	tell
demand	urge
instruct	warn

QUESTIONS

ask
inquire
question
want to know
wonder

14 Verbs and Expressions Commonly Used Reflexively

amuse oneself	be proud of oneself	dry oneself	introduce oneself	remind oneself
ask oneself	behave oneself	enjoy oneself	kill oneself	see oneself
avail oneself of	believe in oneself	feel sorry for oneself	look after oneself	take care of oneself
be hard on oneself	blame oneself	help oneself	look at oneself	talk to oneself
be oneself	cut oneself	hurt oneself	pride oneself on	teach oneself
be pleased with oneself	deprive oneself of	imagine oneself	push oneself	tell oneself

15 Some Common Transitive Phrasal Verbs

(s.o. = someone s.t. = something)

Note: *Separable phrasal verbs are shown with the object between the verb and the particle (call s.o. up). Inseparable phrasal verbs are shown with the object after the particle (carry on s.t.). Verbs which must be separated are shown with an asterisk (*) (do s.t. over). Other separable verbs can take the noun object either between the verb and the particle or after the particle (call Jan up OR call up Jan). These verbs must, however, be separated by a pronoun object (call her up NOT ~~call up her~~).*

PHRASAL VERB	MEANING
ask s.o. **over***	invite to one's home
block s.t. **out**	stop from passing through (light/noise)
blow s.t. **out**	stop burning by blowing on it
blow s.t. **up**	1. make explode
	2. fill with air (a balloon/water toy)
	3. make something larger (a photograph)
bring s.t. **about**	make happen
bring s.o. or s.t. **back**	return
bring s.o. **down***	depress
bring s.t. **out**	introduce (a new product/book)
bring s.o. **up**	raise (children)
bring s.t. **up**	bring attention to
burn s.t. **down**	burn completely
call s.o. **back**	return a phone call
call s.o. **in**	ask for help with a problem
call s.t. **off**	cancel
call s.o. **up**	phone
carry on s.t.	continue
carry s.t. **out**	conduct (an experiment/a plan)
charge s.t. **up**	charge with electricity
cheer s.o. **up**	cause to feel happier
clean s.o. or s.t. **up**	clean completely
clear s.t. **up**	clarify

PHRASAL VERB	MEANING
close s.t. **down**	close by force
come off s.t.	become unattached
come up with s.t.	invent
count on s.o. or s.t.	depend on
cover s.o. or s.t. **up**	cover completely
cross s.t. **out**	draw a line through
cut s.t. **down**	bring down by cutting (a tree)
cut s.t. **off**	1. stop the supply of
	2. remove by cutting
cut s.t. **out**	remove by cutting
do s.t. **over***	do again
do s.o. or s.t. **up**	make more beautiful
draw s.t. **together**	unite
dream s.t. **up**	invent
drink s.t. **up**	drink completely
drop s.o. or s.t. **off**	take someplace
drop out of s.t.	quit
empty s.t. **out**	empty completely
figure s.o. or s.t. **out**	understand (after thinking about)
fill s.t. **in**	complete with information
fill s.t. **out**	complete (a form)
fill s.t. **up**	fill completely
find s.t. **out**	learn information
follow through with s.t.	complete
get s.t. **across**	get people to understand an idea

(continued on next page)

PHRASAL VERB	MEANING	PHRASAL VERB	MEANING
get out of s.t.	*leave (a car/taxi)*	see s.t. **through***	*complete*
get s.t. **out of** s.t.*	*benefit from*	set s.t. **off**	*cause to explode*
give s.t. **away**	*give without charging money*	set s.t. **up**	*1. prepare for use*
give s.t. **back**	*return*		*2. establish (a business/an organization)*
give s.t. **out**	*distribute*		
give s.t. **up**	*quit, abandon*	show s.o. or s.t. **off**	*display the best qualities*
go after s.o. or s.t.	*pursue*	shut s.t. **off**	*stop (a machine/light)*
go along with s.t.	*support*	start s.t. **over***	*start again*
hand s.t. **in**	*submit work (to a boss/teacher)*	stick with/to s.o. or s.t.	*not quit, not leave*
hand s.t. **out**	*distribute*	straighten s.t. **up**	*make neat*
hang s.t. **up**	*put on a hook or hanger*	switch s.t. **on**	*start (a machine/light)*
help s.o. **out**	*assist*	take s.t. **away**	*remove*
hold s.t. **on**	*keep attached*	take s.o. or s.t. **back**	*return*
keep s.o. or s.t. **away**	*cause to stay at a distance*	take s.t. **down**	*remove*
keep s.t. **on***	*not remove (a piece of clothing/jewelry)*	take s.t. **in**	*notice, understand, and remember*
		take s.t. **off**	*remove*
keep up with s.o. or s.t.	*go as fast as*	take s.o. **on**	*hire*
lay s.o. **off**	*end employment*	take s.t. **on**	*agree to do*
lay s.t. **out**	*1. spend (money)*	take s.t. **out**	*borrow from a library*
	2. arrange according to a plan	talk s.o. **into***	*persuade*
leave s.t. **on**	*1. not turn off (a light/radio)*	talk s.t. **over**	*discuss*
	2. not remove (a piece of clothing/jewelry)	team up with s.o.	*start to work with*
		tear s.t. **down**	*destroy*
leave s.t. **out**	*omit*	tear s.t. **up**	*tear into small pieces*
let s.o. **down**	*disappoint*	think back on s.o. or s.t.	*remember*
let s.o. or s.t. **in**	*allow to enter*	think s.t. **over**	*consider*
let s.o. **off**	*allow to leave (a bus/car)*	think s.t. **up**	*invent*
let s.o. or s.t. **out**	*allow to leave*	throw s.t. **away/out**	*discard*
light s.t. **up**	*illuminate*	touch s.t. **up**	*improve by making small changes*
look s.o. or s.t. **over**	*examine*	try s.t. **on**	*put clothing on to see if it fits*
look s.t. **up**	*try to find (in a book/on the Internet)*	try s.t. **out**	*use to see if it works*
make s.t. **up**	*create*	turn s.t. **around**	*change the direction so the front is at the back*
move s.t. **around**	*change the location*		
pass s.t. **out**	*distribute*	turn s.o. or s.t. **down**	*reject*
pass s.o. or s.t. **up**	*decide not to use*	turn s.t. **down**	*lower the volume (a TV/radio)*
pay s.o. or s.t. **back**	*repay*	turn s.t. **in**	*submit*
pick s.o. or s.t. **out**	*1. select*	turn s.o. or s.t. **into***	*change from one form to another*
	2. identify	turn s.o. **off**	*(slang) destroy interest*
pick s.o. or s.t. **up**	*lift*	turn s.t. **off**	*stop (a machine/light)*
pick s.t. **up**	*get (an idea/a new book/an interest)*	turn s.t. **on**	*start (a machine/light)*
		turn s.t. **over**	*turn something so the top side is at the bottom*
point s.o. or s.t. **out**	*indicate*		
put s.t. **away**	*put in an appropriate place*	turn s.t. **up**	*raise the volume (a TV/radio)*
put s.t. **back**	*return to its original place*	use s.t. **up**	*use completely, consume*
put s.o. or s.t. **down**	*stop holding*	wake s.o. **up**	*awaken*
put s.t. **off**	*postpone*	work s.t. **off**	*remove by work or activity*
put s.t. **on**	*cover the body*	work s.t. **out**	*solve*
put s.t. **together**	*assemble*	write s.t. **down**	*write on a piece of paper*
put s.t. **up**	*erect*	write s.t. **up**	*write in a finished form*
run into s.o.	*meet accidentally*		

16 Some Common Intransitive Phrasal Verbs

PHRASAL VERB	MEANING	PHRASAL VERB	MEANING
blow up	*explode*	burn down	*burn completely*
break down	*stop functioning*	call back	*return a phone call*
break out	*occur suddenly*	catch on	*become popular*

(continued on next page)

PHRASAL VERB	MEANING	PHRASAL VERB	MEANING
clear up	become clear	go over	succeed with an audience
close down	stop operating	go up	be built
come about	happen	grow up	become an adult
come along	accompany	hang up	end a phone call
come back	return	hold on	1. wait
come in	enter		2. not hang up the phone
come off	become unattached	keep away	stay at a distance
come out	appear	keep on	continue
come up	arise	keep up	go as fast as
dress up	wear special clothes	lie down	recline
drop in	visit unexpectedly	light up	illuminate
drop out	quit	look out	be careful
eat out	eat in a restaurant	make up	reconcile
empty out	empty completely	pay off	be worthwhile
end up	1. do something unexpected or unintended	pick up	improve
	2. reach a final place or condition	play around	have fun
		run out	not have enough of
fall off	become detached	show up	appear
find out	learn information	sign up	register
follow through	complete	sit down	take a seat
fool around	act playful	slip up	make a mistake
get ahead	make progress, succeed	stand up	rise
get along	relate well	start over	start again
get back	return	stay up	remain awake
get by	survive	straighten up	make neat
get together	meet	take off	depart (a plane)
get up	rise from bed	turn out	have a particular result
give up	quit	turn up	appear
go back	return	wake up	arise after sleeping
go off	explode (a gun/fireworks/a rocket)	watch out	be careful
go on	continue	work out	1. be resolved
go out	leave		2. exercise

17 Spelling Rules for the Present Progressive

1. Add -ing to the base form of the verb.

   read   read*ing*
   stand   stand*ing*

2. If a verb ends in a silent -e, drop the final -e and add -ing.

   leave   leav*ing*
   take   tak*ing*

3. In a one-syllable word, if the last three letters are a consonant-vowel-consonant combination (CVC), double the last consonant before adding -ing.

   C V C
   ↓ ↓ ↓
   s i t   sit*ting*
   C V C
   ↓ ↓ ↓
   r u n   run*ning*

However, do not double the last consonant in words that end in w, x, or y.

   sew   sew*ing*
   fix   fix*ing*
   enjoy   enjoy*ing*

4. In words of two or more syllables that end in a consonant-vowel-consonant combination, double the last consonant only if the last syllable is stressed.

   admit́   admit*ting*   (The last syllable is stressed)
   whisper   whisper*ing*   (The last syllable is not stressed, so you don't double the -r.)

5. If a verb ends in -ie, change the ie to y before adding -ing.

   die   dy*ing*

18 Spelling Rules for the Simple Present Tense: Third-Person Singular *(he, she, it)*

1. Add -*s* for most verbs.

work	work*s*
buy	buy*s*
ride	ride*s*
return	return*s*

2. Add -*es* for words that end in -*ch*, -*s*, -*sh*, -*x*, or -*z*.

watch	watch*es*
pass	pass*es*
rush	rush*es*
relax	relax*es*
buzz	buzz*es*

3. Change the *y* to *i* and add -*es* when the base form ends in a consonant + *y*.

study	stud*ies*
hurry	hurr*ies*
dry	dr*ies*

Do not change the *y* when the base form ends in a vowel + *y*. Add -*s*.

play	play*s*
enjoy	enjoy*s*

4. A few verbs have irregular forms.

be	is
do	does
go	goes
have	has

19 Spelling Rules for the Simple Past Tense of Regular Verbs

1. If the verb ends in a consonant, add -*ed*.

return	return*ed*
help	help*ed*

2. If the verb ends in -*e*, add -*d*.

live	live*d*
create	create*d*
die	die*d*

3. In one-syllable words, if the verb ends in a consonant-vowel-consonant combination (CVC), double the final consonant and add -*ed*.

```
C V C
↓ ↓ ↓
h o p        hop*ped*
C V C
↓ ↓ ↓
r u b        rub*bed*
```

However, do not double one-syllable words ending in -*w*, -*x*, or -*y*.

bow	bow*ed*
mix	mix*ed*
play	play*ed*

4. In words of two or more syllables that end in a consonant-vowel-consonant combination, double the last consonant only if the last syllable is stressed.

prefér	prefer*red*	(The last syllable is stressed.)
vísit	visit*ed*	(The last syllable is not stressed, so you don't double the *t*.)

5. If the verb ends in a consonant + *y*, change the *y* to *i* and add -*ed*.

worry	worr*ied*
carry	carr*ied*

6. If the verb ends in a vowel + *y*, add -*ed*. (Do not change the *y* to *i*.)

play	play*ed*
annoy	annoy*ed*

Exceptions: pay—paid, lay—laid, say—said

20 Spelling Rules for the Comparative *(-er)* and Superlative *(-est)* of Adjectives

1. Add -*er* to one-syllable adjectives to form the comparative. Add -*est* to one-syllable adjectives to form the superlative.

cheap	cheap*er*	cheap*est*
bright	bright*er*	bright*est*

2. If the adjective ends in -*e*, add -*r* or -*st*.

nice	nice*r*	nice*st*

3. If the adjective ends in a consonant + *y*, change *y* to *i* before you add -*er* or -*est*.

	pretty	prett*ier*	prett*iest*
Exception:	shy	shy*er*	shy*est*

4. If the adjective ends in a consonant-vowel-consonant combination (CVC), double the final consonant before adding -*er* or -*est*.

```
C V C
↓ ↓ ↓
b i g        big*ger*        big*gest*
```

However, do not double the consonant in words ending in -*w* or -*y*.

slow	slow*er*	slow*est*
coy	coy*er*	coy*est*

21 Spelling Rules for Adverbs Ending in -ly

1. Add -ly to the corresponding adjective.

nice   nice*ly*
quiet   quiet*ly*
beautiful   beautiful*ly*

2. If the adjective ends in a consonant + y, change the y to i before adding -ly.

easy   eas*ily*

3. If the adjective ends in -le, drop the e and add -y.

possible   possibl*y*

However, do not drop the e for other adjectives ending in -e.

extreme   extreme*ly*
Exception: true   tru*ly*

4. If the adjective ends in -ic, add -ally.

basic   basic*ally*
fantastic   fantastic*ally*

22 Punctuation Rules for Direct Speech

Direct speech may either follow or come before the reporting verb. When direct speech follows the reporting verb,

a. Put a comma after the reporting verb.
b. Use opening quotation marks (") before the first word of the direct speech.
c. Begin the quotation with a capital letter.
d. Use the appropriate end punctuation for the direct speech. It may be a period (.), a question mark (?), or an exclamation point (!).
e. Put closing quotation marks (") after the end punctuation of the quotation.

Examples: He said, "I had a good time."
She asked, "Where's the party?"
They shouted, "Be careful!"

When direct speech comes before the reporting verb,

a. Begin the sentence with opening quotation marks (").
b. Use the appropriate end punctuation for the direct speech. If the direct speech is a statement, use a comma (,). If the direct speech is a question, use a question mark (?). If the direct speech is an exclamation, use an exclamation point (!).
c. Use closing quotation marks after the end punctuation for the direct speech (").
d. Begin the reporting clause with a lower-case letter.
e. Use a period at the end of the main sentence (.).

Examples: "I had a good time," he said.
"Where's the party?" she asked.
"Be careful!" they shouted.

23 Pronunciation Table

These are the pronunciation symbols used in this text. Listen to the pronunciation of the key words.

	VOWELS				CONSONANTS		
Symbol	Key Word	Symbol	Key Word	Symbol	Key Word	Symbol	Key Word
i	beat, feed	ə	banana, among	p	pack, happy	ʃ	ship, machine, station, special, discussion
ɪ	bit, did	ɚ	shirt, murder	b	back, rubber		
eɪ	date, paid	aɪ	bite, cry, buy, eye	t	tie	ʒ	measure, vision
ɛ	bet, bed			d	die	h	hot, who
æ	bat, bad	aʊ	about, how	k	came, key, quick	m	men
ɑ	box, odd, father	ɔɪ	voice, boy	g	game, guest	n	sun, know, pneumonia
ɔ	bought, dog	ɪr	beer	tʃ	church, nature, watch	ŋ	sung, ringing
oʊ	boat, road	ɛr	bare	dʒ	judge, general, major	w	wet, white
ʊ	book, good	ɑr	bar	f	fan, photograph	l	light, long
u	boot, food, student	ɔr	door	v	van	r	right, wrong
		ʊr	tour	θ	thing, breath	y	yes, use, music
ʌ	but, mud, mother			ð	then, breathe	t̬	butter, bottle
				s	sip, city, psychology		
				z	zip, please, goes		

STRESS
' shows main stress.

24 Pronunciation Rules for the Simple Present Tense: Third-Person Singular *(he, she, it)*

1. The third person singular in the simple present tense always ends in the letter -*s*. There are, however, three different pronunciations for the final sound of the third person singular.

/s/	/z/	/ɪz/
talks	loves	dances

2. The final sound is pronounced /s/ after the voiceless sounds /p/, /t/, /k/, and /f/.

top	tops
get	gets
take	takes
laugh	laughs

3. The final sound is pronounced /z/ after the voiced sounds /b/, /d/, /g/, /v/, /ð/, /m/, /n/, /ŋ/, /l/, and /r/.

describe	describes
spend	spends
hug	hugs
live	lives
bathe	bathes
seem	seems
remain	remains
sing	sings
tell	tells
lower	lowers

4. The final sound is pronounced /z/ after all vowel sounds.

agree	agrees
try	tries
stay	stays
know	knows

5. The final sound is pronounced /ɪz/ after the sounds /s/, /z/, /ʃ/, /ʒ/, /tʃ/, and /dʒ/. /ɪz/ adds a syllable to the verb.

relax	relaxes
freeze	freezes
rush	rushes
massage	massages
watch	watches
judge	judges

6. *Do* and *say* have a change in vowel sound.

say	/sɛɪ/	says	/sɛz/
do	/du/	does	/dʌz/

25 Pronunciation Rules for the Simple Past Tense of Regular Verbs

1. The regular simple past always ends in the letter -*d*. There are, however, three different pronunciations for the final sound of the regular simple past.

/t/	/d/	/ɪd/
raced	lived	attended

2. The final sound is pronounced /t/ after the voiceless sounds /p/, /k/, /f/, /s/, /ʃ/, and /tʃ/.

hop	hopped
work	worked
laugh	laughed
address	addressed
publish	published
watch	watched

3. The final sound is pronounced /d/ after the voiced sounds /b/, /g/, /v/, /z/, /ʒ/, /dʒ/, /m/, /n/, /ŋ /, /l/, /r/, and /ð/.

rub	rubbed
hug	hugged
live	lived
surprise	surprised
massage	massaged
change	changed
rhyme	rhymed
return	returned
bang	banged
enroll	enrolled
appear	appeared
bathe	bathed

4. The final sound is pronounced /d/ after all vowel sounds.

agree	agreed
play	played
die	died
enjoy	enjoyed

5. The final sound is pronounced /ɪd/ after /t/ and /d/. /ɪd/ adds a syllable to the verb.

start	started
decide	decided

INDEX

This Index is for the full and split editions. All entries are in the full book.
Entries for Volume A of the split edition are in black. Entries for Volume B are in color.